RADIO MAN

Even the prospect of early annihilation should not keep us from making the most of our days on this unhappy planet. In the best of times, our days are numbered anyway. And it would be a crime against Nature for any generation to take the world crisis so solemnly that it put off enjoying those things for which we were presumably designed in the first place, and which the gravest statesmen and the hoarsest politicians hope to make available to all men in the end: I mean the opportunity to do good work, to fall in love, to enjoy friends, to sit under trees, to read, to hit a ball and bounce the baby.

ALISTAIR COOKE, INTRODUCTION TO
COLLECTION OF *LETTERS FROM AMERICA*, 1951

RADIO MAN

BRENDAN BALFE ∼

Gill & Macmillan

Gill & Macmillan Ltd
Hume Avenue, Park West, Dublin 12
with associated companies throughout the world
www.gillmacmillan.ie

© Brendan Balfe 2007
978 07171 4239 2
Index compiled by Cover to Cover
Typography design by Make Communication
Print origination by Carole Lynch
Printed and bound in Great Britain by
MPG Books Ltd, Bodmin, Cornwall

This book is typeset in Linotype Minion and
Neue Helvetica.

The paper used in this book comes from the wood pulp
of managed forests. For every tree felled, at least one
tree is planted, thereby renewing natural resources.

The author and publishers have made every effort
to trace all copyright holders, but if any has been
inadvertently overlooked, we will be pleased to make
the necessary arrangement at the first opportunity.

A CIP catalogue record for this book is available
from the British Library.

5 4 3 2 1

For Eileen, Ellie and John,
for all the love,
and
for Ellie most of all,
for encouraging me to do it.

Thank you.

CONTENTS

AUTHOR'S NOTE

An astute reader like you will appreciate that life happens slightly out of sequence. Some of the episodes related are concurrent with each other, but for clarity I have grouped them into chapters.

The world, they say, is divided into two types of people: those who make lists and those who don't. I am one of the former and at the end of the chapters I have included short catalogues of music and information, based on listeners' queries over the years.

So, if you want to know the title of Frankie Byrne's signature tune or Ireland's first Top Ten, look no further. I hope you enjoy the rest of the book as well, a personal chronicle of over forty years in Irish broadcasting.

I am indebted to Sarah Liddy of Gill & Macmillan for her patience and support in turning me into an author, and to the American writer H.L. Menken for a definition of self-respect that may be applicable: the secure feeling that nobody is, as yet, suspicious.

Brendan Balfe
Dublin
2007

Chapter 1 ᨑ

| THE LONG CORRIDOR

When Sir John Barbirolli came to the Radio Éireann studios in 1947, he was already an enthusiastic Dublin devotee. As knowledgeable about architecture as he was about music, he was much taken by the Georgian town houses of Merrion and Fitzwilliam Squares, which reminded him of the great houses of his beloved Bloomsbury.

He was in Dublin that week to conduct his Hallé Orchestra at the Theatre Royal and Eamonn Andrews invited him to come to the studios in the GPO to be interviewed on *Microphone Parade*. This was in the days before portable tape recorders. There was a disc-cutting machine on the premises that could produce a recording on a 78rpm record, but it was not transportable without the aid of six strong men and, possibly, a team of horses. So, the guests came to us; we didn't go to them.

Sir John knew a little about the GPO and Eamonn filled him in on its history. How it had been shelled in the 1916 Rising and rebuilt, how it had become the home of Irish radio since 1928, when the fledgling service had moved from its original base in Great Denmark Street, currently the site of the ILAC Centre. The GPO studios were modest in the beginning—a studio for music, a studio for drama and, on the fourth floor, overlooking Henry Street, a studio for the announcer. Gradually, the studios were expanded: Studios 3, 4 and 5 were added on the fourth floor while down on the third floor, running along the O'Connell Street frontage, were Studios 7, 8, 9, 10 and a dubbing suite.

Connecting the two sets of studios was a long corridor running from the front of the GPO down parallel to Henry Street as far as Moore Street. It was over a hundred yards long and on each side were offices, rehearsal rooms, and the Green Room of the Radio Éireann Players. They were tastefully painted in Civil Service Brown, offset by Public Sector Yellow. Carpets were eschewed, the spartan brown linoleum being more in keeping with the frugal philosophy of the Department of Posts and Telegraphs.

That long corridor was lined, halfway up the wall, with white tiles. The upper half was translucent glass, with its surrounding woodwork in brown. Piquancy was added by the slight hint of Jeyes Fluid and the all-pervasive smell of boiled cabbage emanating from the canteen on the fourth floor. So, on the night when Sir John Barbirolli came to the GPO, the sight of the long tiled corridor and its unique décor prompted him to remark to Eamonn Andrews that it looked like 'the longest row of lavatories in the world'.

But for almost fifty years, that long corridor was the centre of Irish radio. I was there for ten of those years. For me, it was a university, an arts club, a publishing house, a music hub, an asylum for eccentrics and a place where I met some of my best friends.

———

So, there I was in the Continuity studio one Saturday night in the summer of 1968. I was the late announcer and also Station Supervisor, a sort of duty officer, responsible for everything that goes out on the air. The studio was at the far end of the long corridor, on the third floor, and directly overlooked Moore Street. Indeed, such was the poor air-conditioning that the window was sometimes left open during announcements, prompting many a listener to wonder if they had really heard 'Jap Oranges, two-and-six a dozen' during the introduction to *Music for Children*.

Nothing much happens on a Saturday night. I came on at five o'clock, was relieved by the early announcer from 7.30 to 9.00 and settled in to announce the programmes, log the items, and fill in wherever programmes ran short. There was a stack of LP records for interval music, two turntables and a microphone, all of which the announcers operated themselves.

It was 10.15 when the internal phone rang.

'He's drunk. Listen to him. Drunk again,' a slightly hysterical voice said.

'Who is?'

'Ó Murchú. Pissed as a skunk. I can do nothing with him.'

The voice was that of Dermot O'Hara, at one time conductor of the Radio Éireann Light Orchestra and now producer of *Céilí House*, which was scheduled to be broadcast live from the O'Connell Hall in fifteen minutes.

'Let me listen to him,' I said. By means of a pre-fade facility on the Continuity desk, I could eavesdrop on the events in the hall, which was a fully equipped music studio and, at the time, the home of the Light Orchestra and programmes like *The Seventeen Club* and *The Maureen Potter Show*.

Seán Ó Murchú was one of Ireland's most beloved broadcasters. A Galway man, he had joined the announcing staff of Radio Éireann in the 1950s. He had a mellifluous voice, in both Irish and English, plagued occasionally by a touch of emphysema, or a chesty cough. In fact, he claims to have invented the menthol cigarette by smearing Vicks VapoRub onto a Woodbine cigarette. Not a pretty sight, he agreed, but 'it did produce a most productive cough'.

Nor was he, as the euphemism goes, ignorant of the grape. On many an occasion he would arrive into the GPO to read the eight o'clock news smelling strongly of having been out all night. There were usually two announcers scheduled for the early shift—one to read the news and one to act as continuity announcer. The unwritten rule, when Seán was the newsreader, was for the second announcer to mind him. This minding entailed producing strong black coffee and removing any small Baby Power bottles of whiskey he may have secreted about his person. On more than one occasion, the news script was wrested from Seán's fingers by the second announcer, moments before the live broadcast.

Even when apparently sober and authoritative, he had a propensity for commenting on the news as he read it. This had an even more startling effect on the listener than the slurring of words, as in the case when two entirely different stories followed each other. One, about which Seán felt strongly, concerned the American who bought part of Killarney National Park and the other was about the arrival of a papal representative.

'Mr Pat Robertson, the new owner of Killarney, is expected in Ireland tomorrow.

'Mr Robertson's grandmother came from Kerry.'

There was a slight sniff of disapproval. He continued, 'The Papal Legate, Cardinal Agagianian, has arrived in Dublin…'

There was a pause.

'… I suppose his grandmother came from Kerry too,' Seán added.

By the time I became a continuity announcer, Seán had long since left the staff. But whatever death wish he liked to invoke by sailing close to the wind had continued on *Céilí House*. His irreverent, witty approach made for compulsive listening among his many fans. In a pub in Wicklow one Saturday night, I saw the affection in which he was held. *The Late Late Show* was belting out of the television set and the entire pub was riveted by the conversation, until someone asked:

'What's the time?'

'It's half past ten.'

'Well then, turn off that television and put on *Céilí House*.'

As I listened to Seán's attempt to rehearse his opening for the programme down in the O'Connell Hall, I realised that he couldn't be allowed on air. Dermot O'Hara was so exasperated over the years that he washed his hands of the whole affair and so the decision was left to me.

'All right, tell Seán he can't do the programme and to leave the studio. The programme is cancelled. I'll present a programme of céilí band records from here.'

I then looked at the selection of LPS at my disposal. All the great names of Light Music On Gramophone Records were there—Frank Chacksfield, Bert Kaemphert, Stanley Black, Reg Owen, Werner Muller—but not a céilí record among them, and the record library was closed and locked.

'Dermot,' I said, 'a change of plan. Tell me the titles of the pieces and I'll announce the tunes from here.'

'We haven't got the titles. Seán was meant to do a running order and script. But he never did. Just arrived here incapable, stocious drunk.'

It was now 10.25. It dawned on me that, although Dermot O'Hara's main role had been to supervise Seán, there had been no plan worked out in the event of his being incapable of doing the broadcast, other than to let the continuity announcer decide.

So, here is what the continuity announcer decided. At 10.30 I said, 'Radio Telefís Éireann. The time is half past ten. Time for *Céilí House.*'

A red light was given to the O'Connell Hall and, on cue, the céilí band started playing. I then left the Continuity studio and sprinted the hundred yards down the long corridor, down the lift to the ground floor, out the first door of Henry Street, up O'Connell Street to the O'Connell Hall, opposite the Gresham Hotel, into the studio and walked to a small table with a microphone set up for the compere. The band was still playing the selection of reels. I had taken the precaution of noting the name of the band from the programme schedule in the GPO, but that's all I knew. There was no sign of the producer.

Addressing who I thought might be their leader, because he was near a microphone, I asked him to tell me what he had just played. He paled visibly. He had appeared on the programme many times, but no one had ever asked him to speak. He identified the tunes and then I asked him what the next item would be. He rallied and in a more confident voice named the tunes. Likewise when we came to the guest tenor, I had a chat with him and he told me about the song he'd sing. I went on like this for half an hour, the band and tenor warming to the new, if unexpected, approach. When we got to the final selection of marches, I enjoined them to keep playing until they were told to stop. As they launched into the medley, I re-traced my steps down O'Connell Street, into the entrance at Henry Street, up the lift, down the corridor and into the Continuity studio, exactly on the hour, to say, 'The time is eleven o'clock. Here are the news headlines.'

I suppose I could have cancelled the programme and played reams of the Frank Chacksfield Orchestra for half an hour, but I thought of our regular listeners who loved their céilí music and decided that they shouldn't be disappointed. Besides, an element of danger added a certain spice to the long Saturday-night shift. As a result of that escapade, I was asked to finish out the series of about six programmes. Seán was suspended for a while but he came back and presented *Céilí House* from the new Radio Centre well into the 1980s, until he was succeeded by Breandán Ó Dúill.

To this day, I have the greatest difficulty in persuading people to believe that I was actually a scheduled presenter of *Céilí House*. It was never my ambition to do that programme. I could barely tell a reel from a roundelay, but if you aspire to be a versatile broadcaster, you should be able to cover a number of bases.

The sound engineer that night—or, in Radio Éireann parlance, the Balance and Control Officer—was Michael Murtagh. By then, both he and Dermot O'Hara had already played a part in my first broadcast.

| GROWING UP IN DUBLIN

Y ou can tell an authentic male native of Ireland's capital city by what he calls himself. He is a Dublinman, rather than a Dubliner. I am one of that vanishing breed of the species, unaffected by any rural strain.

My mother was Vera O'Toole from Mountjoy Street on the north side of the River Liffey. It was a quiet residential street with Victorian-style houses. At one end was Upper Dominick Street and at the other, the infamous Black Church near Broadstone. Walk three times around the church, they said, and you'll meet the Devil. Or maybe protect yourself from meeting the Devil; I can never remember.

My mother's name was actually Farrell, the daughter of Joseph and Mary Farrell of 33 Wellington Street. When Mary died early in their marriage, Joseph Farrell left the family home and my mother was effectively raised by her maternal grandmother, who lived nearby at 32 Mountjoy Street. She adored her granny and, to solidify the relationship, she reverted to the family name of O'Toole. She had a brother, Dermot, and a sister, Carmel. Her father, like the defunct leaders in the Soviet Union, was erased from the family history.

To balance the northern influence, my father was from south of the Liffey. James Balfe, always known as Jimmy, was born and raised at 33 Thomas Court, in the heart of the historic Liberties area. He was the eldest of six children born to Edward and Brigid Balfe. Edward, a distinguished-looking gentleman with a military bearing and white moustache, was 'Ned' to his friends but to us he was our beloved 'Granda'. My grandmother was originally Brigid Aspel and before her marriage was 'in service', that is, working as a domestic servant.

The houses at Thomas Court were, by today's standards, tiny: two bedrooms upstairs and a parlour/dining room downstairs, leading to a scullery. A kitchen extension made of wood had been added and a flush toilet, although you still had to go outside the door to access it. The only refrigeration was provided by a meat-safe out the back, the cold air keeping food fresh.

The Guinness family had built the houses to accommodate the employees of the Guinness Brewery at James's Gate, which took over acres of land around James's Street, Thomas Street and a warren of tall, sombre buildings backing onto Thomas Court and Pimlico. The smell of hops and barley roasting could be detected all over the area, a tangible reminder that much of the economy of the neighbourhood was dependent on the Guinness Brewery. It was a sort of circular business model: Guinness paid the men to make the stout and they, in turn, paid Guinness as they drank the stuff. Nonetheless, Guinness were model employers, supplying healthcare, dinners and a free pint per day. A job at the Brewery was much sought after in Dublin.

My grandfather worked there as a storeman. Two of his sons, Eddie and Jackie, followed him into the company, working as a cooper and a labourer respectively. Another son, Tommy, joined the Civil Service and worked for the Revenue Commissioners, while also managing the National Ballroom by night, thereby putting him in the position of having to report his part-time work to himself. There were two daughters: May, who died young, and Bridgie, who married a forestry worker, Charlie McCoy, and settled in Glendalough, Co. Wicklow, one of Ireland's most celebrated tourist attractions.

My father took a different route and went into the business of building supplies. He took technical exams and joined Baxendales of Capel Street, Dublin, as its youngest manager, in charge of the large ironmongery department and became a leading expert in his field. He sold anything made of metal, but was particularly adept at dealing in architectural ironmongery—locks, hinges, window fastenings, door-closers—required for large buildings. Jimmy Balfe devised a method, still used today, whereby he could look at an architect's drawings for, say, a large hospital and assess exactly how many locks, hinges and door-closers were required, and of what type. It enhanced many an architect's reputation, but, as a result, Baxendales kept getting the business.

My parents married on 22 February 1943 in St Michan's Church and went to live in 141 Herberton Road, Rialto. It was a rented house, roomy, two-storeyed, with large bay windows. My sister Joan was born first and I followed on 19 September 1945. Around the time I was due, my mother's granny was dangerously ill and I was a little dismayed to learn (much later) that my mother had offered God my life in exchange for Granny's. I'm glad to say God didn't take up the offer and I was born in Holles Street Maternity Hospital by Caesarean section, partly because my mother had contracted rheumatic fever at Joan's birth. It would result in heart problems for the rest of her life.

My second sister followed a couple of years later and one of my earliest memories is of seeing this small person lying on a red bedspread in the bedroom in Herberton Road and wondering what all the noise was about. She was christened Jacinta, as my mother was much taken at the time by the film *Miracle of Fatima*.

There are early memories of radio. Whenever I hear 'Till I Waltz Again With You' by Teresa Brewer, I am back immediately in Herberton Road. I remember being much taken with 'Young at Heart' by Frank Sinatra and *Dick Barton, Special Agent* on the BBC, although I, apparently, insisted on calling him Special 'Angel'. He may have been the inspiration for me pulling some dangerous stunts myself—like walking across from one side window to another on the upstairs window ledge. On the outside. Luckily, my dad on his way home spotted me. That same week, I swallowed a few brown sweets that turned out to be my mother's digitalis heart tablets. They were extracted forcibly by the simple expedient of a parental hand down the throat. Maybe I really had a Special Angel.

Then, in 1950, we moved from Rialto to Lower Kilmacud Road, Stillorgan. Our new house was a bungalow, with a large elm tree in the front garden, ideal for falling out of. It was a newly developed area, the road essentially joining Goatstown village with Stillorgan village. Behind us was Mount Merrion and in front, beyond the new Redsdale Estate, wide tracts of land leading up to the foothills of the Dublin Mountains.

Like any new suburb, there were children everywhere. I was enrolled in Mount Anville National School, first as a Low Baby graduating to High Baby and on into First Class. Nuns with traditional black-and-white garb ran the school. One, in particular, had a small jewellery box that she used to make a clacking sound to discourage talking. It was an early automated classroom— no words were required, just one click and the room fell silent. They supplied lunch, too: the most delicious soup and the most awful sandwiches, made from thick brown bread spread with stewed rhubarb. No butter, just stewed rhubarb.

I made my First Holy Communion in Mount Anville, walking down the aisle with Mary Doyle, who was suffering from a runny nose. I was then transferred to Kilmacud Boys' National School, a tougher place entirely, with a rougher type of clientèle. The mix of boys included those from the newer estates, mixed with those from the established Stillorgan village and Beaufield Estate, mainly comprising local authority housing. They didn't always get on with the more recent recruits and it was advisable to go around in groups for protection. Ironically, the boy to be most wary of was the headmaster's son, who seemed to think that his station entitled him to behave with impunity towards those of smaller stature. He has since become a Senior Counsel.

But I was making friends with the boys nearer my house: Michael and Matthew Forkin, two cousins who lived in adjoining houses, Barry Houston, Billy Brown, and Canice Hayes, the son of David Hayes. David was the nearest we had to a celebrity on our road. He was the writer of the popular Radio Éireann serial *The Foley Family* and on the wall in his living room was a signed cartoon of Ben and Bebe Lyons, stars of the BBC Radio series *Life with the Lyons*, leading me to assume that David Hayes had also contributed material to that programme. *The Foley Family*, incidentally, ran for years on radio but when a move to television was mooted, its leading actor, George Greene, who played the much put-upon Tom Foley, turned it down. Being a radio actor, he was adamant that he shouldn't be photographed because it would break the illusion for listeners when he was playing other parts. Moreover, Tom Foley featured in a regular series of cartoons by Pyke in the *Evening Press*, and George Greene didn't look remotely like him.

Two doors down, my particular pals were Brian and Jimmy O'Connor. They were the youngest of a family of five boys. Their mother had a part-time job and wasn't normally there when they came back from school. She used to make toast before she left and that would be there to keep the boys going until teatime. They shared it with me every day, even though I had to walk only twenty yards to my own house, but it was more fun eating in someone else's house. Their father, Jack O'Connor, was a kindly man who ran silent films of Laurel and Hardy and Charlie Chaplin on birthdays and special occasions. He also introduced me to radio serials like *The Shadow* and *The Third Man* being broadcast from AFN (American Forces Network) in Germany and from Radio Luxembourg. In the O'Connors' back garden, I learned how to smoke dry leaves as a tobacco substitute and lived to tell the tale. Brian once threw a bamboo spear at me, which caught me in the eye. There was a lot of blood, but it missed any vital working parts by a hair's breadth.

The summers were long and sunny. In memory, they always are. In the school holidays, we would be up and about by nine o'clock, leaving the house clad only in shorts and bearing our provisions for the day—a sandwich and a drink made from orange cordial. There could be a dozen of us from our immediate area and we were armed with our bamboo spears, purloined from the Bamboo Woods, part of a private house on Sweetbriar Lane. We would gather in the Mount Merrion Woods, which were thick with undergrowth at the time, so you could hide very effectively, as well as get lost very effectively. We broke into gangs and played war games of attack and defence, half of us being the soldiers in the fort and the other half being the Indians.

Then more boys joined us, so that we now numbered over fifty. The following day, the fifty had become a hundred, so some command structure was required. Leaders were appointed and every day we played games from early morning until it got dark.

They were closely worked-out games—a few of us would devise the scenario, setting out a series of challenges to be achieved before lunch and designating tasks and commands. Eventually, Mount Merrion Woods became too small for the number of boys playing the game, so we moved to the huge open space off the Upper Kilmacud Road. It had hills and ditches, divided by the Harcourt Street railway line, and contained the ruins of an old manor house. It was like something from a John Ford Western: over two hundred boys appearing on the brow of a hill, acting as the attacking Indians, and an equal number defending the fort and sending out raiding parties. No injuries or bad temper blighted the exercises, but they lasted the entire day, until dusk. Our parents weren't worried about where we were or what we were doing. They knew we were safe.

I did acquire some injuries, though. All boys do. I split my head open when I fell from the tree in the garden, but most of my scars are on my left leg. The first was earned when Eamon Morrissey, a rough diamond whose family ran the farm for the nuns in Mount Anville, ran me down with his bicycle. He had seen me coming out of Mackey's shop with my copy of *The Beano* and pulled it out of my hand. Having read somewhere that the best approach to dealing with bullies was to stand up to them, I grabbed the comic back and ran for home, about a hundred yards away. Morrissey followed me on his bike. I was almost there when his bike connected with me, I fell on the loose shingle on the footpath and his bike ran over my leg. Not only did it break the bone, but it also caused an eighteen-inch lesion between my ankle and my knee, as I slid on the sharp shingle. I was in plaster for months and complications ensued when the wound became infected. My father later went to remonstrate with Mr Morrissey, the culprit's father, but got no satisfaction or apology.

The left leg also featured in a scalding accident. I was standing in the back of the bath as my mother was refreshing the luke-warm water with boiling water from a kettle. I lost my footing on the slippery surface and fell under the jet of water. Mam was so shocked that she couldn't stop pouring. For weeks, I slept with a fireguard over my legs, acting as a frame so that the bedclothes didn't touch the area. Later, a toe infection I picked up in Blackrock Baths ran up my leg and turned gangrenous; there was even talk of amputation. Many years later, it was sprained, twisted, bitten by a dog (one of Twink's infernal mutts) and only a year ago, I fell off the garden wall while fixing a clothes-line. Where was the injury? My Left Leg. They have made movies about less.

Even though we lived in suburbia, regular contact had always been maintained with our city relatives. At an early age, when my mother had been ill, I had been despatched to live with my Aunt Carmel and Uncle Phil at Mountjoy Street. The family name was Gregan and they had two sons, David and Anthony, my first cousins. They lived in the upstairs of No. 32, while my Auntie Kathleen lived downstairs with her daughter, Gretta, who worked as a waitress in Bewley's Café in Grafton Street. My sister Joan was much impressed with the black uniform and white cap worn by Gretta and expressed an ambition to work in Bewley's herself. My uncle Dermot lived on the middle floor, or 'return', and Uncle Phil kept pigeons and chickens in the small back yard. There was a big kitchen with a range downstairs, a typical old Dublin house that hadn't changed since it was built, a hundred years before. There was a dairy across the road on the corner where I was sent for butter and milk, bringing a two-pint jug to be filled from a milk-churn. Smells are as evocative as sights or sounds and whenever I smell bull's-eyes and clove drops and sherbet, in my mind I am back in the sweet shop around the corner, looking again for lucky bags and red ice pops.

I must have been there for an extended stay at some time, because I joined my cousins at their school in King's Inn Street. It was rough, with poor sanitary conditions, and the children were generally pasty-faced and thin, but everyone got a small bottle of milk each day; it was the early 1950s and nourishing food was still hard to come by.

I added another scar to my collection when my cousin David threw a chocolate fish, a present from my dad, into the fire. I retrieved it, getting a nasty burn on my wrist. But honour was satisfied and the fish was shared.

My first visit to the pictures was to the Plaza Cinema in Dorset Street, virtually around the corner from Mountjoy Street. Much later it became the National Wax Museum, but even its most grisly exhibits couldn't match the excitement of seeing *Superman* in the fifteen-part serial, or, in local parlance, 'the follyin-upper'. Kirk Alyn played the Man of Steel, but when he had to leap tall buildings in a single bound, he mysteriously became a cartoon figure, like Mickey Mouse. You really couldn't believe a man could fly. Space travel was even more exotic as Flash Gordon, played by Larry Buster Crabbe, battled Charles Middleton in the character of Ming the Merciless, the villain whose headquarters seemed to be made entirely of curtains and a single throne. There, as he plotted his dastardly deeds surrounded by space maidens in skimpy costumes, the whole cinema would cheer as Flash arrived in what looked like a large tin can with someone blowing smoke out the back of it. Admission to the matinees was a penny, but if you hadn't the cash, the management would accept two jam jars.

Close contact was also kept with Thomas Court. My grandfather, who was by now retired, was an active man and regularly walked out to Kilmacud from the centre of the city. We in turn would collect him and Nana in our recently acquired Morris Minor and go for drives and picnics. My sisters and I hated these jaunts, with four adults and three children squeezed into a small saloon. The grown-ups would stop for a drink in Ashford or Newtownmountkennedy or Avoca, leaving us to be content sweltering in the car outside with a bottle of orange. Most feared was the drive to Glendalough, which meant enduring the Long Hill between Kilmacanogue and Roundwood. The Morris came with a faulty petrol pump or carburettor and when the car was off the horizontal for any length, petrol would drain away, stalling the engine and bringing the car to a complete stop. We could time when it would happen almost exactly—it was halfway up the Long Hill—so it became the organised picnic break. Passing round sandwiches and tea, we would look on approvingly as my father manually pumped the petrol back into the business end of the engine. And off we would go again, onward and upward.

As a special treat, we grandchildren were invited to stay for the weekend at Thomas Court. I loved those visits: going shopping in the friendly shops of Meath Street and Francis Street, walking along the Liffey with the Guinness barges still plying their route to the docks, Henry Street and Moore Street teeming with life and laughter, the noble buildings of the city, the width of O'Connell Street, the shops that had remained unchanged for decades, wine shops, grocery shops with slabs of butter and cheese, the immense size of Arnotts and Clerys department stores and the Theatre Royal. They were imprinted on my mind as I walked the streets of Dublin, holding my grandfather's hand. We met Bang Bang, the local character who used a large key as a pistol and 'shot' selected passers-by. Invariably, Dubliners responded to the shouted 'bang-bang' with the agreed etiquette, by clutching their sides and teetering on their feet. I even saw a garda clutch his chest, utter a gasping sound and fall flat to the ground, in an elaborate mime. Love-Joy-Peace was another much loved character, who did nothing more dangerous than chalk the words 'Love, Joy, Peace' on any available surface. No one minded. They left the marks until they were erased by time and weather.

The Phoenix Park was one of the favourite walks, with stops for background on the Wellington Monument, the Gough Monument, the Zoo and Áras an Uachtaráin. One morning we met Seán T. O'Kelly strolling along the main road, alone and without escorts. 'Good morning, Seán T.,' said Granda. 'A fine morning indeed, thank God,' said the President.

I recall an important lesson from one of those visits to Thomas Court. I was up in my grandparents' room looking out the window, when I noticed the blind was too far down for a clear view. I was trying to adjust it when, to my horror, the whole thing came away in my hand. I put it back as best I could. Later, Nana asked me had I been interfering with the blind. I denied it. She asked me again. I denied it again. And so it went on, she pointing out that I was the only other person in the house, and suggesting that I might want to reconsider my answer. The whole episode lasted half an hour, but in the end, I relented and admitted my guilt. It taught me a lesson I have never forgotten—tell the truth, no matter how embarrassing. I have since become a sort of pathological truth-teller, which has also got me into trouble, but it's better to be direct.

Apart from the occasional weekend visits, we would regularly visit Thomas Court for Sunday tea. It was usually ham and salad and apple pie, known as high tea in the days when you had your dinner in the middle of the day. Afterwards, we listened to the radio—and the ritual was always the same: *Question Time* with Joe Linnane from Radio Éireann, followed by *Opportunity Knocks* with Hughie Green and *Take Your Pick* with Michael Miles from Radio Luxembourg. Later, my uncles Eddie and Jackie would wander in for their tea, clasping large brown bags whose clinking noises betrayed their contents. My mother played the piano and at the request of Nana ('Vera, play your masterpiece'), rendered 'In an Eighteenth-Century Drawing Room', the popular name for one of the Mozart sonatas. Soon the party would be in full swing. Granda's party piece was 'Phil the Fluter's Ball'; Eddie would perform 'The Rose of Tralee' (but only with the lights out); Nana, with the aid of a small whiskey, could be persuaded to sing 'Genevieve'. My own speciality was 'Copenhagen', Jacinta gave her version of 'Softly Softly', while Joan avoided the vocal arts completely, contributing instead an Irish hornpipe. There was talk of the old days, of a family shop in Pimlico that sold pea soup from the windowsill; of a Balfe who had married Alec Byrne, who in turn was a relation of Gay Byrne; of cousins in New York and Bridie Velden and May O'Brien and aunts who weren't really aunts, just family friends.

Those Sunday-night parties cannot have been very different from gatherings all over Dublin during the previous fifty years. They were called 'hooleys' and on Christmas night, neighbours and family friends would crowd in, one in particular in blackface make-up who did a 'My Mammy' act. She subsequently appeared regularly on radio on the old-time variety show *Town Hall Tonight*. The small house was then filled to capacity when Uncle Tommy, Auntie Jean and their seven children, our first cousins, joined us. Marie, the eldest of the cousins, had spent some time in England and came back one Christmas with her boyfriend. They told tales of how Rock 'n' Roll was sweeping Britain and decided to put on a demonstration of jiving in front of the fire. My mother didn't have any rock tunes in her repertoire but 'Mountain Greenery', played slightly faster than Mel Tormé's current hit version, fulfilled the requirements.

The jiving was wonderful, with back flips, splits and over-the-shoulder throws, and it served as my introduction to the world of Rock 'n' Roll, long before I heard any records. I was, after all, only eleven.

It was, nonetheless, the beginning of Youth Culture. Dublin wrote herself into the history books in 1956 when the first pop riot in Europe occurred at the Carlton Cinema during the playing of 'Rock Around the Clock'. Seats were torn up and furnishings damaged by a small group of 'blackguards', as the cinema manager described them in a wonderful report for radio by Kevin O'Kelly; a report I've used many times subsequently in documentary features. 'Rock 'n' Roll has arrived,' Kevin announced ominously, and talked to clients of the local ballrooms who were ejected because of jiving. 'I told him I was only doin' the Charleston,' said one disgruntled patron, 'but he said "That's jivin' and out you go"'. These were the Teddy Boys, a species peculiar to Britain and Ireland, but never seen in the USA, the birthplace of pop music. They sported long jackets, drainpipe trousers, string ties, fluorescent shirts and socks. The hairstyle was the pompadour style inspired by Tony Curtis and the shoes were Bungees, with inch-high soles. The Teddy Boys were viewed with some suspicion, certainly in Thomas Court, but they were the first to pro-claim that they were different, that the times were changing, and that after the grey days of the post-war era, youth was coming into its inheritance.

Back home in Kilmacud, I saw my first Rock 'n' Roll record in our neigh-bours' house. Bill and Anna Price were a young couple with two small children. Bill worked 'in stamps' and they were British. They asked us in occasionally to see their television set. There was no Irish station at that time, but they had installed a roof aerial to pick up BBC coming from Wales. We watched this snowy haze with oblique figures barely discernible and convinced ourselves that the shadows we saw were Eamonn Andrews and Gilbert Harding and Lady Isobel Barnett on *What's My Line?* Bill took out an LP of 'Rock Around the Clock' by Bill Haley and The Comets, a red sleeve with cartoon graphics as I remember, and played it. I don't recall it making much of an impression on me, because whatever music chip in the brain activates music appreciation hadn't yet been turned on. I preferred 'The Ballad of Davy Crockett' and Jimmy Young's 'The Man from Laramie', to my ears a cowpoke who seemed to eat and drink adventure ('Danger was his Special Tea'). Across the road, on Matthew Forkin's gramophone, I preferred Victor Borge doing his 'Phonetic

Punctuation' and 'Oklahoma!' from the familiar soundtrack album with Gordon McCrae and Shirley Jones in the surrey with the fringe on top, against an orange sunset. It seemed that every house in the country had a copy, except ours. We hadn't even got a record player.

On the other side of our bungalow lived the Karrachs, an Austrian couple who had fled to Ireland when the Nazis invaded their country. Herbert was a jolly rotund man with excellent English. He was an importer of, as far as I could figure, novelty items, of the kind you used to find in Hector Grey's and can now purchase in your nearest convenient two-euro shop. In short, toys and trash. He was an ideal neighbour for young kids, though, and always brought little gifts on his visits. His wife was a more dour personality but to this day I can smell the odours of Jewish cooking emanating from her kitchen: strudels, goulashes, pickles, bagels. One Christmas Eve, my dad came home from an office party slightly the worse for wear, unusually for him. Mistaking the Karrachs' drive for his, he drove in and was surprised to find that his key didn't fit the hall door. He rang the bell and was even more surprised to find Mrs Karrach in her dressing gown, answering his door. When he saw the inside of the house, the penny dropped. He tried to recover, saying: 'I've come to wish you the compliments of the season. We don't see enough of each other. Why don't you come in to us for a drink tomorrow?' She thought he was mad.

This combination of suburban and city life continued, the rolling hills and woods of Kilmacud and Mount Merrion contrasting with the regular forays into the Liberties of Dublin City. Those happy and carefree days that were saddened when my best pals, Brian and Jimmy O'Connor, announced that the family was emigrating to Canada. It was the first time I had to say goodbye to people I liked and I was heartbroken.

∽ SOUNDTRACK ∽

Signature tunes gave programmes an instant identity, even though some tunes changed over the years. Here are some of the most famous.

- 'Someone to Watch Over Me'/Percy Faith Orchestra
  Hospitals Requests
- 'Fish and Sticks'/Eric Delaney Band
  Music on the Move
- 'Le Jet d'Eau'/Sydney Smith
  The Foley Family
- 'Three Little Words'
  Living with Lynch
- 'Gaîté Parisienne' (Offenbach)/Monte Carlo Symphony Orchestra
  Who's News?
- 'Candid Snap'/Frank Chacksfield Orchestra
- 'Winter Walkin''/Chet Atkins
  Morning Melody
- 'Lulu's Room'/André Previn (from the soundtrack of *Elmer Gantry)*
  Woman's Page with Frankie Byrne
- 'Perpetuum Mobile' (Strauss)/Mantovani Orchestra
  Question Time
- 'Cotton Candy'/Al Hirt
  Pop Call
- 'Holiday'/André Brasseur
  Terry Awhile
- 'Ja-Da'/Floyd Cramer
- 'Soul Limbo'/Booker T. and the MGs
- 'If I were a Buddy Rich Man'/Kenny Clare
  Saturday Spin
- 'Tico's Tune'/Geoff Love Orchestra
  The Gay Byrne Show
- 'L-Dopa'/Maynard Ferguson and Orchestra
  Discs-a-Gogan
- 'On the Street Where You Live'/Ray Conniff Orchestra
  On Balfe Street

Chapter 3 ~

SCREENS, SWIMS AND SCOUTS

Hollywood came to Kilmacud in 1955 with the opening of the Ormonde Cinema in Stillorgan village. I was there at six o'clock on the first night, for the first showing of the first picture. It was *The Grace Moore Story*, a film biography of the opera singer who was played by Kathryn Grayson. It was a dismal picture, certainly for a ten-year-old, but the cinema was beautiful with a wide CinemaScope screen and a lighting system that changed the colours of the transparent curtains. With enormous loudspeakers, music sounded like nothing I'd ever heard before. Winifred Atwell's Piano Party medleys blared out with a crispness and clarity that radio couldn't reproduce, notwithstanding the old singalong tunes being played on her 'other piano', the jangly one she left out in the rain.

The projectionist also favoured an organ version of 'In the Chapel in the Moonlight', a tune that was burned into my consciousness from constant exposure before the serial *Mysterious Island*. It was played on the lower octaves of the instrument, producing a sound that could rattle the teeth, an effect I tried to reproduce on our newly acquired piano at home. My mother was a fine pianist—she had also studied trombone in the school orchestra— and I had been persuaded to take piano lessons from Mrs O'Dwyer on Trees Road, Mount Merrion. Constant five-finger exercises and endless renditions of 'Wonderland Waltz' left me longing for something more exciting. Despite having been told that I would regret not continuing, I gave up after a while, on the basis that I wanted to be taught 'In the Mood' and not 'The Blue Bells of Scotland'. And sure enough, I regret not continuing, but to this day I can pick out any tune on the piano. I have a limited range of keys and accompanying chords, so I'm closer to Phil Coulter than to George Shearing.

The six o'clock show at the Ormonde during the week and the afternoon matinees at weekends were our chance to see the best gangster films of the 1950s. Today, they are called *film noir*, but to us they were just exciting police adventures, starring the then stalwarts of the B-Movies—Robert Mitchum, Lee Marvin, Richard Widmark, Raymond Burr and Edmond O'Brien. Susan Hayward, Lana Turner and Gloria Graham provided the female interest. The plots were engaging and seemingly authentic, although I was always a little sceptical of the lieutenant barking out orders like 'Get me a list of all the five-foot-two blondes in the Chicago area who were given a mink coat with matching hat in the last five years.' To this day, my loyalty to gangster thrillers is unswerving: give me a picture that opens with a black-and-white police car, siren wailing, racing through the dark streets of Manhattan or Los Angeles, and I care not who writes the nation's laws.

Occasionally, my father would take me to the later show at eight o'clock and I sat with the grown-ups watching Paul Newman, in his first major role, playing the boxer Rocky Graziano in *Somebody Up There Likes Me*, Marlon Brando in *On the Waterfront* and Russ Tamblyn in *High School Confidential*, notable for its explosive opening sequence with Jerry Lee Lewis pounding the piano during the title song. It was issued in 1958 and was a poor imitation of *Blackboard Jungle* three years earlier, the film renowned for introducing 'Rock Around the Clock' over the titles.

All these films were in black-and-white and their harsh lighting and exaggerated shadows added to the feeling of suspense and, occasionally, terror. From the British studios came the half-hour series *Scotland Yard*. 'Just a stone's throw from the Houses of Parliament, lies the Criminal Records Department of Scotland Yard,' intoned the narrator, before Edgar Lustgarten introduced each episode based on real cases and usually featuring Russell Napier as Superintendent Duggan. Short, efficient, low-budget pictures with a repertory company of regular actors, they were staple fare in the 1950s as a prologue to The Big Picture. Occasionally, we'd spot an Irish actor—Eddie Byrne or Joe Linnane—in the role of a policeman.

The film that scared me most was also in monochrome. *The Spiral Staircase* came out our way long after it had been made in 1946. It was a thriller, set in a large mansion around 1915, in which Dorothy Maguire played a deaf mute who had attracted the attentions of a serial killer, whom, we suspected, was now one of the residents of the house. We didn't know the identity of the murderer, but to indicate him observing his intended victim, the camera focused on a single eye in the darkness. Slowly the eye got bigger and bigger, until it filled the entire screen. It was terrifying. For years afterwards I had nightmares, often waking up in a cold sweat thinking that the eye was coming to get me. Some nights, the effect was exacerbated by two cats wailing on the wall outside my bedroom. Cats and eyes. Don't like 'em.

The Ormonde wasn't the only institution to arrive in the area in the mid-1950s. The Christian Brothers had set up shop in 1951 by opening a secondary school with a single class in Oatlands College, Mount Merrion. In 1955, they built a new primary school, Saint Mary's, beside the old house that served as a monastery, and I was enrolled in Third Class. It was opened by the Archbishop of Dublin, John Charles McQuaid, who stayed for lunch that mysteriously appeared in a classroom, served by a group of nuns who had equally manifested themselves from out of nowhere.

I wasn't sorry to leave Kilmacud Boys' National School for a brand new school in pleasant grounds, with bright and airy rooms, working toilets and a large hall. I was there on the morning of 1 December 1956 when the whole school celebrated Ronnie Delaney winning a Gold Medal in the 1,500 metres race in the Melbourne Olympic Games. My father had stayed up all night to hear the race on the radio. It seemed to be the first time that Ireland had made any impact on the world stage and the Christian Brothers rightly made sure we understood its import.

My father had been a well-known soccer player for St James's Gate, but the football gene had skipped a generation in my case. Despite the best efforts of Brother Power to encourage me, I could see no value in getting my shins kicked or shoulder dislocated to satisfy school policy that all pupils should play Gaelic football. Brother Power was probably only in his twenties at the time, but some-how—like many before and after him—seemed to share Éamon de Valera's dictum that true Irishness was manifest only in 'the contests of athletic youths'. My view was that Irishness was equally manifest in going to the pictures, or reading, or listening to the radio, or lying in bed. Of course, being eleven years old, I kept my opinions to myself. It was as well not to challenge the Brothers with contrary views, lest their vocation (or my well-being) be compromised.

Academically, I did well. Every term, Brother Magee put up cash awards for the Christmas exams and I regularly walked away with the first prize of ten shillings. I was good at Irish and Maths, better at English composition. The constant drilling of the basics of English grammar and construction is responsible for thousands of past pupils of the Christian Brothers being able to express themselves efficiently, in both spoken and written English. In a world obscured by business-speak and psychobabble, it's still hard to beat the simple declarative sentence.

My first public performance was in the qualifying rounds for a Feis Ceoil in the Parish Hall, Mount Merrion. Brother Power tried to calm me before I went on stage, by encouraging me to breathe deeply. He settled for just breathing, as I was apparently holding my breath for minutes at a time. In some sort of trance, I sang 'Báidín Fheidlimidh', my boyish treble echoing around the dusty hall. It was my first time on a stage and it cannot be said that my efforts were crowned with success. I was placed well down the field. Nor was I attracted to a life on the stage. It seemed to be a dangerous business, particularly for the respiratory system.

Some physical exercise was achieved by swimming. I learned to swim in Poulshone, about a mile south of Courtown, on the coast road to Wexford. It was so far away from Stillorgan that the Morris Minor underwent a complete service before undertaking the arduous journey of some fifty miles. The journey, complete with enforced picnic on the Long Hill, seemed to take the entire day, but the first sight of the sea at the pretty resort town of Courtown Harbour was joyous. Poulshone was a magical place, a small cove with cottages and holiday bungalows and a sandy beach. It wasn't quite Malibu, but it had its own celebrity in Paddy Crosbie, who spent entire summers there, developing a Hollywood tan. (Paddy was an early radio personality who had parleyed his experience as a teacher in North Brunswick Street National School into a schoolboy act in places like the Theatre Royal and the Capitol, not unlike the 'Bottler' act since done by Brendan Grace. That, in turn, led to his devising and presenting conversations with school children in *The School Around the Corner* on Radio Éireann, one of many unique radio formats to come out of Ireland, later transferring to Telefís Éireann to become Irish television's highest rated programme in the first week of its service.)

We stayed a few hundred yards up the road from the beach in a guesthouse run by the Hobbs family. It was a fine manor house, with a gravel drive and a large tree outside. There was a swing attached to the tree and, to get first place ahead of my sisters and the other children staying there, I would rise at first light and swing away uninterrupted for hours on end. In my mind, I can still see a startlingly blue early-morning sky with the sun beaming down on the gravel path, the field of hay to the side and the lush green trees. In the house, Mrs Hobbs was preparing breakfast and the smell of frying bacon mingled with the smell of freshly mown hay. From the farmyard beside the house came the sounds of the cows being milked and the hens complaining as eggs were collected from the henhouse. A whole day of sunshine and swimming lay ahead and all was right with the world.

Summer nights were a ritual in themselves. My sisters and I would be dropped off at the carnival in the town while my mother and father went for a drink in the Bayview or Taravie Hotel with some of the other parents. As Kay Starr belted out 'The Wheel of Fortune' on the loudspeaker system, we swung on the chair-o-planes, got dizzy on the roundabout or crashed into each other on the bumpers. We ate candyfloss and rounded off the night playing Pongo, an early version of Bingo. My parents would join us for a while, mainly to see that we were in one piece, and my mother would use the opportunity to place orders for prizes in the event that we won anything at Pongo. So it was that the three of us eschewed highly desirable items like the *School Friend Annual* or cowboy outfits or talking dolls in favour of double saucepans, clothes brushes and dressing-table sets made from pink glass. We made our way back to Poulshone in the descending darkness, walking in the middle of the road with all the other child residents of the Hobbs house. Cars were rare and we felt perfectly safe and very grown up. Back in the dining room, supper for the children was laid out: a big jug of milk, slightly warm from the evening milking, and plates of soda bread spread with the farm's own country butter.

I don't think I tasted food as delicious as that in Wexford in the 1950s. The beef didn't taste like it did at home, the soups were of a kind not encountered in Dublin. Even the vegetables tasted different. It was, I suppose, the kind of pure food we now call Organic. The food was equally good north and south of Courtown. Occasionally, we went to a guesthouse run by the Grace family in Ballymoney, just north of Courtown, probably because we left it too late to get a place in the Hobbs house. The food there was also wonderful, as well as plentiful. I'm intrigued as to why food is such a memory of those times and why it made such a strong impression on me. It may be that we were always slightly hungry at home. We were well fed, but certainly not stuffed. It's a curious thing that in the comics we read in the 1950s, *The Beano* and *The Dandy*, the best reward for good work by the Bash Street Kids, or Lord Snooty, or Dennis the Menace was a good feed of egg and chips. Desperate Dan's favourite treat, of course, was a large portion of cow pie. Food was to be prized.

One year we ventured down as far as Blackwater, a few miles beyond Poulshone. It was a working farm, with a large farmhouse set close to the beach. I helped to make butter, going through the process of churning and shaping the finished product in the dairy. I even drank the buttermilk, agreeing with the woman of the house that while it was very nourishing, a little went a long way. The house had not yet been electrified, and the farm was as it had been for the previous hundred years. There were oil lamps and a huge fire in the kitchen, even in the height of summer, as much for light as for heating and cooking.

They had just finished building a henhouse of concrete blocks, no more than twelve feet square, and, to celebrate the event before the new residents took over, a céilí was held. It was like something out of Percy French's time; a fiddler and accordionist squeezed into one corner, fortified with bottles of stout, while the neighbours came from all over. Along the road, as evening fell, you could see them approaching from the nearby houses and farms, with the occasional torch lighting the way along the dusty roads and tracks. They squeezed in and danced jigs and reels, waltzes and foxtrots until the early hours, dozens of happy people in their best clothes, the women in their floral dresses and open white sandals, the men in their suits with the tie left out over the jumper, to look smart. The musicians were encouraged with fresh supplies of drink, to ensure 'the better would the music be for batterin' the floor'. Whenever my grandfather sang 'Phil The Fluter's Ball' at those Sunday-night parties, I was transported back instantly to the new henhouse in Blackwater, with its music and laughter and Tilley lamps to light the darkness.

There was some kind of *cause célèbre* that year in Blackwater, about which my father never spoke much. It seemed to involve the men of the farmhouse, a few drinks in the village pub with my father, a walk home along a river, the procuring of a salmon by means not approved in The Fisheries and Gaming Act, the arrival of a bailiff and subsequent consultations with the local sergeant. The name of Donagh McDonagh was invoked in that connection, either as the complainant or as a responsible officer of the court. I got the impression that a fine was paid at a later stage, but the whole episode was shrouded in mystery. As a postscript, a clue may be garnered from the subsequent appearance of Donagh McDonogh on Telefís Éireann presenting a quiz game. He was instantly turned off, as 'we don't want to watch that bowsie.'

Back home, we swam in Killiney, White Rock and Seapoint. On summer evenings, after tea, my father would round us up and head for the water around eight o'clock. The sun had died, but the water was certainly refreshing, often to the point of numbness, bordering on frostbite. At weekends, there were picnics to Brittas Bay and Silver Strand.

Otherwise, my pals and I went to Blackrock Baths in the long hot summers of the late 1950s. I cannot hear Bobby Darin singing 'Dream Lover', one of the best pop records ever made, without conjuring up an image of those sparkling whitewashed walls, the high diving boards in a tower and the three-, four- and six-foot pools. Out of the loudspeakers came the pop hits by Cliff Richard and Connie Francis and Craig Douglas. Sitting in the sun and listening to the music felt to us a little like California, the first awareness that maybe it was going to be a good time to be young. The main problem with Blackrock Baths was that they were in Blackrock. From Kilmacud, it took a good hour to walk there, all the way down the interminable Mount Merrion Avenue, and back up again in blazing sunshine, relieved only by an ice pop from the Lido Café.

I was becoming a good swimmer, though, my prowess enhanced by further swimming practice during school time. To keep the Brothers off my back as much as anything else, I had signed up for swimming lessons, and every Saturday morning some of the class trooped into Tara Street Public Baths. A Victorian building, it provided bathing facilities for Dubliners without their own baths, many coming from nearby tenement houses. It housed a number of pools with an overpowering smell of chlorine. There were separate baths for washing, but we always got the impression that some customers used the swimming pools as much for hygiene as for recreation. Some even brought soap, an unnecessary luxury, as the amount of disinfectant in the water would have eliminated the bubonic plague, never mind body odour. We came out of the pool with skin shrunk like prunes and eyes blazing red from the near-toxic water.

The star swimmer was my new pal, Liam Donaldson, who eventually ended up as a diver in the Irish Naval Service and rose to high rank as a senior officer. Liam's father, Bill, was a friend of my father and they regularly walked down to Boland's Pub in Stillorgan for an evening pint or two. We used family friendship to good effect when I successfully got money for the six o'clock show in the Ormonde, by pointing out that Liam was going and I should be able to go too. He, likewise, pitched the same argument to his mother, using me as the excuse. It worked well until we got a phone and the facts could be checked. My other friend was Barry Gillen, a neighbour of Liam on Clonmore Road, Mount Merrion. We were all pupils of St Mary's Primary School and we also became founding members of the 86th Dublin Troop of the Catholic Boy Scouts of Ireland.

I had been training as an altar boy at Kilmacud Church, memorising the De Profundis and Hail Holy Queen and the exact sequence of the bells at the Elevation. The Mass was still in Latin and the priest still had his back to the congregation. Some people are still nostalgic for the Latin Mass, and its slightly arcane ceremony was certainly impressive, but when the vernacular was introduced it was widely welcomed, even if it reduced the prestige of the priest by making his utterings understandable to the common folk.

My father gave me a choice: the black soutane and white stole needed for altar duty or a scout uniform, but he could not afford both. The decision was easy and so on 5 October 1958, I was invested into the Beaver Patrol, along with Barry Gillen as Patrol Leader, Finbarr Devine as Assistant Patrol Leader, with Liam Donaldson, Tony Branagan, Philip Heneghan, Leonard Fowler and me making up the foot soldiers. Resplendent in grey shirt, navy corduroy shorts and beret, neckerchief in the troop colours of brown and white, fastened with a woggle, we looked a picture.

Our headquarters was a damp dungeon under the old church in Mount Merrion. There our scoutmaster, Joe Coghlan, with occasional support from Commissioner Willie Potts, trained us in knot-making, semaphore, first aid, cooking, compass points, knife and axe expertise, thrift, tracking, observation and all the skills needed to be model citizens. I can still make a reef knot, signal sos in semaphore and execute a fireman's lift, although no set of circumstances so bizarre has yet arisen as to prove them necessary.

Great emphasis was placed on hygiene and internal cleanliness, with the literature containing dire warnings about drinking and smoking: 'Alcohol in excess has a depressing effect and dulls the senses and is responsible for a great deal of sorrow and unhappiness—even madness. Nicotine, the poison in tobacco, is dangerous to growing boys.' Whatever impression these admonitions made on thirteen-year-olds, they were happily ignored when we became all growed up.

We went on lengthy hikes walking the byways of Wicklow in all weathers. There were regular visits to Larch Hill, a large estate in the foothills of the Dublin Mountains originally owned by Lord Glenavy, the father of the writer Patrick Campbell, and donated to the Scout movement as its national campsite.

Our first annual camp, in July 1959, was to Glenstal Abbey in Murroe, outside Limerick City. Our first time away from home was shared with a troop from Westland Row, Dublin. I became the cook for our patrol, serving roast beef, potatoes and cabbage from an open fire and presenting, as Commissioner Potts publicly averred, 'the best and most lump-free custard' he had ever had. Unfortunately, doubtless due to an unenlightened hierarchy, there was no Scout Badge for custard making.

Between the two troops, there were probably forty boys present. We swam in the mud-coloured lake and walked deep into a jungle-like wood to find, unexpectedly, a rushing river with a waterfall, like something out of the Tarzan films. It was icy, but exhilarating. At night, we sat around a huge campfire singing 'There were rats, rats, big as bloody cats in the Quartermaster's Stores' and all the many verses of Slim Dusty's current hit, 'The Pub with No Beer'.

One afternoon, we hiked into Limerick City to visit the cinema. On the outskirts, we asked for directions.

'Turn left at the traffic lights,' a local said.

'Which traffic lights?' we asked.

'Don't worry,' said he, 'there's only the one.'

The biggest adventure was akin to a military manoeuvre. After dark, twenty of the boys were taken by one of the scoutmasters to a secret location. They left discreet markings, so the other contingent could eventually track them.

They had taken possession of a hill and placed sentries all around it. I was in the second company, whose task was to rescue their flag. For added effect, when we reached and took over one of the enemy sites, there was a maroon in place, a firework which exploded with a loud bang when hit with a mallet. Well after two o'clock in the morning, we crept up like Apache Indians and, accompanied by loud explosions, secured the top of the hill.

By 1960, four of the original members had become Patrol Leaders. I was in charge of the Wolf Patrol, whilst also acting as Scribe at the grandiosely named Courts of Honour. These were leaders meeting to sort out disciplinary matters and troop business. One minute taken from the meeting of 2 April 1960 admonished a certain Richard Ryan, who was 'to buck up, as he had no respect for Patrol Leaders'. The same Mr Ryan presented me with a signed bookmark from Lourdes bearing the legend 'At the Blessed Grotto I have prayed for you'. Whether this proof of divine supplication was prompted by repentance of his attitude toward his betters, or was a large hint that he viewed our disciplinary regime with some disdain, was not clear. Such creative ambiguity could, perhaps, have been an early indication of his vocation. Richard Ryan subsequently became a poet and a diplomat, serving his country in embassies all over the world and distinguishing himself particularly in the Irish Embassy in London, working on the Northern Ireland settlement while, in his own words, 'dining for Ireland'. He was latterly appointed as Ireland's Ambassador to the United Nations.

∽ SOUNDTRACK ∽

Ireland's First Top Ten Chart

Ireland's first chart show was introduced by Harry Thuillier, compiled by Jimmy Magee and produced by Róisín Lorigan. It was broadcast on Monday, 1 October 1962 at 6.45 p.m. on Radio Éireann.

1. 'She's Not You'/Elvis Presley
2. 'Wolverton Mountain'/Claude King
3. 'Things'/Bobby Darin
4. 'You Don't Know Me'/Ray Charles
5. 'Sheila'/Tommy Roe
6. 'Spanish Harlem'/Jimmy Justice
7. 'Roses are Red'/Ronnie Carroll
8. 'Adios Amigo'/Jim Reeves
9. 'Speedy Gonzales'/Pat Boone
10. 'It'll be Me'/Cliff Richard

Ireland's First No. 1 Hits by Irish Artists

It took almost a year for an Irish act to reach the No. 1 spot in Ireland's Top Ten. All were showband singers, the unlikely founders of Ireland's successful music industry.

- 06.09.63 'Kiss Me Quick'/Brendan Bowyer and the Royal Showband
- 27.12.63 'No More'/Brendan Bowyer and the Royal Showband
- 03.01.64 'There's Always Me'/Dickie Rock and the Miami Showband
- 29.05.64 'Fallen Star'/Eileen Reid and the Cadets (Joint No. 1) with:
- 29.05.64 'I'm Yours'/Dickie Rock and the Miami Showband (Joint No. 1)
- 03.07.64 'Bless You'/Brendan Bowyer and the Royal Showband
- 30.10.64 'Candy Store'/Dickie Rock and the Miami Showband
- 11.12.64 'Down Came the Rain'/Butch Moore and the Capitol Showband
- 18.01.65 'The Hucklebuck'/Brendan Bowyer and the Royal Showband
- 08.03.65 'Born to Be With You'/Butch Moore and the Capitol Showband

Chapter 4 ❧

| ROCK, RECORDS AND RADIO

On 3 February 1959, Barry Gillen told me that he had heard terrible news on the radio: Buddy Holly had died in a plane crash. I didn't admit at the time that I wasn't quite sure who Buddy Holly was. Barry was slightly ahead of me in the finer points of Rock 'n' Roll and had even acquired a long-playing record of Buddy and the Crickets. The date was famously immortalised by Don McLean as 'the day the music died', but that year marked the genesis of music awareness on my part.

Rock 'n' Roll music was a great liberating force for youth. Up to then, the impetus was with the record companies and the song publishing houses, who, between them, formed the music establishment. The term 'Tin Pan Alley' described them, so coined by a journalist, Monroe Rosenfeld, who thought that the incessant sound of tinny pianos in the song publishing houses in New York's 42nd Street resembled the clatter of tin pans. When, in a dispute about royalties, the song publishers banned their songs from being played on radio in the 1940s, local broadcasters turned to non-copyrighted music, clearing the way for white country music and black Rhythm 'n' Blues to prosper. And so, Bill Haley, Elvis Presley, Buddy Holly, Chuck Berry, Fats Domino, Jerry Lee Lewis and scores of others filled the gap, proving that the newest trends came from the street or the country roads, not from the professional writers and performers in the high-rise buildings. In time, Tin Pan Alley integrated, bought out, or blatantly copied the trends—but they never started them. It's a cycle that continues to this day, but while the new arrivals have the initiative, it's a confirmation that amateurs can take on the professionals. Besides, it's always well to remember that 'amateur' comes from the Latin verb 'to love', describing people who do things because they like doing them.

Of course, in 1959 we didn't know this; we had just become teenagers and, like millions before and since, were at the age when youngsters begin to notice pop music. Back in the scout den, we had ended our decorating efforts by banging empty paint tins with trowels and paintbrushes to provide a percussion accompaniment to our vocals on 'Last Train to San Fernando' and 'Does Your Chewing Gum Lose its Flavour on the Bedpost Overnight?', the big hits of the Skiffle Era by Johnny Duncan and Lonnie Donegan, respectively. Skiffle was a do-it-yourself kind of music, characterised by rhythm guitars, washboards and a tea-chest bass, ideal for noisy music making. We were also much taken by Dee Clarke's 'Just Keep it Up' and 'Hoots Mon' by Lord Rockingham's Eleven.

The scout den was under the Old Church in Mount Merrion, recently vacated when the huge new church, St Theresa's, was completed on the top of the hill. The whole complex had originally been the site of a manor house and estate so large that the entire mile-long Mount Merrion Avenue was its drive-way. Some of the outbuildings survived and one of them became the Parish Hall, the same spot where I sang in the Feis. Because of its original use, the hall became known to most of south Dublin as The Barn.

We would climb the outside fire escape of The Barn to peep through a hole in the door at the Saturday Night Dance. The scene was magical: young men in their best suits and girls in their wide skirts jiving under red-shaded lights to real musicians. The Bob Ormsby Band, a motley outfit sporting a Hawaiian guitar, was a regular attraction as were The Viscounts, probably the most popular group of the time. The Viscounts, named for the sleek planes recently acquired by Aer Lingus, were the last word in cool. Their leader, who fronted the band as both vocalist and drummer, was Paul Russell, and John Curran, Tommy Ellis and Jim Doherty made up the balance. They favoured the pop hits of the day, all performed with a high degree of musicianship and flair. All the members carved long careers in the business and Jim Doherty, later one of Ireland's most accomplished jazz musicians, remembers that the last arrangement he did for The Viscounts was in October 1962. It was 'Love Me Do', a minor hit in Britain for a new group called The Beatles and, as Jim put it, 'We left and let them take over.'

The dance hall eventually moved across the car park to take up residence in the Old Church and, in an early example of brand management, retained the name The Barn.

Instead of peeping through the hole in the door, we now had a bird's-eye view of the merriment as the scout den provided access to the ceiling space over the stage. We could now listen to the bands in relative, if slightly dizzying, comfort. We were still too young to attend formally, having acquired long trousers only recently. The dances were run under the auspices of the Espoir Youth Club, inaugurated by the local curate, Fr Paddy Devine. The club also had branched into marine sports by forming the Espoir Canoe Club in Seapoint. When they weren't dancing or canoeing, they were singing in the church choir. My sister, Joan, was a member and the committee members were common to both wings of the club; essentially the Canoe Club ran the dances.

But if I couldn't go to the dance, the dance could come to me. One weekend in 1959, Joan had persuaded our parents to hold a party in our house. The dining room was cleared of furniture and a red bulb installed to provide a sultry ambience for dancing. Vast quantities of egg rolls, cocktail sausages and chocolate Krispies were prepared for the guests, with nothing more stimulating than orange drink to quench the thirst.

The missing ingredient was the music. We had no record player, but a solution was provided by the loan of a pick-up from one of the guests. It was only a turntable and needed to be plugged into the radio to amplify the sound, but I was fascinated by it, intrigued by the record changer that allowed you to stack six 78rpm records and watch them drop onto the turntable with a clunk. And they were loud: Elvis belting out 'I Need Your Love Tonight' and 'A Fool Such As I' and 'I Got Stung'; Bobby Day chirping 'Rockin' Robin'; Buddy Holly averring bravely that 'It Doesn't Matter Anymore'; Pat Boone assuring us that everyone's gonna have 'A Wonderful Time Up There' and Connie Francis accusing her beloved of infidelity with 'Lipstick on Your Collar'. Everyone knew the words and sang along happily as they bopped. There were Frank Crowley, John O'Gorman, Aileen Cronin, Ruth Richardson, Andy Maher, Ted Carroll and others. Andy later became a lifelong friend, and Ted Carroll, for a time a boyfriend of Joan's, entered the music business subsequently, managing Thin Lizzy and founding Ace Records. Much the same crowd came to an almost identical party on the snowy evening of 31 December 1961, to watch the crisp pictures at the opening of Telefís Éireann.

But that weekend, I was still fascinated by the record player. It stayed in our house for a few days and I was trying to figure out an important conundrum. Listening to the radio, I had noted that as soon as the announcer had stopped talking, the record would start immediately. At home, it had to be stacked and dropped and then the arm would snake out and drop the stylus on the record, taking its own sweet time while it found the first groove. There had to be a better way, so I experimented by placing the record directly on the turntable, dropping the arm onto the record and winding it forward by hand until I heard the first notes of music. Then, to avoid the slowness of the turntable coming up to speed, I wound back the turntable by a complete revolution. By turning on the motor, the music was on speed by the time the stylus hit the first note. This, I later found, was pretty much what radio stations had been doing for years.

Then, in time for Christmas 1959, we got our own record player: a Bush turntable in a Plessey mahogany cabinet. The speakers were small, so you couldn't get wall-shaking volume, but it did the job. The first record in the family collection, chosen by my father, was 'Mack the Knife' by Bobby Darin, which turned out to be the best-selling single of the Rock 'n' Roll era, out-selling Elvis, Fats Domino, Bill Haley and all the other rockers. I was much taken by its style and verve, with Bobby at the top of his game and a splendid big band arrangement by Richard Wess disguising the limitations of the song, essentially four lines repeated. It's a record I've loved ever since and it still sounds as fresh as when I first heard it, which is, I suppose, the definition of a true classic.

More big band music arrived with the first long-playing record acquired for the family collection. It was the soundtrack to *The Glenn Miller Story*, in which James Stewart played the bandleader who perished in a plane crash at the end of the war. It was my mother's favourite film at the time, and it may have been the endless playing of 'In the Mood' and 'American Patrol' that gave me a love for big band music. Perhaps it was the sheer value of hearing eighteen musicians playing orchestrations that were mathematically worked out, while leaving room for improvisation and passion, that appealed to some logical and creative chips embedded in my brain.

My musical education was enhanced by a set of twelve long-playing records of classical music acquired from *Reader's Digest* and featuring all the popular classics by Rossini, Brahms, Bizet, Liszt, Mozart, Smetana... and that crowd. A satisfying startle could be achieved on visitors to the house by ask-ing them if they liked Tchaikovsky and then suddenly dropping the needle onto the last part of the 1812 Overture, the bit where loud cannons and gun-fire almost drowned the orchestra. Many a china cup, as well as the walls of Moscow, bit the dust during those musical recitals.

The first record I paid money for was 'What do You Want?' by Adam Faith, with its distinctive string accompaniment by the John Barry Orchestra. The little pizzicato string motif after the first verse always sent a tingle down my spine, just as George Shearing's key change in Nat King Cole's 'Let There be Love' and the modulation into the bridge of 'Say I Won't be There' by The Springfields did later. Emile Ford and the Checkmates expanded the col-lection with 'What Do You Want To Make Those Eyes At Me For?' and Michael Holliday brought my record library to three with 'Starry Eyed', an attractive ditty that (for trivia fans) became the first No. 1 record of the 1960s. Later, I saved up my pocket money to buy two records that I had to have: 'Cathy's Clown' by the Everly Brothers and 'Apache' by The Shadows.

The only record shops were in Dublin City and I traipsed in most days after school to the record shop in Switzer's department store to enquire. I even remember the record number of the Everly Brothers song—wb1—the first single issued on the Warner Bros. label. The fragrant, if slightly mature, assistant told me that they would be getting it in when there were enough orders for it. They had, however, got 'Apache'. I encouraged her to produce it instantly. When it arrived, it wasn't on the green Columbia label it should have been on; it was on the orange Top Rank label. It was, horror of horrors, the Bert Weedon version and not the authentic reading by The Shadows. Declining to enter an argument about the obvious merits of the original version compared to one by the hack who spent his time writing amaze-your-friends-by-learning-the-guitar-in-three-days tutors, I took my business elsewhere and tracked down the required pieces in a shop more attuned to the requirements of the discerning music devotee.

But if we couldn't afford to buy many records—they cost five shillings and threepence, after all—we could get them for free on the radio. Radio Éireann had virtually ignored pop music, not through any sense of malevolence but, rather, through plain indifference. It was a civil service organisation, a branch of the Department of Posts and Telegraphs, and there was no one there to promote the cause of pop music. Radio Éireann had been stung by the outcry against jazz music in the 1930s, when even Bing Crosby was banned as being 'slightly decadent'. Jazz records were occasionally played, but when the Gramophone Library purchased them, they were not catalogued and put on the shelves as other records; instead they were put in a box under a desk and, at the end of the year, they were donated to charitable institutions.

The bbc Light Programme was not much better. It had a couple of hours at the weekend on *Saturday Club* and *Easy Beat*, both introduced by Brian Matthew, where you could hear pop music, but in a peculiar bbc hybrid of live performances and records. It was prompted by needle-time restrictions, an agreement with the Musicians' Union that gave work to its members. So, instead of hearing, say, 'That'll be the Day' by Buddy Holly, you could hear it by paid-up union members like The Dallas Boys with the Oscar Rabin Band. Dire.

The most attractive programmes for listeners to the home station were the sponsored programmes. Fifteen minutes long, they ran in the mornings from 8.15 to 9.00 and in the afternoons from 1.00 to 2.30. They were produced by commercial firms who paid airtime to Radio Éireann and undertook to supply the programme through its advertising agency. Some programmes were live, with facilities supplied by the station, while others were pre-recorded in the few recording studios around town. The programme styles were varied—they had to be, to distinguish them from the other sponsors—and the station had final editorial say in the content. The formats covered music of all styles, beauty advice, farming information, cookery, quiz shows, short stories, agony aunts and drama serials, like *The Dalys of Honeydew Farm* and the daddy of them all, *The Kennedys of Castleross*.

Long before audience research gave us statistics on listener reaction, *The Kennedys* was undoubtedly the most popular radio programme in Ireland. It was sponsored by Fry-Cadbury and written by Hugh Leonard, under his real name of John Keyes Byrne, and Mark Grantham, an American studying in Ireland. Marie Kean played the shopkeeper and matriarch, Mrs Kennedy, while T.P. McKenna and Vincent Dowling played her sons, Brian and Christy. An indication of its popularity may be gathered from one famous episode, 'The Reading of the Will', a *denouement* that had been presaged for weeks. As the programme went out at one o'clock, we were let off school ten minutes early to be home in time. There were few people on the streets and country roads, and offices were deserted as everyone got near a radio to hear who got the goodies in the divvy-up of the will. Only episodes in television programmes like the capture of the one-armed man in *The Fugitive* and the revelation of who shot JR in *Dallas* came near to the effect a radio drama had on an Irish audience. A water-cooler moment, if we had had them.

The different signature tunes for sponsored programmes acted as both a clock and a calendar. The music would tell you what time it was and what day it was. Mondays, though, were a drag; they had saved the most turgid offerings for the worst day of the week, when a little uplifting entertainment or music might have helped with the blues. At 8.15, Micheál O'Hehir, with a voice like a laser beam, would present the *Vaseline Sports Parade*, followed by *Clár Gael Linn*, a programme of Irish music introduced by Pádraig Ó Raghallaigh, an ex-announcer with one of the most beautiful voices in radio. The music wasn't to my liking, although I still have a soft spot for Seán 'ac Donncha's unaccompanied singing of 'Bean Pháidín'. One brave experiment was the ill-starred 'Gael Linn Pops', songs in the modern idiom sung in Irish, and audiences who were subjected to 'Bí Liom' by Seán Fagan or 'An Bhfuil an Fonn Sin Ort?' by Sonny Knowles have rarely been the better for it. The latter song, which translates as 'Are You in the Mood?' with music by Ian Henry and words by Niall Toibín, marked the recording debut of Louis Stewart, ace jazz guitarist.

Only when Pádraig started playing the music from *Mise Éire* by Seán Ó Riada, with its haunting theme on French horn, did I take notice of Irish music.

The arrangements by Ó Riada of Irish folk tunes in an orchestral setting were most attractive and, far from diminishing them, revealed their inherent stature and beauty. If there had been an Irish Top Twenty at the time, I've no doubt that this landmark recording would have been No. 1 for months on end. The extended-play record appeared to be in every house in the country.

Monday sponsored programmes continued in the afternoon with *The Fruitfield Information Desk*, a programme of household hints that answered listener queries (somewhat testily, I've often felt) with bizarre recipes that invariably included 'the white of an egg, bicarbonate of soda and vinegar' as the answer to most complaints, including How to Get Bloodstains Off a First Communion Dress or How to Remove Footprints From a Georgian Ceiling. That programme was followed by *The Mitchelstown Programme* featuring Richard Fitzgerald and his céilí band, while the compere, Noel Andrews, exhorted us to consume Three Counties, Mandeville and Calvita Cheese in increasing quantities, all the better to be 'slim, trim and brimful of energy'. Cheese makes you slim, eh?

Over the rest of the week, other sponsored programmes were presented by a succession of established radio comperes: Harry Thuillier, Joe Linnane, Eddie Golden, Val Joyce, Bart Bastable, Roy Croft, Ronnie Walsh, Denis Brennan, Pat Layde, Terry O'Sullivan and Cecil Barror, with his famous slogan for Bird's Custard and Bird's Jelly-de-Luxe, 'After all, you do want the best, don't you?' But for teenagers like us, looking for a supply of pop music, the programme not to be missed was *The Donnelly's Programme* on Saturday lunchtime at 1.15. It was based on the new record releases and was introduced by Niall Boden with his catchphrase 'Hello There'. Niall sounded like a real disc jockey, with his slight Newry accent sounding almost transatlantic. He had been in radio for years, producing sponsored programmes and radio features like *Who's News?*, and discovered Val Doonican, singing on the seafront in Bray. He hired him to sing the jingle for Donnelly's sausages, to the tune of 'The Mexican Hat Dance':

Well, it's true it's the talk of the nation
A sausage excitingly new,
So new that it's caused a sensation
And Donnelly's make it for you.

Another must-hear Niall Boden programme at one o'clock on Friday lunchtime was *Top Ten Tips*, a pop record review programme sponsored by Chivers and obviously aimed at the younger jelly-maker. The panel comprised a dour character call Bill, a girl whose name I've forgotten and John McColgan, whom I later discovered had been hired by Niall Boden on the long corridor in Radio Éireann where John worked as a boy messenger.

Sponsored programmes were also indirectly linked to the most successful comedy programme ever broadcast by Radio Éireann. *Living with Lynch* came on the air in 1955, based around the multi-talented Joe Lynch, written by Dermot Doolan and Michael McGarry and produced by Ronnie Walsh. The overall influences on the programme were decidedly American and British and the cast and company were insistent that it would not be produced or recorded under the auspices of RÉ; they didn't want the dead hand of the civil service on their comedy. So, using the expertise gathered from the commercial programme sector, they recorded the show in front of a live audience in places like the Ballerina Ballroom and presented the tape to the station, just like a sponsored programme. Its popularity has never quite been matched and it became an indispensable part of Sunday lunchtime, its catchphrases like 'Ah, ya heard it before Joe' and 'What about the workin' man?' and 'Not on your nanny!' becoming common currency all over the country. In those pre-television days, Joe Lynch—actor, comedian and singer—became the biggest thing in Ireland.

Apart from sponsored programmes, the only place you'd hear a bit of pop music was on *Hospitals Requests*. Its origins go back to the time after the war and it was designed as a service to listeners who wanted to keep in touch with relatives and friends in hospital. At a time when cars were scarce, public transport skimpy and telephones almost non-existent, it came into its own during the outbreak of tuberculosis in the 1950s when relatives could be a hundred miles away from their loved one in hospital. The station announcers presented the programme between 1.00 and 2.30 on Wednesdays and it was obvious that many of their own choices were included. John Skehan, Una Sheehy and Terry Wogan always included some good pop songs, but the old chestnuts, 'Go Thoughts on Golden Wings', 'The Humming Chorus' or 'Bring Flowers of the Rarest', usually outnumbered them. We discovered the names of the announcers only later; but in those days they were anonymous, referring to themselves only as 'your *Hospitals Requests* announcer'. The Cult of the Personality wasn't exactly rampant in Radio Éireann.

So, daytime radio listening was confined to the morning and lunchtime sponsored programmes from Radio Éireann and weekend programmes from the BBC Light Programme. At night, though, from six o'clock on, a whole new choice opened up. A gong sounded, then Barry Alldis said the magic words: 'For all that's worthwhile, your radio dial is on 208—Radio Luxembourg'.

Their theme tune, 'The Luxembourg Waltz' played by Frank Chacksfield, struck up and for the rest of the evening we were in heaven.

Luxembourg had changed since the days of *Take Your Pick* and *Opportunity Knocks* and *The Ovaltineys*. It had become a pop music station, broadcasting its English-language service towards Britain and Ireland and all around Europe from a large manor house in the Grand Duchy of Luxembourg. It struggled to be heard in Ireland through the atmospheric haze of the ether, but somehow it was all the more exciting for that, as if we were listening to something illegal. We weren't, of course, but the Station of the Stars had a slight taint of piracy about it, with its racy style and friendly approach. The record companies now sponsored most of the programmes, the larger organisations like Decca and EMI alternating with smaller companies like Philips, Pye and Top Rank. These programmes, recorded in London and then flown out to the station for transmission, were presented by disc jockeys such as Pete Murray, Tony Hall, Jack Jackson, Sam Costa, Muriel Young, Ray Orchard, David Gell, David Jacobs, Keith Fordyce, Alan Freeman, Jimmy Young and Jimmy Savile with his *Teen and Twenty Disc Club*. Kent Walton introduced *Honey Hit Parade* with 'music the sweet way and the beat way, courtesy of Fleetway and their hit magazine, Honey', Cliff Richard presented *Me and My Shadows* and the dreaded Horace Bachelor with his Infra-Draw Method for winning the football pools seemed to be everywhere. Whatever the method was, we never discovered—but we knew his address: Horace could be contacted at Keynsham: 'That's K-E-Y-N-S-H-A-M, Bristol,' as Geoffrey Everett solemnly intoned every evening. Ted King, Don Moss and Barry Alldis were three resident disc jockeys who announced the programmes, presented their own shows, compered the nightly request programmes and gave time-checks on their H Samuel Everite watches.

I particularly liked Pete Murray, originally an actor who had done service as an announcer in the station itself and was now presenting pre-recorded programmes for Decca. His funny, irreverent and self-deprecating approach was a master class on how to be an entertaining broadcaster. Barry Alldis was originally from Australia and had a unique warm voice with the mildest Aussie twang to add colour. He presented the *Top Twenty Show* every Sunday night at eleven o'clock and intense negotiations were required at home to allow me to stay up to listen. I may be wrong, but my memory is that at one stage Barry Alldis began the countdown by starting at No. 1 and working down. That was soon reversed, however, and the No. 1 became the last record to be played. The compromise at home was that I could listen until midnight, as long as I was in my pyjamas, ready to jump into bed at midnight precisely, before Steve Conway and the Hastings Girls' Choir sang the closedown music, 'At the End of the Day'.

Radio Luxembourg became the soundtrack to my early teens. As I did my homework at the dining-room table, 208 was belting out on the radio— proving that teenagers could always do different things at the same time. I could do arithmetic, listen to the finer points of the string arrangement on the new Drifters record, eat a sandwich, read a comic, carry on a conversation, and listen closely not only to what Pete Murray and Barry Alldis were saying, but also how they were saying it. And somewhere at the back of my mind, a thought occurred: I could do that.

By now, I had moved down the drive to the secondary school in Oatlands College, fronting the Stillorgan Road, as it still does. The principal was Brother Kennedy, who was fond of misquoting 'my namesake in America' who would certainly concur with 'ask not what Oatlands can do for you, ask what you can do for Oatlands'. Brother Spellacy, a large man with a booming voice and an actor's flair for theatrics, succeeded him. When he used the traditional Christian Brothers' weapon, the leather strap, he went to great lengths to convey that it hurt him more than it hurt me. This emotion, I soon detected, was not based on scientific fact; most people who implement corporal punishment suffer no discernible disadvantage. Another brother, 'Spud' Murphy, taught us Science, Physics and Chemistry. He had a number of favourites, whom he would bring to the top of the class and question, while he ran his hand under their jumper to pinch them. Luckily, I was not on his list, thinking it discreet to keep a low profile.

The lay teachers were more agreeable, most of them realising that they were dealing with bright young adults and treating them accordingly. Patrick O'Driscoll, a droll countryman with a laconic sense of humour, taught us Irish. Michael 'Tich' Courtney taught me Latin so effectively that I was one of the few students ever to get 100 per cent in the subject in the Leaving Certificate. It's rarely, if ever, taught now, but Latin did teach a basic knowledge of logic and language. Because I seemed to have a flair for it, I was seldom asked to read translations of Virgil's *Aeneid* in class, on Tich's assumption that I, one of his star pupils, would have done the necessary preparation the night before and would, of course, be word perfect. On the odd occasions when he would call on me unexpectedly, I would flick to the back of the book and read the English translation conveniently placed there, all the while making slight, but understandable, mistakes to ensure authenticity. How does that old saying go?—If you get up at dawn once, you get a reputation as an early riser.

A number of younger teachers were on the staff also. One in particular was quickly christened 'Cisco' for his cowboy-like appearance and the impression that he was about to go for his six-guns. He looked as if he couldn't have been much older than his pupils. Another, Mr Shannon, taught French and drove a powerful motorbike. He was staying in digs off the Lower Kilmacud Road and would regularly pass me on his way back to school after lunch. One day, he offered me a lift on the pillion, which I accepted with some trepidation, as I had never been on a bike before. It wasn't that I was concerned for my safety, it was more a question of bike etiquette: what did I hold on to? I couldn't put my arms around the waist of a teacher. There was no handle or grip to cling to and nowhere to put my feet. So, panicking slightly, I put my hands on my lap and one foot on the exhaust pipe and balanced my weight as I imagined Red Indians did while shooting from a galloping horse. And so, we arrived noisily through the school gates under the bemused gaze of my fellow pupils, some hating my guts and others merely undecided. From then on, I got a lift from Mr Shannon whenever he was passing me, but I don't remembering him ever talking to me. He'd stop, I'd hop on and would then say a quick 'thank you' when we reached school. Conversation was almost impossible over the sound of a 500cc bike. Mr Shannon was a kindly man. He did not stay long at Oatlands.

Michael Murtagh was our teacher of English, Maths and Music. One of his yearly functions was to organise the school opera, always one of the works of Gilbert and Sullivan. I auditioned for *Iolanthe* and was offered a spot in the Fairies' Chorus ('Tripping Hither, Tripping Thither...'), a part I declined. By the next year, my voice had broken and I became one of the Chorus of Sailors in HMS *Pinafore* ('We sail the ocean blue and our saucy ship's a beauty...'). That was more like it, although executing the 'Sailor's Hornpipe' required some convincing on the part of the producer that this was not girly stuff. Michael's nickname was 'Bunty', bestowed affectionately because of his slight corpulence around the equator, and on the week of the performances in the school hall, he would appear in a tuxedo to conduct the small orchestra. We all wondered how he managed to look thinner for his public appearances. His music classes during the year were always thoroughly enjoyable. The music curriculum was flexible, comprising choral singing and the odd bit of theory. One day, near the holidays, not wanting to burden us too much, he just said: 'Have you ever seen this before?' and proceeded to demolish the piano. Not as Jerry Lee Lewis might have done, he just disassembled the whole instrument and laid it out neatly on the floor—cabinet, pedals, frame, hammers—then put it back again and checked the tuning. 'So now you know how a piano works,' he said and left.

A teacher once told me that the three best things about teaching were June, July and August. Michael Murtagh spent some of his holidays working in Radio Éireann. When the Archbishop of Dublin, John Charles McQuaid, authorised the broadcast of Sunday Mass on radio, he suggested that those involved should be of sound character, knowledgeable about the rituals and religiously beyond reproach. Such a man was Michael Murtagh. He became the regular balance and control officer with responsibility for the Sunday Mass. Only required on weekends during the school terms, he would travel to the location on Saturday, rehearse the ceremony in the church and stay over for the transmission on Sunday. During the summer holidays, he would also join the regular roster to facilitate holiday leave among the full-time staff. Which is how he came to be doing *Céilí House* that night.

When I joined Oatlands College, most of my primary school colleagues came as well. Peter Keane and Paul Kilcullen became good friends, as did Philip Hannigan, Des Connolly and Des Donegan. Philip was the son of a bookmaker who came from the Liberties of Dublin. (The family was the inspiration for Cecil Sheridan's famous song, 'Hannigan's Hooley'.) A fine athlete, Philip went to sports meetings all over Dublin as he represented Oatlands, mainly in the hundred-yards sprint, and we went to cheer him on. We were there when he broke the Irish record for the race. In typically generous style, his father invited some of his pals out to celebrate Phil's triumph and he took four of us to the Gresham Hotel for dinner. I still remember the silver service, the attentive waiters, the chicken dish... and my first taste of red wine. It looked like Ribena and should have tasted sweet and fruity. Discovering that red wine was dry and bitter was a shock that took my breath away. It was like eating a tomato for the first time and expecting it to taste like a plum. The sudden surprise, however, did no lasting damage and I've since got over it.

The Hannigans lived on The Rise, Mount Merrion, and like their forebears, kept open house. I was there in October 1962, the night John F. Kennedy announced that he would regard any use of the Russian missiles in Cuba on any country in the Western Hemisphere as an attack on the United States, 'requiring a full retaliatory response on the Soviet Union'. I started to leave, saying that I had homework to do. 'Don't bother,' Mr Hannigan said gaily. 'Sure, we won't be here tomorrow. Have a rasher sandwich.'

But the threat of nuclear attack notwithstanding, the days passed civilly enough. For recreation, the Stella Cinema opened in Mount Merrion and Philip, Des Connolly and I formed a sort of cinema-going trio. We always went to the front row of the stalls, craning our necks to see the enormous screen. I don't know why we took the worst seats in the house. Bravado, probably; but more likely so that we could talk and comment on the pictures without disturbing the rest of the patrons. Des was blessed with a dark sense of humour and a facility for spotting the ridiculous; a witty fellow, still is, he was known as Torrio. We had all taken Mafia pseudonyms in class—Philip was Big Al—just to confuse the Brothers, more than anything. But it was all very innocent and harmless. Our biggest adventure was the running of illicit booze into an unexpected location: a retreat house in Tallaght.

It was a live-in retreat, where fire and brimstone was threatened if we dared to depart from the ways of righteousness. It lasted only a couple of days and, to add a little spice to the rituals, we borrowed some alcohol from the Hannigan cocktail cabinet. It was a sickening mixture of sherry, vermouth and brandy poured into a bottle that was known as a Baby Power; in other words, the capacity of one glass of whiskey. I don't remember ever getting a taste of it, but at one stage during the night, a group gathered in one of the bedrooms after lights out and the bottle was shared between us. The whole thing lasted no more than five minutes. But there was a stool-pigeon in our midst, and word reached the authorities. We were cross-examined individually and admitted the crime. The worst part was telling our parents that the Brothers wanted to talk to them, and having to suffer the ignominy of having let them down. The whole episode ended with an apology to the entire school in the hall, a toe-curling embarrassment on our part, particularly when most of our audience heartily approved of our scandalous behaviour. The stoolie was known to us, however, and even as late as a class reunion in 2003, he was ostracised vociferously. Luckily for him, he wasn't present.

A little trace of show business entered our lives when Ardmore Film Studios opened in Bray. For a time, as I walked the Stillorgan Road to Oatlands in the morning, a black limousine regularly passed bearing the glamorous blonde film star Kim Novak on her way to Ardmore to make the film *Of Human Bondage*. Following later, her co-star Laurence Harvey whizzed by. I waved at Kim occasionally and usually got a mild, almost regal, wave in response.

Eventually, the long summer holidays were interrupted when, in 1961, my father arranged for me to join Baxendales. He was manager of the ironmongery department and I worked in the stores, in the office and occasionally at the counter. I was subject to the usual initiation rites of being sent to the plumbing department to get a bubble for a spirit-level and a glass hammer, and was often mystified by the prices tied with little labels on to the merchandise. They were in the form of letters and usually I had to ask an old hand to translate, as they wouldn't tell me the secret code. My dad explained that it was a closely guarded secret, so that the staff always knew the price, but the customer didn't, thereby allowing a greater mark-up if they felt they could get away with it, particularly with trade customers. The department code was 'Rusty Bacon', each letter corresponding to the figures 1 to 10; hence RS/N/B equated to 13 pounds, 10 shillings and 6 pence.

Across the street, Dolphin Records blared out Gene Pitney singing 'The Man who Shot Liberty Valance', as a workman from a building site came to the counter. Everyone else was on a tea break and I was the lone server. It was a little like the famous *Two Ronnies* sketch, 'Four Candles'. I asked what I could do for him.

'A bastard file,' he said.

Thinking that his language matched his rough demeanour, I went around the back and brought back two files, a ten- and a twelve-inch.

'No. Bastard,' he said.

Not knowing what I had done to upset him, I went searching for more files. I brought back another brand.

'No. A bastard file, for Jaysus' sake,' said he, getting more heated.

'They're all the files we have,' I said, starting to panic. This could end in tears.

'Are you sure you have no bastards?' he said, decidedly unhappy. 'I've come all the way in from Ballymun.'

Just then, my father's assistant manager, Cecil Martin, passed by and saw my pained expression. He went around the back, produced the required implement and sent the customer on his way. He explained that there are male files, where the grooves go one way, and female files, where the grooves go the opposite way, and there are bastard files, where the grooves go both ways. After that, I kept to the office chores, trying to match invoices to delivery dockets and occasionally checking figures with one of the clerks in Accounts, Paddy Moloney. A man of small stature, he was regarded as something of an oddity for his interest in playing the uilleann pipes and tin whistle. His hobby became his living and, perhaps because of his way with an accounts ledger, has been spectacularly successful, financially and artistically, as leader of The Chieftains.

My interest in radio was advanced when my friend Peter Keane, who lived behind me on Thornhill Road, acquired a tape recorder. Actually, it was a family tape recorder, but we had the use of it, the Keane household being one of the many locations where we were always welcome. Peter's father, Donie, was a delightfully outgoing man who reminded me of Dean Martin. He was in charge of the Men's Department in Clerys and every time I'd visit the house, he would unconsciously adjust my jacket and lapels as if supervising the fitting of a suit. I would record programmes on the tape recorder, acting like the DJs I heard on Luxembourg. It was the first time I heard my own voice back. The effect was startling, to hear yourself as others hear you. It sounds different, until you eventually realise that you hear yourself with the inner ear, whereas the recorder reproduces what others hear on the outside. I got used to it eventually and recorded entire programmes with music and commercials in the Keane front room.

We had noticed a new voice on Radio Éireann too. A younger, slightly American voice that introduced 'Dantro, Mystery Man From Mars' on *The Urney Programme* at one o'clock on Saturday afternoon, just before the beloved *Donnelly's Programme*. He was also to be found on *Jazz Corner* in the darkest recesses of night-time radio, and rumour had it that he also appeared on Granada Television in Manchester, but we couldn't see it. Occasionally, he could be detected doing continuity announcements between programmes. Even then, he was blowing the dust off Radio Éireann. He was Gay Byrne and we regarded him as the Great White Hope of Irish radio. This guy, whoever he was, spoke to us.

Telefís Éireann started on 31 December 1961. The first Chairman of the Authority, Eamonn Andrews, had promised that he would have the service on the air during 1961, and he got there with five hours to spare. We watched the crystal-clear pictures as President de Valera warned of the dangers of mishandling the medium, we saw a young Kathleen Watkins introduce the night's programmes, including a variety show introduced by Micheál O'Hehir, and marvelled as Patrick O'Hagen dodged the snowballs as he sang to the crowds in O'Connell Street. The first quiz show came a few weeks later as Gay Byrne presented *Jackpot*, a quiz devised by the variety comedian Cecil Sheridan.

Then, on the evening of Friday, 6 July 1962, with little fanfare, Telefís flashed up an announcement on screen, saying that there would be a new live show going out that night and if anyone would like to be in the audience, they should just come along. So we did—Phil Hannigan, Des Connolly and I. Like anyone who visits a television studio for the first time, we were fascinated by the machinery—the lights, the cameras, the microphone booms. Noel Kelehan and his trio played the theme tune live (a tune I can still play on the piano), Michael Lindsay-Hogg was the Floor Manager, and cameramen like Barry Kelly pointed at the first guests—the comedian Danny Cummins, the model Verona Mullen and, for the brains, Professor Liam O'Briain. Off camera, Harry Thuillier announced the programme, 'It's *The Late Late Show*... and here is your host and compere, Gay Byrne.' That's how I came to be at the first night of the longest-running talk show in the world; I have Gay's autograph to prove it.

We went back again and again through that summer as we realised that, for the first time, Ireland had just found a real star who came not from variety (although he knew the performers), nor from the old-fashioned radio station (although he worked there), but seemed to drop, fully formed, into our lives and into the spirit of the age. It was the 1960s and the times they were a changin'.

Looking back, there were a number of clues to my future that I didn't fully appreciate during my school years in Oatlands: going on a Mystery Train to climb Croagh Patrick and being fascinated by the compere in the booth playing records for the passengers on turntables that seemed to float, to avoid the movement of the train; spending a day with Phil Hannigan in Butlins Holiday Camp in Mosney and looking for hours at the Redcoat announcer on Radio Butlin; the attraction of the mechanics of how broadcasting was done; the playing with the Keane tape recorder; the interest in music; the disc jockeys on Radio Luxembourg and the tiny sparks on the sponsored programmes that might lead to more pop music on the worthy, but dull, home station.

I left Oatlands College in 1963. For the Oral Irish examination in the Leaving Certificate, Mr O'Driscoll warned us that we would probably be asked what career we wanted to pursue. If we gave him the job title, he would give us the Irish for it. I had no doubt in my mind as I told him, and the class, what I wanted to be. Nobody laughed as he gave me the Irish version: 'bolscaire craolacháin'—radio announcer.

～ SOUNDTRACK ～

The Top 30 Oldies as voted by listeners to *Six O'Clock Rock* on RTÉ
Radio 2 on 9 November 1979

1. 'Rock Around the Clock'/Bill Haley and The Comets
2. 'Jailhouse Rock'/Elvis Presley
3. 'Runaway'/Del Shannon
4. 'Summertime Blues'/Eddie Cochran
5. 'Dream Lover'/Bobby Darin
6. 'It Doesn't Matter Anymore'/Buddy Holly
7. 'Don't Be Cruel'/Elvis Presley
8. 'I Need Your Love Tonight'/Elvis Presley
9. 'Heartbreak Hotel'/Elvis Presley
10. 'Oh Boy'/Buddy Holly and the Crickets
11. 'That'll Be The Day'/Buddy Holly and the Crickets
12. 'All I Have To Do Is Dream'/Everly Brothers
13. 'Blueberry Hill'/Fats Domino
14. 'Apache'/The Shadows
15. 'Move It'/Cliff Richard
16. 'Diana'/Paul Anka
17. 'Oh Carol'/Neil Sedaka
18. 'Rave On'/Buddy Holly
19. 'Good Golly Miss Molly'/Little Richard
20. 'Three Steps to Heaven'/Eddie Cochran
21. 'At the Hop'/Danny and the Juniors
22. 'Hound Dog'/Elvis Presley
23. 'Wooden Heart'/Elvis Presley
24. 'Whole Lotta Shakin' Goin' On'/Jerry Lee Lewis
25. 'Blue Suede Shoes'/Elvis Presley
26. 'Great Balls of Fire'/Jerry Lee Lewis
27. 'Living Doll'/Cliff Richard
28. 'Oh, Pretty Woman'/Roy Orbison
29. 'All Shook Up'/Elvis Presley
30. 'Cathy's Clown'/Everly Brothers

Chapter 5 ∾

| BREAKING IN

The startling thing was his red hair. We had seen him on black-and-white television, but to see him in the flesh was to feel some of the charisma that had put him in the White House. With his tanned good looks and his toothy smile, John Fitzgerald Kennedy had the aura of a film star. I was reluctant to go into Dublin to see him, as I didn't think I could get near, but I joined the throng on St Stephen's Green opposite the Department of External Affairs in Iveagh House. As the president came out, the crowd greeted him in typical Dublin fashion by singing the television jingle for Kennedy's Bread:

K for Kennedy
E for Energy
N's for Nice and Nourishing
E for Enjoyment
D for Delicious
YS means You're Satisfied.

I'm sure the president had no idea what the tune meant, but he broke from his security men and walked smiling across the street to the crowds. We, in turn, walked towards him. He shook a few hands and was bundled into his limousine. The car ran over my foot, not enough to damage my toes, but enough to leave tyre marks on the tip of my shoes. It was a sort of privilege, really, to be accosted by the presidential motorcade.

The singing crowd had shown the same mixture of respect and irreverence as Kennedy had in his speeches around the country. In his speech to Dáil Éireann on the role of small nations, he gave the land of his forefathers a shot in the arm, an injection of self-confidence, as he recounted Ireland's contribution to the arts and culture of the world, as well as its role in peace keeping, 'not that Ireland is unmindful of its place in the world, but it's important that you know that we know.' He quoted for the first time George Bernard Shaw, 'who, writing as an Irishman, defined an approach to life: Some men see things as they are and say why; I dream things that never were and say "why not?"' That quotation virtually became the Kennedy family motto, used later by his brothers, Bobby and Edward.

It was the summer of 1963. I was seventeen years old. Baxendales provided pocket money, but I wanted to work in radio. I knew, however, that I would have to do something else until I was old enough to be a real broadcaster. I got some practice in by doing record hops in The Barn. To my surprise, I had been voted Dance Secretary of the Espoir Youth Club, a job that that gave me control of the weekly dance, assisted by a committee. When I took over, I decided that the panel of bands needed refreshing and sought out new ones: The Cyclones, The Vampires and one group in particular that was guaranteed to fill the place, The Caravelles. They were managed by Ted Carroll (my sister's one-time boyfriend) and they had developed a reputation all over south Co. Dublin, particularly in Longford Tennis Club and The White Cottage on Killiney Strand. If we could get them, we would fill The Barn, but they were expensive: twenty pounds for a Saturday night. It doesn't sound much now, but in 1963 it was a week's wages for many households, including ours. By doing a record hop every third week or so, where the only charge was the hire of the public address system, I could afford to hire The Caravelles regularly.

They were a fine group with a unique sound and the nearest thing we had to The Beatles: Mog Ahern on drums, Paul Williams on guitar, Brian Lynch on bass and John Keogh on piano and vocals. John played piano like Jerry Lee Lewis and was a born showman, standing up on the piano during the final number, 'Shout'. It was the first time I saw people coming to listen to the band, rather than to dance. They would group around the bandstand, both in The Barn and Longford, mesmerised by Mog's drum solos or John's pumping piano on 'What'd I Say?' Later, they were asked to play The Cavern in Liverpool, and because there was already a girl vocal group in England called The Caravelles (who had a hit record with 'You Don't Have To Be a Baby to Cry'), they changed their name to The Greenbeats.

But for all of John Keogh's artistry, musicianship and gift for mimicry, I was much more impressed by the fact that he worked in Radio Éireann. He was an effects operator, or in local parlance, a disc-man, the person who played the records while the announcer talked. I had, in fact, heard his name mentioned on *Overseas Requests* by the announcer Denis Meehan, who started his programme with the Gallowglass Céilí Band wheezing through 'Oft in the Stilly Night', followed by a standard opening announcement: 'Fond memories, céad fáilte róimh isteach; as always you're more than welcome to the musical mementoes your friends abroad want you to hear and that it's our very great pleasure to bring you.' Not the snappiest of openings, but stuck in my mind forever.

So, knowing my interest in radio, John gave me a name to write to and I applied for a position as Effects Operator in July 1963. I was politely declined, as it was subject to public advertisement and competition. Likewise, in August, a post of Studio Trainee in Telefís Éireann proved equally tough to crack. I wrote to Jack White, Assistant Controller of Programmes, Television, with suggestions for a number of television series, including one called *Behind the Scenes,* a series of documentary features looking behind the public façade of the Garda Síochána, the Army, a casualty department, the Lifeboat Service and similar institutions. Mr White wrote back to say that 'the subjects you mention are certainly of a type that makes excellent television... we now have certain programmes of this kind at the planning stage for autumn.' (I think they eventually made those programmes, because I'm sure I saw them during the last year or so.) My failure to make an impression on the radar of the state broadcaster made me suspect that they weren't treating a seventeen-year-old seriously.

The early days of Telefís Éireann were fascinating. It seemed the entire country was watching all the programmes, all the time. It was noticeable that the streets and neighbourhoods were quieter than ever during transmission hours, few though they were. *The Late Late Show* continued to thrive; there was a pop show of sorts called *For Moderns,* consisting of the actor T.P. McKenna introducing records on a Bush record player with occasional contributions from the Ian Henry Quartet (at the time, the epitome of grooviness), while pale teenagers danced around the tiny studio; *Tolka Row* mirrored parts of Dublin life as a weekly serial, although nothing much ever happened, and *The Riordans* broke new ground in television by being the first ever serial shot completely on location with the Outside Broadcast Unit. *The Showband Show,* introduced by ex-Viscount Paul Russell, gave a shop window to the newest dance outfits, eventually giving a national platform to The Greenbeats when they became the resident beat group. The daily news magazine, *Broadsheet,* put faces on many of the voices already familiar from radio—Ronnie Walsh, John O'Donohue, P.P. O'Reilly and John Skehan. Terry Wogan replaced Gay Byrne on the quiz game *Jackpot* and announcers like Michael Herity and Andy O'Mahony read news at the weekend. Gay also read news on the weekend shift, as well as taking over the live *Donnelly's Programme* on Saturday lunchtime and recording *The Seventeen Club* on Saturday afternoons in the O'Connell Hall. The programme featured live showbands and new record releases, with a studio audience. I joined them one Saturday afternoon in June 1963, which I can date accurately because one of the new releases Gay introduced that week was 'Confessin'' by Frank Ifield. (*The Seventeen Club* was modelled on an earlier packaged programme, *The Downbeat Club,* produced by Fred O'Donovan and presented by Noel Andrews.) Radio Éireann was showing small signs of modernisation, having introduced its first dedicated pop programme in October 1962 when Harry Thuillier presented *Ireland's Top Ten,* compiled by Jimmy Magee and produced by Róisín Lorigan.

Meanwhile, I soldiered on, doing the intermittent record hops in The Barn alongside the live bands. It was good practice, as it was the only way to play records for the public without being on the radio. It taught me a few important lessons in structuring a set, allowing for contrasts and vetting records for 'danceability'—a solid, unchanging rhythm. Luckily, the era of The Beatles, Gerry and the Pacemakers, Dave Clark Five, Searchers, Tremeloes, Tornadoes and Hurricanes provided good thumping hits to rattle the dance floor. The trick, then as now, was getting the running order right. It also gave me a certain facility to link records and maintain contact with the dancers, particularly as I had to talk while changing the record on the single turntable.

Other microphone experience came when Barry McAneany, a school friend, acquired a real microphone. Unfortunately, he had nothing to plug it into. Undeterred, we drove around Kilmacud and Redesdale Estate in his father's car, stopping to ask the local citizens their views on the issues of the day. They spoke into the microphone, assuming, no doubt, that the trailing lead actually went into a recording machine in the car. It didn't, but it showed me that if you act like it's real, they believe it is real.

It also demonstrated the almost magical power of a microphone; point it at them with confidence and most people respond by answering questions that they would never contemplate answering if asked by their best friend. Barry also wrote to Radio Éireann asking for a tour of the facilities. We turned up at the GPO and were shown around by Denis Meehan, the Station Supervisor. It was there that my theory of cueing records was proven correct as the announcer on duty, David Timlin, showed us how it was done in the Continuity studio. David, a former effects operator and boy actor (Brendan in *The Foley Family*), went on to become one of Telefís Éireann's most accomplished newsreaders. I wondered how Barry got such easy access to the hallowed corridors of RÉ. 'I told them I was setting up a large business and was contemplating buying advertising space on radio,' he replied suavely. Barry did as he had promised, eventually, without the advertising space. I just hoped that I wouldn't be remembered as a con artist.

Still, gainful employment was required. I asked Mr O'Driscoll for a reference and, while at his house, discussed career prospects. My exam results showed a leaning towards the arts and languages, and my father had said that money would be found for university, but Mr O'Driscoll advised against it, on the basis that I would end up as a Bachelor of Arts. 'BA degrees are ten a penny,' he said, 'and you'd only end up teaching. Do you want that?' Not for me, I thought, so I'd find any job until I was about twenty-five and then apply for broadcasting, which was the age I'd imagined to be the minimum. The reference was nice, though: 'He enjoys the popularity of his classmates, on whom he has a beneficial and steadying influence.' Ah, shucks.

I applied to all the usual firms—Esso, Cement Ltd, Roadstone—all to no avail. A career in banking was suggested, but was conditional on passing the Bank Exam.

To prepare for the Bank Exam, I enrolled in an Academy on St Stephen's Green, run by an Anglo-Irish gentleman who rejoiced in the appellation A.H. Sparkhall-Brown. He was, as you would imagine him to be, like something out of the Billy Bunter comics. He introduced us to the exotic mysteries of ledgers, balance sheets, and double-entry bookkeeping. The mind-numbing tedium was relieved by the presence of a fellow student who was also a colleague from The Barn and Canoe Club, Andy Maher. Andy was a dry and laconic individual, and we became great friends. We both failed the Bank Exam, Andy went to Spain, and I turned eighteen and went back to more job applications.

If the banks didn't want me, I'd try insurance. In November, I fired off letters to all the insurance companies, hoping that there might be a place for me, but also hoping that there might not. Then, inspired perhaps by JFK's 'why not?' motto, I asked my former English teacher, Michael Murtagh, for a name to write to in Radio Éireann. He gave me another nice reference and a name— Kevin Roche, Assistant Head of Music.

One night, having written more letters to more insurance companies, frustrated and in dread of a career in insurance, I wrote to Kevin Roche, a one-page letter on blue Basildon Bond paper. I didn't keep a copy, but I did see it many years later and was quite surprised by its cheeky tone. It said that I was an experienced record-hop DJ and that I had a huge career ahead of me and that if they played their cards right, I might be persuaded to do an audition for Radio Éireann. The letter was dated 12 November 1963.

Ten days later, we were sitting having our tea and listening to *Sports Stadium* with Philip Greene. I wasn't paying much attention, other than wondering why they used Mitch Miller's march from the film *The Longest Day* as a signature tune. Philip interrupted the discussion for a special news announcement (they didn't use the words 'news flash' in those days). A newsreader came on to give the dreadful news—John Fitzgerald Kennedy had been shot in Dallas. No further news, more details later. We went into the front room to see what the television was saying. It was playing an American detective serial, *Checkmate*, if memory serves, which was eventually faded to reveal the sombre face of newsreader Charles Mitchel. The president was dead. You could feel a hush descend on the country. Our Bonny Boy was gone.

My mother suffered from a heart condition. In the 1950s, she had undergone one of the first-ever heart operations performed by the sainted Mr Keith Shaw. She was also susceptible to chest infections, exacerbated by cold weather. So, in the days following the assassination of President Kennedy, she was in hospital. I was alone in the house and it was freezing; even the breakfast crockery lying in the sink was frozen over with solid ice. Sitting on a paraffin oil heater for warmth, I watched the funeral and obsequies of the president, described by Micheál O'Hehir for Telefís Éireann. Michael had been in the USA for a sporting fixture and stayed on to do the commentary. It was heartbreaking to see little John Kennedy Junior salute the cortège while his mother carried herself with impressive dignity. President de Valera represented Ireland, walking the funeral route with other world leaders and, even in death, John Fitzgerald Kennedy gave recognition to his ancestral home as, at the request of Jackie Kennedy, a group of Irish Army cadets in full dress uniform formed an Honour Guard at the graveside. He didn't succeed in doing all he promised, but he brought to the 1960s a spirit of optimism and hope: the feeling that the old ways would not do, that anything was possible.

Six days after the death of Kennedy, I got a reply to my letter to Kevin Roche. It read:

Dear Sir,

Thank you for your letter of November 12th. We will arrange a voice test for you, but due to the heavy demands on us from now until the New Year, it will not be possible to do so until early January. In the meantime, should you have any ideas for a record programme perhaps you would let us have your draft script.

Yours faithfully,
Róisín Lorigan
Programme Assistant
Music Department

I have the letter still, as you probably gathered, and St Paul's Epistle to the Romans paled into insignificance compared with the import of that letter, typed on Radio Éireann notepaper. A voice test. A draft script for a record programme. This was the real thing.

I hadn't anticipated being asked for programme ideas, though. I thought they hired voices and gave them things to do, little realising that, at the time, Radio Éireann was more a commissioning, rather than a producing, organisation. I wrote back to Róisín and suggested a number of formats for the voice test. One in particular found favour: I was asked for a draft script of 'Now and Then', a programme contrasting current records by popular singers with their earlier efforts. This was not as easy as it sounds. I had a limited record collection and could choose only records that were familiar from the radio, because, as yet, I had no access to the Radio Éireann record library. The programme required some knowledge of musical trends and changes in style, but somehow I cobbled together a script, typed by my sister Joan, and sent it in. The voice test was set for Monday, 10 February 1964 at 4.00 p.m.

Róisín Lorigan met me. A friendly blonde of about thirty-five (I guessed) with a slightly scattered air about her, she gave me some of the discs for the programme and handed me over to Pádraig O'Neill, a producer with the Features Department who also acted as Talks Officer. The moustache was familiar: he was also Paddy O'Brien, the greyhound-racing commentator who regularly read the sports results on television. He had also been a teacher and an actor, so he was certainly qualified to audition a prospective broadcaster. He brought me down the long corridor, past all the lavatorial offices, up to the fourth floor and into Studio 5, overlooking the internal offices of the GPO. It was a small studio with a desk holding three turntables and a small table with a microphone. Pádraig introduced me to the crew—Charlie Clegg would play the records while Brendan Roche would balance the programme in the control room. He explained that I would speak when the red light went on and that, as this was an audition, they would merely 'top and tail' the records, playing only the beginning and the end. There was no advice that I remember from anyone; I read the script without any mistakes, thanked everyone and was shown out. The whole thing lasted half an hour.

One month later, on 11 March, a letter from Radio Éireann arrived. I opened it with some trepidation. It was from Róisín:

Dear Mr Balfe,

     With reference to your recent voice test, I am glad to inform you that your microphone audition has been adjudged successful. As soon as we are in a position to offer you a broadcasting engagement, we shall get in touch with you immediately.

Joy was unconfined. But the weeks passed and nothing was heard from the GPO. On 5 May, I wrote to 'Miss Lorigan', observing the niceties of formal correspondence, thanking her for the news of my audition but pointing out that 'since then, I have heard nothing and I must confess I have begun to wonder whether I have been overlooked'. Two weeks later came Róisín's response:

Dear Mr Balfe,
    Thank you for your letter of May 5th. We had not forgotten you but we were waiting for a suitable programme slot. We have now programmed you for a series of six 30-minute broadcasts commencing on Sunday July 5th (11 to 11.30 pm) and concluding on Sunday August 9th. We can offer you a fee of £10 per programme. We intend pre-recording programmes 1 & 2 on Monday, June 29th from 2 to 6pm in our Henry Street studios. We have switched the title of your programme to 'Then and Now', and we hope you have no objection to this.

No objection whatever. Whatever you think yourself, Miss Lorigan. It made more sense anyway, as I was starting with the 'Then' record and leading to the 'Now'. In my reply accepting the offer, I wondered naïvely, 'if you could advise me as to whether I write the script, or yourselves'. Oblivious to broadcasting practice, I somehow thought that, having floated the idea as an audition piece, it would be passed to some scriptwriting department where professional wordsmiths would polish and hone my work until it shone.

Dear Mr Balfe,
    Yes, we intend to pre-record all your programmes. With regard to the script, we naturally assume that you will supply your own scripts.

Oops. I had been hard pressed to come up with enough examples for a half-hour programme; now I had to find enough material for six of them. But, as a forthcoming broadcaster, I now had access to the Gramophone Library. Kathleen Evans, aided by Phil Donnelly and John Shine, ran the library with commendable efficiency and was always helpful, particularly when I didn't really know what I was looking for. There were four or five listening booths and I spent happy hours there assembling programmes and looking up singers and musicians on the index system. All song titles were on a card index and folders devoted to the recording artists supplemented them. So, you could trace a song by its title or by its singer. Different sections carried different categories of music: A was solo singers, B was popular (or 'Variety') singers, C was classical, D was solo instruments, E was jazz and dance music and F was film and light instrumental music, of the type only radio stations buy. It became a standard answer when I'd ask for a particular song:

'Have you got "Please Please Me" by The Beatles?'

'No, but we have it by Stanley Black and His Two Pianos, Manuel and his Music of the Mountains and The Ron Goodwin Orchestra.'

The library kept the Top Twenty Chart always in stock, but was a little light on slightly older pop songs; they hadn't, for instance, a copy of Cliff Richard's 'Living Doll' and a copy had to be acquired from a record shop in Henry Street.

I was looking mainly in the B and E Sections to find material, and compiled programmes featuring The Beatles, Cliff Richard, Elvis Presley, Louis Armstrong, Gerry and the Pacemakers, Joe Loss, Steve Lawrence and Eydie Gorme, Gene Pitney, Ted Heath, Dusty Springfield, the Everly Brothers ('Cathy's Clown', what else?), The Dave Clark Five, Nat King Cole, Connie Francis, The Beach Boys, Count Basie and many more who had changed their style to keep ahead. The first record in the first programme was the first record I had bought five years earlier—'What Do You Want?' by Adam Faith. I contrasted it with his then current single 'We are in Love' by illustrating the change between the John Barry string backing and the Beatle-like influence of Adam's new backing group, The Roulettes. (Mr Faith, incidentally, since proved to be a versatile performer, holding his own under the grilling of John Freeman on BBC TV's interview programme *Face To Face* and moving into acting, management and property development when his pop career came to a natural end.)

Technically speaking, Adam Faith was the first featured singer, but not the first piece of music; before him came thirty seconds of the signature tune. Most programmes have a 'sig tune', to identify the programme musically and also to act as a buffer in case of an under-run. When it came to choosing a signature tune for *Then and Now*, I had decided on a catchy piece by the Reg Owen Orchestra, *Manhattan Spiritual*, a minor hit from 1959. But between the choosing and the doing, I came across an LP in what was now my record shop of choice—Murray's on Ormond Quay—called 'This Time By Basie', wherein the Count Basie Band took on some recent pop hits and re-interpreted them as exciting showpieces in arrangements by Quincey Jones. The first track was a dazzling *tour de force* that became my signature tune, not just for its sound, but also for its title. So it came to pass that the first record I ever played on the radio was 'This Could Be the Start of Something Big'.

It didn't feel like the start of Something Big on that Monday afternoon, 29 June 1964. It may have been the long-dreamed-of day of my radio debut, but its significance was somewhat lost on the management of Radio Éireann. For them, it was part of the daily schedule, just one more recording session to be conduced in a business-like and professional manner. I was familiar with the Gramophone Library and some of the offices but, apart from my audition in February, I had not been in a studio since. Róisín Lorigan took me down to Studios 7 and 8. They were the most recent additions to the facilities and were to the front of the GPO, rather than parallel to Henry Street.

These studios were of an odd design. Imagine a box divided into four square rooms, with glass panels linking them. One of the squares was Studio 6, a second Continuity studio, suitable for spilt wavelengths. It looked into Studio 7, a talk studio with a big round table. Across from that was Studio 8, with a microphone and three turntables, suitable for operation by a compere or by a disc operator. Both Studios 7 and 8 were linked to the fourth square, a small control booth operated by a balance and control officer. That day, Brendan Roche manned the desk in the booth, Jimmy Wogan spun the discs in Studio 8 and I was placed in Studio 7 to read my prepared script. Somewhere upstairs, in a tape room, another operator was waiting to record the programme, communicating with the control booth by telephone. All that was missing was the producer, a rare enough breed in RÉ as producers were confined mainly to the Drama Department. Traditionally, the compere or writer who had been commissioned took care of the content and got on the air through the assistance of the operational staff, so programme production was effectively a group effort. As Róisín had seen my scripts in advance, the presence of a producer wasn't required but I suspect that, as it was my first broadcast, a formal presence was deemed necessary. That baleful presence was Dermot O'Hara.

Dermot was a small man who had been conductor of the Radio Éireann Light Orchestra since 1948, having come through the Army School of Music. With the advent of a new Director of Music in the shape of Tibor Paul, new changes were introduced to refresh the RELO, particularly for its television appearances. Frank Chacksfield was seconded from London to take up the baton, while Bobby Murphy (later Colm Wilkinson's father-in-law) was appointed arranger/conductor. Dermot was appointed Music Producer, but didn't take his loss of prestige well; he blamed his demise on Tibor Paul, whom he always referred to as 'that man'. With his acerbic tongue and loud voice, Dermot was not shy in letting you know his views on music, particularly of the pop and rock variety. He regularly burst through the door of the studio while a record was playing to upbraid the singer or the recording: 'That

Dusty Springfield has too much echo on her voice,' he shouted in my ear, castigating 'I Just Don't Know What To Do With Myself'. 'And the orchestra's much too loud.'

'Was that Everly Brothers drummer a special friend of the recording engineer?' he inquired. 'Because he's drowning out the singers.' So much for my beloved 'Cathy's Clown'.

These interruptions were a little startling to a neophyte broadcaster. Trying to present my first programme while also justifying the music I was playing to a slightly manic producer was disconcerting, but the two programmes were recorded successfully.

The first broadcast, on the following Sunday, 5 July 1964, was a sort of out-of-body experience. It was certainly me, but it didn't really sound like me. It wasn't the usual surprise people feel when they hear back their recorded voice for the first time: that is simply the difference between the inner ear (as you hear yourself) and the outer ear (as others hear you). No, I was familiar with the sound of my voice from Peter Keane's tape recorder, but hearing myself on the radio was a little different, as if it was someone else talking. The fact that I was now inside the radio set, so to speak, added an element of authority or, perhaps, status and joined me unconsciously to all those broadcasters who had gone before. Ringo Starr expressed a similar reaction: 'When we heard "Please Please Me" played back in the recording studio, it sounded good. But when we heard it played on Radio Luxembourg, it sounded even better. We couldn't believe it was us.'

Nonetheless, I was now a broadcaster. And I got my first professional newspaper critique in a radio column written by Desmond Fennell:

> Another interesting new series, again musical, is Brendan Balfe's 'Then and Now' in which he is comparing recent recordings by popular singers and bands with their earlier successes. This is not merely playing 'pops'. It provides an opportunity to observe changes of techniques as artists have developed, either in maturing or keeping up with the current trends. The idea is good and it is being well developed.

The series ran for the six weeks, ending on Sunday, 9 August. The RTV *Guide*, with its uncanny timing, did a short article on the programme on 7 August, two days before it ended. Under a picture of a bespectacled adolescent, it described the programme and then profiled its originator:

> The programme was devised and scripted by Brendan Balfe, a newcomer to radio. Brendan is 20 years old and was educated at Oatlands College,

The Long Corridor.
RTÉ

Brigid Kilfeather in the Continuity studio, Henry Street, with John Walsh at the controls.
RTÉ

Studio 10 in Henry Street, the Drama Suite, with two actors at the far end and sound-effects man Brian Halford, waiting for his cue. Note the white door for practical effects. *RTÉ*

With two pals on Lower Kilmacud Road,
Jimmy O'Connor and Canice Hayes.

With Granda in O'Connell Street, on one of
our marathon tours of Dublin.

With my mother and sisters, Joan and
Jacinta, during a bracing summer holiday.

My father and mother in Lourdes.

My grandparents' Golden Jubilee in Thomas Court, with aunts, uncles and cousins. (I'm top left, Joan is in front of the hanging portrait and Jacinta is directly below her. Mam is fourth from left, Dad is third from right.)

The investiture of the first patrol in the 86th Dublin Troop, Mount Merrion, October 1958. L-R: Liam Donaldson, Leonard Fowler, Philip Heneghan, Scoutmaster Joe Coughlin, Tony Branagan, Chaplain Fr Rogers, me (back row), Finbarr Devine and Barry Gillen.

With two good friends from Oatlands, Des Connolly and Phil Hannigan, in O'Connell Street. All were present at the first *Late Late Show*.

Gay Byrne on the set of *The Late Late Show*, 1963. The floor manager is Michael Lindsay-Hogg, later a noted film and TV director. RTÉ

My mentor and friend, Denis
Meehan. *RTÉ*

Terry Wogan, controlling his nerves in 1963. *RTÉ*

A youth of 22, to publicise the first
radio broadcasts from the RDS.

The sweetest voice in radio, Una Sheehy. Note the crane for dropping the needle onto the disc.
RTÉ

The Captain, the imperturbable John Skehan. That's me at the back, out of focus.
RTÉ

The Dean of the DJ Corps, Joe Linnane.

Get an earful of those happy funsters,
Rosaleen Linehan and John Keogh. RTÉ

Avondale Studio, 1967: recording *The Yardley
Programme*. The Client, Paula Healy, BB,
Gay Byrne.

Presenting a sponsored programme in
Avondale Studio, with Paddy Gibbons in the
control room.

Twenty DJs and announcers at the launch of Pat McGeegan's Eurovision entry, 'Chance of a Lifetime', April 1968. L-R: Arthur Murphy; Noel McCaul, Des Keogh, Cecil Barror, Jimmy Magee, Maurice O'Doherty; Frank Kelly, Mike Murphy, Eddie Golden, Chris Curran, Noel Andrews, B.P. Fallon, John Murray-Ferguson, BB, Val Joyce, Peter Murphy, Terry O'Sullivan. (Seated) Frankie Byrne, Lorna Madigan, Una Sheehy.

Mount Merrion, where he took part in many of the school's dramatic productions. He went into insurance on leaving school, also joining the Espoir
Dramatic Society. When he is not writing scripts or rehearsing plays, he is
most likely to be found at Seapoint, indulging in his favourite pastime—
canoeing.

In the interests of verisimilitude, that slight varnishing did put a more
positive gloss on reality, but such is the way of public relations. My parts in
the chorus of two school operas took on a weight I never intended, as did my
'joining the Espoir Dramatic Society', which, as I recall, comprised one
appearance in a Christmas pantomime called *Snow White and the Seven
Corkmen*, directed by Tom Barry (I was one of the magnificent seven south-
erns). So, everything was true, if embellished, apart from my age. I must have
given my age as twenty out of a fear that if Radio Éireann knew I was younger,
they wouldn't let me near the place. In fact, when I made my broadcasting
debut, I was still eighteen years old.

And that 'went into insurance' bit? Well, one of those letters to insurance
companies also had a positive response and somewhere between applying to
RÉ and getting on the air, I joined the Insurance Corporation of Ireland. As
with Eamonn Andrews and Gay Byrne before me, it seemed to be a condition:
if you wanted to reach the promised land of radio, first you had to endure the
dry desert of insurance.

As the prophets had foretold.

∿ SOUNDTRACK ∿

A Collection of 'Firsts'

↜ **First Recorded Words:** 'Mary Had a Little Lamb', spoken by Thomas Alva Edison to test his new 'phonograph or speaking machine' on 15 August 1877.

↜ **First Million-Selling Record:** Enrico Caruso's recording of 'Vesti la Giubba' ('On with the Motley') from the opera *Pagliacci* by Leoncavallo. Recorded 1903 and re-recorded after electrical recordings were introduced in 1925.

↜ **First Disc Jockey:** Generally agreed to be Christopher Stone on the BBC in 1926, the first to construct a programme entirely out of gramophone records.

↜ **First Chart Radio Show:** *Your Lucky Strike Hit Parade*, featuring the best-selling songs of the week in sheet-music sales, began on 20 April 1935. The MC was Fred Astaire and the first No. 1 song was 'Cheek to Cheek'.

↜ **First Record by Frank Sinatra:** 'From the Bottom of My Heart', accompanied by the Harry James Orchestra, recorded 13 July 1939.

↜ **First Actual Gold Disc:** RCA Records presented a disc sprayed with gold lacquer to bandleader Glenn Miller for his recording of 'Chatanooga Choo Choo' on 19 February 1942, to celebrate over 1,200,000 copies sold.

↜ **First No. 1 on 208:** The first No. 1 on the first Top Twenty on Radio Luxembourg, introduced by Teddy Johnson, was 'Galway Bay'. It was based on sheet-music sales, so the records played alternated between versions by Bing Crosby, Anne Shelton and Josef Locke.

↜ **First Long-Playing Hit Record:** Columbia Records introduced the microgroove long-playing vinylite disc on 26 June 1948. The first LP to sell a million copies was the Broadway Cast recording of *Oklahoma!*, while the film soundtrack of *South Pacific* was the first No. 1 in the British LP Charts in November 1958, holding its position for all of 1959 (seventy weeks in total).

↜ **First Irish Rock 'n' Roll Record:** 'The Irish Rock', coupled with 'Santa Claus Rocked and his Reindeer Rolled' recorded in 1956 by The Mountaineers, a country and western group from Drogheda, well-known on radio variety shows.

- **First Irish Pop Riot:** Inside the Carlton Cinema, Dublin, during the showing of *Rock Around the Clock* in 1956. Because the film was released in Ireland before Britain or the Continent, it was also the first pop riot in Europe.

- **First Record on RTÉ Radio 2:** The first record on *Pop Around Ireland*, presented by Larry Gogan on 31 May 1979, was 'Like Clockwork' by the Boomtown Rats. 'Rat Trap' by the same band was more recent but was considered unsuitable.

- **First Record on RTÉ Lyric FM:** The Hallelujah Chorus from *Messiah* by Handel, first performed in Dublin in 1742.

Chapter 6 ∿

| INSURANCE DAYS

The Insurance Corporation of Ireland was situated on Dame Street, Dublin. It was typical of the cement, steel and glass edifices that were beginning to proliferate all over the city, most notably Hawkins House, built on the site of the much-loved Theatre Royal. With their banks and insurance offices, Dame Street and College Green formed the nearest we had to a financial district in Dublin.

The ICI offices were clean and bright, if a little stuffy, due to the absence of any air-conditioning system; someone forgot, apparently. Although modern in look, the practices hadn't changed since the days of Charles Dickens. We wore suits during the week, but on Saturday mornings we were allowed casual wear—a blazer or sports jacket. I worked on the ground floor in Fire Endorsements, altering existing fire insurance policies when customers made adjustments to the buildings or goods insured, and calculating the revised premium. Copies of the policies were kept in huge ledgers along the walls and details of correspondence with clients were kept in files in the basement. When a client increased the value of a house from, say, £1,300 to £1,500 (those were typical values of a suburban house in the mid-1960s), I had to change the policy and the file by hand and send a note to the accounts department, so that the client could be billed (they weren't called 'clients' or even 'customers' then; they were always known as 'the Insured', as in 'I have an Insured on the phone…'). It was tedious work, not made any easier by having to explain the intricacies of the Average Clause to the Insureds who rang up demanding an explanation of this new imposition which, as always, favoured the Insurance Company. I can, incidentally, still explain it, but I'll spare you.

The Fire Endorsements section was run by Jimmy Mullarkey, a likeable and helpful man. The Chief Clerk, who had originally interviewed me for the job, was Jack Doherty, a dour Northerner who always reminded me of P.G. Wodehouse's maxim that 'it is never difficult to distinguish between a Scotsman with a grievance and a ray of sunshine'. He had a habit of prowling around our desks during lunchtime to see how we were progressing with the work. In particular, he was looking for Accounts Queries: little green memos from upstairs looking for details of alterations, which were deemed to be highly urgent. I tended to file these under my blotter, intending to get around to them eventually. To my surprise, I discovered a new law of nature: paperwork, left to itself, eventually becomes out of date and can be disposed of safely in the rubbish bin.

I made new friends there. Jim Ahearn and Tony Harkness were the best of company, while Dermot Herbert became one of my best friends. My radio debut was made while I was in the ICI and Jack Doherty was aware of it, but made no acknowledgment thereof. To enhance his lunchtime prowling manoeuvres, Jim and Tony would leave fictitious phone messages for me on my desk in plain view: 'Ring Eamonn Andrews ASAP', or 'The London Palladium wants to know if you're free on Tuesday night', or 'The BBC says they agree the new fee'. No reference was ever made to these missives, but I suspect they gave Mr Doherty something to ponder of an evening.

The manager of the department was Mr Brennan, and his assistant manager was Jimmy Edwards, who, like his namesake, was English, a snappy dresser and sported a moustache. He had a certain style, demonstrated by his reply to a strongly worded letter addressed to him from another insurance company:

Dear Sir,
    I must inform you that someone has stolen a supply of your headed notepaper and is writing abusive letters in your name. I enclose an example, received today in this office. Perhaps you would care to investigate.

No more was heard from the other company but, whilst he sent back the offending letter, Jimmy kept a copy of the original on file. Just for insurance, so to speak.

I was doing some overtime one evening and at around six o'clock, a phone rang. It was the broker for Aer Lingus looking for cover for a new hangar, which had just been transferred to the airline by the building contractor. The call was due for the New Business section, but as there was nobody there, I dealt with it.

'So, can you hold the hangar on cover overnight?' he asked.
'Absolutely', I agreed. 'What is the value?'
'Half a million pounds.'
'Done,' I said.
'Can I have your name, please?'
'Balfe, Fire Endorsements.'

'So, it's Aer Lingus, new hangar, half a million pounds... and you're confirming that the ICI will cover overnight.'

'No problem,' I said. 'Consider it done.'

'And your name is Balfe?'

'Right.'

Now, it's important to know that an insurance company, just like a bookmaker's office, sets off large bets by spreading the risk. Insurance companies re-insure large risks among other companies in Ireland and abroad by offering percentages of the total sum insured. In no circumstances would a company expose itself for such a large sum as I had just agreed to; no wonder the broker couldn't believe his luck and was so anxious to get the name of the guy who had agreed to the insane cover. I left a note for New Business and went home. The following morning, Jimmy Mullarkey explained through gritted teeth that if anything had gone wrong, we would have been liable for all of the half-million pounds. Luckily, they had re-insured the risk first thing that morning. I defended my initiative by pointing out that I was only being agreeable.

'Be agreeable with your own money,' he suggested. 'You could have bankrupted the company'. As it happened, they were perfectly capable of bankrupting it themselves—and did so in 1985. The Insurance Corporation of Ireland had been taken over by Allied Irish Banks and required a huge government subvention of public funds to avoid a crash, brought about by the cavalier way in which it conducted its insurance business. So, as I was a taxpayer like any other, agreeable or not, it was some of my money that rescued them.

One day, a form came around asking us to indicate our prowess in the Irish language. As an honours graduate in Irish in the Leaving Certificate the previous year, I put my name down as having a 'working knowledge'. A bad mistake, I discovered. The background to the search for Irish speakers was a recent court ruling that citizens were entitled to conduct their business through the First Official Language. A week later, I was horrified to see my name listed as the Designated Irish Speaker for the Fire Department. Not long afterwards, I got my first customer. The receptionist came round, gloating mildly. 'One of yours, I think,' she said, as she led me out to the public counter. And there, waiting to alter his policy through the medium, was a man small in stature, but loud of voice. I recognised him: he was Eimear Ó Broin, a man of strong views, conductor of the RÉLO and the son of León Ó Broin, Secretary of the Department of Posts and Telegraphs, who was keenly influential in the development of Radio Éireann. I had just endured six programmes with Dermot O'Hara, and here, to my dismay, was another diminutive conductor sent to thwart me. If an effort was made to speak in Irish, I thought, honour

would be satisfied and we could conduct our business in English thereafter.
Which is exactly what happened.

'Dia dhuit,' says I. 'Nach breá an lá é?'

We exchanged pleasantries 'as Gaeilge' and then I got down to business.

'Anois, cad mar gheall ar an phoilisí seo?' I continued, guessing that the Irish
for 'policy' was probably the same word in an Irish accent. 'Sé an rud táb-
hachtach ná an Average Clause, which I'd better explain 'as Béarla', because it's
quite complicated and we don't want your house under-insured, do we, because
you'd be liable for a lot of money....' Any suggestion of a financial disadvantage,
I found, concentrates the priorities wonderfully. And so, we finished our business in the language of the old oppressor and the insured went away happy.

The days passed in a civil fashion and there were many enquiries from the
management concerning my ambitions in insurance. An indicator of my
future career intentions would be my studying for the examinations of the
Insurance Institute, which I had deferred (indefinitely, I hoped). From my
perspective, I was merely passing through the insurance industry and my real
intention was to get into radio.

I kept in touch with Róisín Lorigan, but there were no new programme
openings in the late summer of 1964. I wrote to Máire Nic Eoin in Children's
Programmes looking for work as a compere, to Tom McGrath in Telefís
Éireann, to Peter Hunt recording studios (who recorded sponsored programmes and whose technical operator was Morgan O'Sullivan, later to
become a first-class broadcaster himself)—all to no avail.

A major advance in broadcasting, and the indelible sound of the summer
of 1964, was Radio Caroline, set up by Ronan O'Rahilly, grandson of The
O'Rahilly, one of the 1916 rebels. It was named after Caroline Kennedy, the
daughter of John F. Kennedy, whom Ronan saw in a photograph scampering
around while her father tried to conduct a formal cabinet meeting. He felt
that if she could disrupt the business of the nation, she was an apt model for
what he was trying to do: run a pirate radio station and disrupt the business
of the staid national broadcaster, the BBC. Just like the rebels of his grandfather's time, he chose Easter Weekend to begin, broadcasting off the coast of
England from a ship, the *Mi Amigo*, which had been fitted out in the port of
Greenore in Co. Louth. We had never heard anything like it. It was fast and
funny and frantic, playing pop music twenty-four hours a day, introduced by
personality disc jockeys using the American and Australian radio style. They
advertised on air for announcers and I applied. I didn't get it.

Back on dry land, I decided that if the state sector didn't want me, I would
try the commercial sector. Parallel to Radio Éireann, a commercial sector had

grown up to produce and record sponsored programmes for advertising agencies. There were two main suppliers: The Eamonn Andrews Studios in Henry Street, who both produced and recorded programmes; and Harry Thuillier, who, with his associate Jimmy Magee, was responsible for at least three programmes a day—almost twenty per week. Harry and Jimmy worked out of ACT Studios in Upper Mount Street, but I wrote to Thuillier at his home in Donnybrook applying for work as compere/scriptwriter/producer in sponsored programmes, 'as one can quite safely predict that they have a big future,' I added with some insouciance. That was on 29 September, ten days after my nineteenth birthday.

Then, one month later, I was startled to receive a telegram from Harry Thuillier with mysterious instructions: I was to call a certain telephone number at 9 a.m. on Wednesday 28 October. I had never received a telegram before and was impressed by its clandestine contents. I rang at the appointed time and Harry asked if I would be interested in writing some scripts for a programme sponsored by Murray Rent-a-Car. It was called something like 'Stars of the Week' and comprised biographical sketches of two musical stars per programme, illustrated by five records. Harry explained that his usual writer/producer, Jimmy Magee, was unavailable, and asked if I would take on the job of researching, writing and supplying the music for each programme.

I would be delighted, I assured him, and asked when I would start. Immediately. The only other slight hitch was that he was going away for four weeks to record material for his famous Jacob's *Come Fly with Me* programme and he'd need four Murray scripts by Friday morning, two days away. 'No problem,' said I. 'They'll be there.' It was only after I had hung up that I realised why he had sent me a telegram. I had put no telephone number on my letter.

I called in the help of my pal, Dermot Herbert, and between us, with the aid of articles from magazines, the backs of LP covers and general knowledge about popular music, we cobbled together four scripts, complete with records acquired from friends, family and record companies, to whom we went begging. Dermot's school friend from Terenure College was Peter Blake, who now worked in O'Keefe's Advertising Agency, and he joined us in our sponsored programme endeavours. He was the account executive for Urney Chocolates, and Harry Thuillier also produced their programme, which was a half-hour show broadcast on Saturday nights, comprising a comedy record, a postal quiz and a particular focus on ballad groups like The Dubliners and The Clancy Brothers. So, the upshot of it all was that I was soon writing both the Murray and the Urney programme for Harry Thuillier every week. The money was not over-generous—about four guineas per script—but, more importantly, I was getting valuable experience of writing for radio and assembling a programme from minimal resources.

Meanwhile, I continued my role as the grandiosely titled Dance Secretary in The Barn, hiring bands, introducing record hops, counting the receipts from the sale of Club Orange and Tayto Crisps and occasionally adjudicating at altercations at the door. There was a slightly rough and troublesome crowd from Beaufield in Stillorgan, who would arrive in groups of ten or twelve and had an intimidating effect on the committee. Technically, it was a club and therefore required membership. My predecessor had simply refused them entry, but I tried a new tack. I issued two memberships each week and told each of them that if they behaved themselves, I would issue two more cards the following week for their friends. I had prompted both male and female members of our committee to welcome them and they made sure that they had dancing partners and someone to chat to. Over the weeks, the entire group was accommodated and they integrated perfectly well with other members. It was an important lesson for me, that groups can indeed be scary sometimes, but if you break them into individuals, you can establish a rapport.

Between The Barn and Longford Tennis Club, I became great friends with The Greenbeats—John Keogh, Mog Ahern, Brian Lynch and Paul Williams— who would become nationally known on television from *The Showband Show*. They also had their own radio series, *Not So Green*, written by one of their friends, Eanna Brophy. It was a comedy series, a sort of forerunner of *The Monkees*, based around the fictitious exploits of a pop group, interspersed with musical performances. Two real actors, David Kelly and Jim Norton, added to the cast and the series proved a particular showcase for the vocal talents of John Keogh, not just as a singer but also as an accomplished mimic. I went to most of the recordings in the O'Connell Hall and felt obliged to go to the defence of the group in a letter to the *Irish Press* when, in his radio column, Augustine Martin opined that The Greenbeats 'refrained from joining in the comedy', but went on to praise 'the impeccable impersonations of Eoin O'Mahony, Harry Thuillier and Paddy Crosbie' without giving credit to John Keogh, who was responsible for them all; a versatile performer, he combined his musical and comedy career with his day job as an effects man in radio.

It was all very well being a spectator, but I wanted to be a practitioner, so I continued my assault on Radio Éireann. I wrote to Francis McManus, the General Features Officer, probably at the instigation of his son Pat, who had been in my class in Oatlands and also served with me on the dance committee of The Barn. Francis was a well-known novelist and a promoter of new writers, as well as instigating and producing the Thomas Davis Lectures, those talks on the arts, history and sciences that have continued on radio since 1953. I have kept his replies to my letters and they should serve as an exemplar of how to treat embryonic broadcasters with tact and courtesy:

Dear Mr Balfe,

Thank you for your letter of February 8, 1965. I sympathise with you. You are young, eager to learn and work, anxious to get on fast—and here you are in what seems a slow world. Please believe me that you will get on but you must have patience—and you must have fortitude to suffer the apparent delays.

Your programmes were liked. I heard one myself. But the unfortunate thing is that in my bailiwick I have no programme in which, at the moment, I could use a Brendan Balfe. I have inquired on your behalf in the Music Department. They are overwhelmed with ideas and comperes. All I can do is to keep on making inquiries. It looks hopeless but I have been too long in radio not to know that there is no such thing. I can distinctly recall Gay Byrne (as a very young man like yourself) becoming hopeless, too.

Meanwhile, don't confine yourself to compèring. Think, at least, of other skills. Interviewing, for instance, which is difficult, demands thought and must have dignity and maturity. Read like mad—science, philosophy, history (especially of Ireland)—but enlarge your dialectic all the time.

Please forgive me for this sort of letter.

Yours sincerely

Francis McManus

General Features Officer

I replied gratefully, but I never kept a copy of my letter of 19 February. I had probably asked how to acquire interviewing skills. He replied on 22 February with the same gentle touch:

Best thing for us to do is let you go through the process of interview training which is sometimes carried out by the producer of the General Features Department, Mr Padraic O'Neill. He will show you how to use a portable machine and will give you some pointers about interviewing. There are a lot of little rules which are worth noting, small points such as, for instance, avoiding the repetition of words like 'well' or 'I see'; avoiding questions to which you will get a mere 'yes' or 'no' answer; avoiding questions which are merely impertinent or inquisitive. After Mr O'Neill has finished with you, you can, if you like, come along and talk to me.

Padraic O'Neill was, of course, the same producer who had given me my voice test a year before. The other colleagues of Francis McManus in Features, I later found out, were Cathal Ó Gríofa, a virtuous if slightly naïve man, and Mervyn Wall, giving rise to the trio being known affectionately to one and all as 'Frank, Innocence and Mer'. I did try to contact Padraic O'Neill, but events overtook my interview training.

To my great regret, I never met Francis McManus face to face. He died that same year, 1965. His immense contribution to Irish radio is remembered today in the Thomas Davis Lectures and, in particular, the Francis McManus Short Story Awards, which for the past twenty years have done what he did best— promote and encourage the development of newcomers.

But the prediction of Francis McManus ('Please believe me that you will get on…') came to pass in 1965. The Children's Department, in the person of Máire Nic Eoin, responded to my overtures with an offer to present *Records for Children*, a quarter-hour music programme on Wednesdays between 5.15 and 5.30 p.m., starting on 31 March for four weeks. A fee of £6 was offered. In the past, the programmes had largely comprised kiddie records of the Burl Ives and Chipmunks variety, but any children I knew liked The Beatles and Sandie Shaw too, so I also included a few accessible pop songs every week. It was my first live broadcast and it was odd to sit in Studio 5 listening to the announcer downstairs introduce me by name.

Odder still was the coincidence that another overture to RÉ had also borne fruit that same day. I had also learned that they hired relief continuity announcers from time to time and had applied previously to Denis Meehan, the Studio Supervisor. The job was never advertised, but (by osmosis, possibly) a wide range of people knew about the practice and applied to be announcers. When he had assembled enough names, about three hundred, Denis ran auditions to separate the wheat from the chaff. My winnowing process was an audition test at 2.15 p.m. on Wednesday, 31 March, the same day I was to present *Records for Children*.

Brigid Kilfeather, the Assistant Studio Supervisor, dressed in a startling yellow suit, met me. Her jet-black hair was relieved by a single streak of white, and I recognised her voice immediately; she was one of the woman announcers who presented *Hospitals Requests* and announced programmes with the slight air of a Reverend Mother reading the Altar List of the Dead. She took me to Studio 5, handed me a script, gave me a couple of minutes to prepare and recorded me reading some announcements. I gathered that Denis Meehan and others would listen to the tapes later.

I was on a half-day from the ICI, so I left the GPO with nothing much to do, hung around town for a while, and returned to the studios for the *Records for Children* rehearsal at 4.45 p.m. I met Brigid in the corridor. She seemed surprised to see me again. 'I'm doing a live broadcast,' I explained. She continued to look nonplussed, but said nothing.

My overture to television was getting a reaction, too. During my correspondence with Tom McGrath about compering work on Telefís Éireann the previous year, I had offered to appear as a panel member on *Pickin' the Pops*, presented by Larry Gogan. Inspired by the BBC's *Juke Box Jury*, the programme had a panel which reviewed the new record releases. The producer, Adrian Cronin, wrote to me and asked me to meet him in the studios in early May. As a result, a month later, I made my television debut in Studio 1, long familiar from my visits to *The Late Late Show*. The fee for the appearance was £10. It was my first time to meet Larry Gogan. I was flattered that he knew who I was, that I'd presented a music series and that I'd even done *Records for Children*.

I don't remember much about the records reviewed, apart from a record by Declan Ryan called 'I Need You', a cover version of a Ricky Nelson song, about which I was less than enthusiastic, predicting a miserable failure. Needless to remark, it subsequently became a big hit for him, proving that my opinions are like straws in the air, to show the direction in which the wind is not blowing.

The TV show was recorded in the afternoon for teatime transmission. Again, it's weird seeing yourself for the first time. Unlike a mirror image, you see yourself as others see you, but your face looks the wrong way round. Again, there's that slight disconnection between you and the fellow on the screen. That television programme was broadcast on Saturday, 12 June 1965. It was a sort of red-letter day, but it was surpassed in my mind by the anticipation of what would be happening on the following Monday. On 2 June, I had got a letter from Brigid Kilfeather:

Dear Mr Balfe,

As a result of your recent audition with us, we are pleased to offer you a training course of five or six weeks' duration, beginning on Monday, 14th June. The sessions will be from 7.15 p.m. to 10.30 p.m. (approx.) Monday to Friday of each week.

At the end of the training session you will be given a further audition to assess your suitability or otherwise to be placed on our panel of relief announcers.

At last, things were looking up.

∼ SOUNDTRACK ∼

Favourite Jazz Tracks

- 'Cotton Tail'/Benny Carter and his Orchestra
- 'I Dig Ed'/Shorty Rogers
- 'Tennessee Firebird'/Gary Burton and Friends
- 'Round Midnight'/Miles Davis
- 'Mercy Mercy Mercy'/Cannonball Adderley Quintet
- 'Hey, Johnny One Note'/Kenny Clarke–Francy Boland Band
- 'Pussy Wiggle Stomp'/Don Ellis Orchestra
- 'Exodus'/Manny Albam Orchestra
- 'Take Five'/Dave Brubeck Quartet
- 'The Atomic Mr Basie' (album)/Count Basie Band
- 'Hobson's Hop'/Jimmy Smith (organ)
- 'Straight No Chaser'/Thelonious Monk
- 'Four Brothers'/Woody Herman Band
- 'The Train and the River'/Jimmy Giuffre
- 'The Preacher'/Quincy Jones Orchestra
- 'Portrait of Louis Armstrong'/Wynton Marsalis
- 'She Moves Through the Fair'/Wayne Shorter (tenor sax)
- 'Bye Bye Blackbird'/Billy May Orchestra
- 'I've Got My Love to Keep Me Warm'/Les Brown Band
- 'My Favourite Things'/George Shearing

Chapter 7 ⌒

| MEEHAN AND WOGAN

W e were gathered in Studios 3 and 4 that Monday evening, an expec-
tant band of candidates who had been shortlisted for announcer
training. They came from all walks of life—the bank, the civil
service, teaching, business—as well as a couple with connections to Radio
Éireann. There were Pádraig Dolan, Brian Reynolds, Valerie McGovern, Donal
Marren, Diane Lonergan, Frank Delaney, Michael Caslin, Nuala Robinson,
Annette Andrews (recently married to a young politician, David)—and me.

Our tutors introduced themselves. We all knew Terry Wogan, the Senior
Announcer; his dark brown voice, still redolent of his native Limerick, was
familiar from his jolly approach to *Hospitals Requests* and his face was familiar
from his compering of the television quiz *Jackpot*. He was friendly and funny
and was dressed as if he had just played a round of golf—or was about to.
Brigid Kilfeather was also on hand, a formidable presence at first sight,
perhaps to counterbalance Terry's casual approach.

The man in charge was Denis Meehan. He had joined Radio Éireann as a
part-time announcer in 1950, was made permanent in 1952 and was appointed
Assistant Station Supervisor to Síle Ní Bhriain in 1953. Four years later, he
succeeded Síle when she left to teach in Nigeria (a short tenure, as it turned out;
the climate didn't suit her and in 1959 she returned to take over from Seán Mac
Réamoinn as Regional Officer in the Cork studios). As Station Supervisor, Denis
was responsible for recruiting, training and rostering announcers, as well as the
administration of the department. He was, essentially, Head of Presentation.

Denis Meehan's grey hair belied his comparative youthfulness. He was
forty years old when I met him and I took to him instantly. A slightly rotund
figure, he had a voice that was both mellifluous and authoritative, while his
personality was good-humoured and learned: the personification of the sound
of Radio Éireann. A native of Ballyfin, Co. Laois, he was educated locally in
Knockbeg and spent a year studying for the priesthood in Maynooth College.
A bout of tuberculosis led to his leaving for University College Dublin, where

he studied English Literature. He acted in some college plays and, as Auditor, ran the English Literature Society. His first paper to that august body was on fantasists in Anglo-Irish literature, illustrated by such authors as Myles na gCopaleen and James Stephens. His conversation, with its purposely arcane references and maddening puns, was a delight to listen to. He loved words and, as well as being an accomplished announcer, newsreader and compere of request programmes, he was a proficient commentator on national events and state occasions. On the visit of President Kennedy, for example, he co-ordinated all the other commentators, supplying them with briefing material, and when he wasn't describing the scene himself, he was in the Continuity suite synchronising the coverage and music intervals, as one conducts an orchestra. He was on duty on the fateful night when the news came in from Dallas and he handled the emergency coverage. He was quietly proud of his ironic little footnote in Irish radio history: with the advent of Telefís Éireann, the radio and TV news operations were combined to supply both services, so the first live transmission from the new television studios in Montrose was the 1.30 p.m. radio news bulletin on Sunday, 10 December, read from the Sound studio by Denis Meehan, three weeks before the TV service opened. All radio news, ever since, has come from the Television Centre, delivered by a new species, the newsreader, with varying degrees of competence.

So, not only had we a formidable team of broadcasters, we had a fine team of teachers as well. Denis had done some formal teaching after leaving UCD, but his approach to announcer training was quietly low-key. There were no lectures; it was learning-by-doing. After we had met them as a trio, our coaches took turns over the weeks. Brigid seemed to concentrate on reading skills, giving us wads of scripts, in English and Irish, ranging from continuity intro-ductions and programme signposts to announcements for plays and classical music recitals and concerts. It was a vital element of radio announcing; we had to get it right, particularly on the occasions where a formal approach was needed. We were, after all, training to be the Voice of the Nation and standards must be maintained. All these exercises were recorded and played back by an operator, and discrepancies pointed out in a gentle fashion. I learned the general rules of pronunciation of foreign names, particularly the classical composers, and could read scripts on sight, if a tad warily. Denis gave me a tip on pronunciation that I use to this day: most mistakes are made by a wrong emphasis on a particular syllable of a word, so if you're not sure which part of a word to lean on, stress each part equally. For example, if you meet Shostakovich for the first time and are not sure which of his four syllables to stress, equal weight on all four comes out close.

Terry Wogan, if not actually contradicting them, sometimes put some of Brigid's rulings in perspective the following evening, particularly in less solemn settings. His more informal approach was already evident from his presentation of *Hospitals Requests*, which, he said, was the reason he had joined. He would borrow the newest pop records from the sponsored programme producers and bring to the programme a little levity for the sick and worried. Terry also had a warm and personal approach that addressed the listeners as individuals, rather than as part of a crowd. We did record programmes with Terry, wrestling with the gramophone decks in Studio 3, which were extraordinary contraptions. Unlike the EMT grams, these were Garrard turntables with a crane-like device holding the pick-up arm in the air over the spinning record. A manual lever on the side literally (as DJ parlance went) dropped the needle onto the record. They were designed for 78rpm records with bigger grooves and faster speeds, but using the same technique on Long Playing Microgroove records was like throwing a dart with a blindfold on— sometimes you hit the target, sometimes you didn't. I found that by ignoring the crane, and starting with the needle already dropped on the disc just before the first note (like I did at home), I achieved a better result.

Gradually, over the weeks, the skills took hold: the ability to 'talk against the clock', that is, to look at a clock while speaking and end exactly on the target time; to be prepared for breakdowns and to fill in with a degree of aplomb; to be ready for any eventuality and deal with it calmly; to be technically competent in operating the equipment. Then there was the problem of the letter 'T'. My theory was that because there was no comparable 'Th' sound in the Irish language, we are not conditioned to pronounce that sound. Hence our propensity to infest our speech with dis and dat. Likewise, there is no hard 'T' in Irish, so we tend to soften the letter after a vowel: we give it its value in the word 'hurt', but not in the word 'hut', which comes out as 'hush'. It is not a hanging offence, but if you put yourself forward as a broadcaster, you should be able to speak correctly and take some pride in your work. Just like the music profession: if you're training as a singer, you should be able to hit the note spot on, not out of tune. If you're not in the business, however, it doesn't really matter.

I suspect that Denis was aware of the two complementary approaches taken by Brigid and Terry. It was the mixture of the formal and the informal that he was looking for. Irish radio had suffered from a comparison with the BBC. It could not match its resources, but for some years it did ape its style. To listen to old recordings of news broadcasts by announcers like Patrick Holland, Bernadette Plunkett, Kathleen Dolan or Síle Ní Bhriain, is to be amazed at how anglicised they were. There was a distinct air of the Home

Counties about the approach by Denis's predecessors that, I believe, he was determined to change. Hence his championing of Terry Wogan as Senior Announcer and his recruitment of younger announcers like Gay Byrne (a part-timer who, according to Denis, was the best reader of a script he had ever heard), Mike Murphy and Maurice O'Doherty.

Denis liked people with an authentic, natural approach and particularly eschewed people who had taken elocution lessons or come from an acting background. Actors make lousy announcers, he believed, because they tend to act the part of an announcer, rather than be one. He was also wary of those 'who tried to sound like the man on the wireless', in other words, those who imitated or reproduced the style of another broadcaster, in an attempt to sound like the real thing. The best advice to any new broadcaster is 'be your-self'—a slightly tidied-up version of yourself, perhaps, but you nonetheless. Some of the trainee announcers were afflicted by what Denis referred to as a Speech Tune—a virus caught by some broadcasters that is very hard to shift. (Clive James called it 'plonking' in its BBC strain.) It's reading a script in a pre-determined way that bears no resemblance to the sense of the material. It's starting on a high note, using a singsong approach to navigate the peaks and valleys of the script, and always coming down on the end of a sentence. It includes those odd pauses. That bear no resemblance. To the sense of the script.

The Speech Tune is endemic, even today; you hear it chiefly on news bul-letins and reports, voice-over narration on television documentaries, and on pop radio. It's an artificial approach, sometimes prompted by nerves, but it's irritat-ing to listen to and, worse than that, tiring; people tend to switch off. The only cure is for the infected person to focus hard on the sense of what they're saying, rather than on the manner in which they're saying it. If the reader concentrates on the sense of the material, the sounds tend to take care of themselves.

All these insights were transferred to us obliquely, possibly by osmosis. There were no formal lectures, but problems were addressed as our three tutors encountered them. We were getting the hang of it and growing in confidence. One evening, we trooped in for our session around half past seven. Denis was seated in the large Studio 4, one of the originals, now used as a multi-purpose studio with its expensive grand piano contrasting sharply with the musty carpet and what looked like old army blankets covering the walls. It took a few minutes for us to sit around Denis and wait for the words of wisdom.

'What', he asked angelically, 'is the first requisite of an announcer?'

Our suggestions were numerous and a little over-confident: a pleasant voice, the ability to be calm under pressure, knowledge of Irish culture, technical know-how, multi-lingual... and other high-flown competences.

'All very important,' he said, 'and all highly desirable. But the first requisite is—to be there.'

Come again?

'To be present. To have your bum on the seat when the red light goes on. You can have the voice of John Gielgud, the stoicism of Gandhi and the artistic flair of W.B. Yeats,' he went on. 'But if you're not there, on time and ready to go, it counts for naught.'

It was Denis's none-too-subtle hint to be on time. Punctuality becomes second nature to radio people. We talk in seconds and when we say that the time is one o'clock, it should be one o'clock, not ten seconds after. Programmes should start and end on time. Sometimes, due to a previous over-run, a programme might start late, but in no circumstances could it start early. It was part of the Contract with the Listener that Denis espoused: we must treat them with deference. While the listeners may be ignorant on certain matters (that is, lacking information or not informed), they are not stupid. If we presume to serve the listener, we must also respect the listener.

And that respect should permeate our every action, not just on the big broadcasting occasions, but also on the daily running of the station. 'Announcing can be exciting,' Denis said. 'But it can also be exhausting. There are few more tiring experiences than being on the alert all the time when you're on duty. That, I think, is an announcer's major problem.'

Denis had done a great deal of serious thinking about his broadcasting vocation, and his philosophical views on the real essence of the job were continued every evening in the Tower Bar, directly across the road from the first door in Henry Street. We went there for our coffee break around nine o'clock those summer evenings and I sat in awe as, with great wit and integrity, Denis talked radio and announcing, answering questions, telling stories and making his dreadful puns. I thought that this must be how the pupils of Socrates felt.

'Even if he starts at half seven in the morning—he often does—he must be calm, authoritative and pleasant. It may be routine, but you must try to appeal to everybody,' he continued. 'Day in, day out, a lot of it necessarily becomes second nature. But that's what you have to guard against most. The day an announcer allows this fact to influence his presentation, the day he is no longer slightly nervous before a major assignment or the day he allows the sense of routine to take over—that's the day he should start thinking about another job. Because any of these things would mean that he had lost that sense of urgency, which alone holds the listeners' interest.'

It was fascinating to hear the job being almost forensically dissected. It was not just the major programmes and events that gave announcers personal satisfaction; it was also the small stuff. Denis was saying, effectively, that the measure of a person is discerned by how well he does the minor things.

'To hold the public ear, he must approach each routine announcement as if it were the only one he has ever made—or will make. Come to think of it, each announcement may be, for at least one listener, the most interesting thing broadcast that day. That's the sort of challenge that makes announcing an interesting job.'

He didn't have to tell me. It was the only job I wanted. But even if I didn't get the job, I wouldn't have missed this for the world. To hear broadcasting discussed at this level was invigorating; to realise that there was a depth and weight and profundity to the role confirmed for me that my ambition to be a broadcaster was no slight thing.

I did another series of *Records for Children* in early July and, at the end of the month, the announcer training course culminated in the final audition. I don't remember much about it, other than that it was in the ancient Studio 4. One by one, we were brought into the studio, given a sheaf of scripts and told that we had five minutes to prepare. There were announcements for continuity, drama, music, pop programmes, Irish language and classical music, as well as public and government announcements. I was on the lookout for a 'ringer', a deliberate mistake or a misprint. And sure enough, Denis had put one in. It was a communiqué from a government department, which gave a list of venues where a service was available—it could have been the mobile X-ray service—and went on to say 'the above are a list of locations where the public can avail of the service', proceeding in the dead language of the Civil Service. The notice was intended to be hung on a notice board, but as it was for speaking, the phrase 'the above are a list' made no sense (notwithstanding that it should be '*is* a list'—as we had learned in Oatlands, the collective takes the singular). I changed the script to read 'here are the venues for the mobile X-ray clinics next week…' and continued with the rest of the script. I was, apparently, the only one to spot it.

I left the GPO, where I had spent all my weekday evenings for the past six weeks, and went home. During this time, I was, of course, still endorsing fire policies with grim determination in the Insurance Corporation of Ireland. My father went home for lunch from Baxendales every day apart from Fridays, when he went up to Thomas Court to see his parents at lunchtime. On 10 August 1964, a week after the end of the training course, he picked me up on the corner of George's Street as usual and we both went home for lunch. My mother was there, as were my two sisters, busying themselves with lunch preparations and pretending that they hadn't noticed that a letter had arrived for me in a Radio Éireann envelope. I took it into my room to read.

Dear Mr Balfe,

I am glad to be able to tell you that as a result of the recent training course followed by audition, your name has been put on the panel on Radio Éireann relief announcers on Sound Radio.

I should be obliged if you would ring Supervisors Office to make an appointment to come in and see us, so that we can take note of the times at which you are available for relief work.

You understand of course that this involves no commitment, and that your retention on the panel will depend on our observation of your standard as time goes on.

Yours faithfully
Brigid Kilfeather
Assistant Studio Supervisor

I came back into the dining room. I must have been slightly shocked, for I seem to have fallen silent. I started to eat. Eventually, my father said, as casually as he could, 'Any word?'

The penny dropped. I had been successful. 'Yes—I got it.'

That evening, after my insuring labours, I was back in the Supervisor's Office with Brigid and Denis, who congratulated me warmly. I was surprised to learn that I was the only candidate going on air immediately, and the only male. Valerie McGovern and Annette Andrews would join later, but they needed an additional course in Irish first; Diane Lonergan and Nuala Robinson, if memory serves, joined later still. As for availability, I worked nine to five, so I could offer only evenings during the week, but weekends were free. I was scheduled for early continuity on the following Saturday morning.

'Don't worry,' Denis said. 'Terry will be there as Early Supervisor to hold your hand.' That's what I was afraid of.

Saturday, 14 August 1965 dawned bright and sunny. Outside public transport hours, we were entitled to a taxi and as I drove through the traffic-free streets of Dublin to the GPO, there were few people about. Ireland was not yet a generation of early risers, particularly on a Saturday. I arrived at 7.30 and made my way through the deserted building to the Continuity suite at the end of the long corridor. As always, there were three technicians scheduled: one in the control room, one to set up tapes and one to man the Continuity desk, on the other side of the announcers' studio. At a quarter to eight, a switch activated a huge capstan in the basement, with magnetic tape in a continuous loop, and the Radio Éireann call sign 'O'Donnell Abú' (officially the Station Interval Signal) rang out across the nation. As I set up records on the two turntables and checked the continuity cue-sheet, Terry Wogan arrived. Putting his arm around my shoulder in a gesture of comradely support, he said, 'Don't worry, Bren, we're in this together. There's no need to be nervous, I'm here to help if anything goes wrong.' I told him that I wasn't nervous, but if he continued to use the word 'nervous', I would be.

'Why don't you go outside and leave me alone?' I said.

'Wouldn't hear of it,' he replied. 'My place is here with you.'

At five to eight, I opened the microphone and addressed the nation.

'Radio Éireann. Mora dhaoibh ar maidin, a dhaoine uaisle. Inniú an Satharn, an ceithre lá déag de mhí Lúnasa, Lá Fhéile Naomh Eusebius, sagart agus mairtíreach.

'Good morning, everyone, on Saturday the fourteenth of August, the Feast of Saint Eusebius, confessor and martyr. The time is five to eight. Over now to the newsroom.'

As I made my way through the supplied script, I noticed a cold and moist sensation on the top of my head. As I read on, a trickle of water ran from my forehead down to my nose and fell onto the script with an audible plop. By the time I got to the end, my head, my shoulders and my script were drenched—but I kept on talking. Terry's idea of helping my nerves was to pour a jug of water over me as I made my first announcement.

'What did you do that for?' I asked him, a little taken aback at the action of my boss, the Senior Announcer.

'Oh, that was the Announcer Initiation Rite. Everyone gets it. Did no one tell you about it?'

'Don't recall it being mentioned, no.'

But I wasn't annoyed in the least. My focus had been on trying not to laugh, rather than on not panicking. Apart from being the job of my dreams, it also looked like fun. And if there was any fun to be had, Terry would find it. He went off to get breakfast and I manned Continuity, introducing the news at eight and filling in before the sponsored programmes started at 8.15. Then, following the news at nine, I introduced *Saturday Spin* and did a signpost to programmes before closing down the station at five past ten.

The next duty was the Sunday play, rehearsed during the week and recorded on Saturday mornings in the Drama suite, Studio 9. Terry brought me down and introduced me to the producer, Séamus Breathnach. They were ready to go when I arrived and Séamus thrust the announcements into my hand and asked me to go into the studio. The usual practice was to announce just the title and author at the beginning of the play and come back later to read the cast list at the end. Not today. I was also required to set the scene, to act as narrator. I shared the same microphone as the actors and, surrounded by the four actors required for the first scene, I read the easy bit: 'Radio Éireann, we present *An Enemy of the People* by Henrik Ibsen.' Then, having had only the most cursory glance at the script, I launched into 'The action takes place in a small coastal town in Norway. Dr Thomas Stockman...' I got through the half page of narration, complete with Norwegian names and locations, and crept out of the studio and back into the control room. 'Well done,' said Séamus. 'See you in about ninety minutes.' At 11.30, I was back to read the cast list in the closing announcement but by then, at least I had had the chance to study the characters and names of the cast.

At five to one, I was back in Continuity to re-open the station for the lunchtime news and announce the sponsored programmes: *The Donnelly's Programme*, now compered by Gay Byrne, *The Bird's Programme* with Cecil Barror, and the Daddy of them all, *The Waltons Programme*, 'your weekly reminder of the grace and beauty that lie in our heritage of Irish songs, the songs our fathers loved', introduced by the indestructible Leo Maguire. Those three programmes were live from Studio 5, the Sponsored Programmes suite, and I popped up to have a look at Leo Maguire. He operated his own turntables, wrote his own scripts, and acted as both presenter and producer. He had been doing the programme live since the 1940s and was a delightful gentleman who loved his music, even though most of the 'songs our fathers loved' were music hall and vaudeville songs from the Irish-American experience.

During the afternoon session, a friendly face popped around the door of the Continuity studio.

'Hi, I'm Mike Murphy. Glad to meet you.' We shook hands. 'Listen, I'm having my stag party tonight in the club. Why don't you come along?'

'Delighted,' said I. 'See you there.' I closed the station at three and headed home.

That evening, I was in the Radio Éireann/Telefís Éireann club in Ely Place celebrating Mike Murphy's imminent marriage to Eileen, who had worked with Fred O'Donovan in the Eamonn Andrews Studios. I knew few people apart from Denis, Terry and Mike. I was ordering a drink at the bar when a deep voice addressed me: 'You must be Balfe. I heard you this morning.'

It was Maurice O'Doherty, a red-haired Limerick man who had been recruited, along with Mike, in the previous intake of announcers. It was the first time I had ever been recognised by my voice alone. Mike and Maurice were to be my new colleagues and, more important, valued friends of long standing.

At the age of nineteen, I had become a Radio Éireann station announcer, the youngest ever. I was honoured to have become part of a national institution, relieved that my first day on duty had passed off with no hitches (jugs of water notwithstanding), and quietly pleased that I had, at least, fulfilled the first requisite of an announcer—to be there.

∿ SOUNDTRACK ∿

Did I really hear that?
Proof that the brain should be engaged before opening the mouth.

✎ 'Until next week, I leave you with just three little words—I like a proper cup of tea.'
HARRY THUILLIER ON *THE LYONS TEA SPONSORED PROGRAMME*

✎ 'Jim Reeves, sadly no longer with us but preserved forever in wax.'
CECIL BARROR ON *THE BIRD'S PROGRAMME*

✎ 'That's the fastest time ever run, but it's not as fast as the World Record.'
DAVID COLEMAN, BBC SPORTS COMMENTATOR

✎ 'Jane Russell's husband said he didn't want his wife to do either cleaning or cooking. He didn't want her to endanger her career by bending over a hot stove.'
US RADIO NEWS STORY ON THE WELL-ENDOWED FILM STAR

✎ 'You don't seem to know very much about The Rolling Stones, do you?'
'No. Should I?'
DONNCHA Ó DULAING REPLYING TO MICK JAGGER DURING RADIO INTERVIEW IN CORK

✎ 'The thieves got away in a fast car. (Well, they'd hardly use a slow one.)'
JOHN SNAGGE ON A BBC RADIO NEWS BULLETIN, FORGETTING TO CLOSE HIS MICROPHONE

✎ 'The weekly Health Talk is given by—a doctor?'
VARIOUS CONTINUITY ANNOUNCERS, INTENDING TO CONVEY SURPRISE THAT IT WASN'T GIVEN BY AN ARCHITECT OR A PLUMBER

✎ 'Red squirrels—you don't see many of them since they became extinct.'
MICHAEL ASPEL ON BBC RADIO

↢ 'I'm from Manchester, actually.'
'Oh, a real Manchurian, eh?'
HARRY THUILLIER INTERVIEWING A GUEST ON THE JACOBS *COME FLY WITH ME* PROGRAMME

↢ 'President Eisenhower today visited the Chocolate City—Hershey, Pennsylvania—to meet all those people who make Hershey Chocolate, with and without nuts.'
LOWELL THOMAS, US NEWSMAN

↢ 'For those of you watching who do not have televisions sets, live commentary is on Radio 2.'
TED LOWE, SNOOKER COMMENTATOR

↢ 'I felt a lump in my throat as the ball went in.'
TERRY VENABLES

Chapter 8 ⌒

| HENRY STREET PEOPLE

I got the first inkling that Radio Éireann was going to be a good place to work when, trying to enter the first door of Henry Street, I had to squeeze past the corpulent figures of broadcaster Seán Mac Réamoinn and genealogist Eoin 'The Pope' O'Mahony talking to the more ascetic poet, Patrick Kavanagh, and all bemoaning the fact that 'since Brendan Behan died, there are no characters left in Dublin'.

But there were plenty, even within the small department of continuity announcers. As I joined the panel of relief announcers, two existing reliefs left: Tony Lyons to go to television and John Henry to return home to the west. Suddenly, relief announcers were in short supply, so I was scheduled on most evenings and weekends. I still worked in the ICI in Dame Street and was supposed to be there until close of business. I was also meant to be in Henry Street in time for the five o'clock opening, so when the Chief Clerk in the ICI asked if that was me he heard the previous evening at five o'clock, I enigmatically pointed out that a lot of what you hear on radio these days is pre-recorded and, anyway, a lot of the announcers sounded very similar. Nevertheless, some fancy footwork was required to achieve the miracle of bi-location. At about twenty minutes to five, I would announce that I was going downstairs to get a file in the basement. I would slip out the back door opposite the Stag's Head, into Dame Lane, across Dame Street, through the pathway beside the Ouzel Gallery, across the Halfpenny Bridge, into Liffey Street and Henry Street and up in the lift to the third floor. The trick then, as now, was never to run. You might arrive on time, but you'd be incapable of coherent speech. A brisk walk—seven minutes, give or take—and I was in Continuity to say 'Dia bhur mbeatha, a uaisle' at five o'clock.

The late announcer would come on duty at five o'clock and cover continuity until half past six. Then another announcer would take over until nine and the late person would continue until closedown at ten to midnight. On Wednesdays, it was slightly different: the late announcer had to read the Cattle

Market Report at half past eight. This preceded *Farmer's Forum* with Patrick O'Keeffe, and for an arcane reason known only to the Irish Transport and General Workers' Union, it was read in the same studio as the programme. Again, Terry Wogan was on hand to ensure that it was made as difficult as possible.

'Come with me, Little One, and I shall bring you to the studio,' he said.

'Leave me alone,' I said.

We went to Studios 7 and 8. There were six burly agricultural types huddled around the table along with Paddy O'Keeffe. I was told that, because of the large panel, there was no seat available in the studio, and asked would I mind just leaning in over someone's shoulder and delivering the magic words. Delivered by courier earlier that evening, it was a closely typed communiqué from the Department of Agriculture and was of vital interest to the farming community, giving the prices achieved at various marts not only by cattle, but also by such exotic creatures as wethers, hoggets, short-horns, fresians and ewes. The latter animal, incidentally, was known as a 'yo' not a 'you'.

As I was walking into the studio, seconds before airtime, Terry opened the door and said: 'One more thing. Remember it's Fat Bullocks, not Fat Bollocks. Good luck.'

The red light went on. I leaned over and started reading. Two of the panel, unused to the disciplines of radio, were whispering away amongst themselves as the chairman tried to shush them. As I came to the fat bullocks, my brain did what Wogan had hoped it would. It asked, 'What was I not to say?' There was a decided pause after each 'fat' as I tried to concentrate on the correct vowel sound. I think I kept them all in the right corral, but the farmers figured out what was happening and became giggly. As I got to the end and said, 'Now over to Patrick O'Keeffe', there was an air of hilarity infecting the panel. No bad thing, I suppose.

The studios of the Irish radio service had changed little since the 1940s. Some new studios had been added along the front of the building and the Continuity suite had been installed in 1956, on the third floor of the GPO facing Moore Street. The studio was efficiently designed with two turntables, a control panel that let the announcer monitor the programmes on headphones or on a huge monitor. The prefade switches matched the eleven studios, enabling the announcer to listen to the output of each studio, whether live or not. (In fact, even today, old radio hands will not have a private conversation anywhere near a microphone.) In the centre of the Continuity desk was a red microphone switch, which gave the announcer access to the air. As it was the only studio that was self-sufficient and permanently live, the announcer could over-ride any programme.

Opposite the studio was the main Continuity desk, manned by the technical staff. All programmes, live or recorded, were routed through the desk on different channels, through the control room and on to the transmitters in Dublin, Athlone and Cork. On one occasion, a senior colleague was showing a young trainee technician how to operate the desk.

'You open the channel to start a programme. That gives a red light to the studio. When it's over, you close the channel. Apart from the announcer's microphone—you never ever close that one. They have complete discretion to say what they want,' he told the young trainee.

'What if the announcer opens the microphone and says "Fuck de Valera" or something like that?' the junior enquired.

'Just see it doesn't distort,' came the reply.

In the caste system of Radio Éireann, operational and technical staffs were sharply delineated and highly unionised, a hangover from the regime of the Department of Posts and Telegraphs. The highest operational grade was 'Senior Balance and Control Officer', a solemn title for the rarefied beings who mixed the channels for drama, live music and concerts. Under them, the basic-model B&Cs operated the desk for record programmes, talks, discussion programmes and announcements. The Tape Men were secreted in dubbing suites and operated the huge green EMI tape recorders, making programmes involving recorded material and committing to tape all pre-recorded programmes from the various studios. Those operational grades required basic technical knowledge but were largely seen as being closer to a production or artistic role.

The technicians, on the other hand, knew how things worked. They had come largely from the Post Office, the Army Signals Corps or the Merchant Navy as Radio Officers. There was a maintenance section, but technicians chiefly worked the main control room, manned the main Continuity desk and covered a mysterious shift called 'inside cubs', referring to the control cubicles in the GPO studios ('outside cubs', incidentally, were those permanent studios off the premises—the O'Connell Hall, home of the RELO; the St Francis Xavier Hall, where the Radio Éireann Symphony Orchestra resided; and the Portobello Studios in Rathmines, the address of the Radio Éireann Singers, all of which demanded a technical presence when in use). Because we spent hours looking at each other through the glass panel, the announcers and continuity technicians developed a strong rapport. At nights, we were usually the only people in the building.

Many of the technical staff became good friends, one of whom was Seán McCasey. He sometimes affected a slightly upper-class accent, belying his roots in Moyne Road, Drimnagh, and earning himself the soubriquet Lord Moyne. He was on the main desk one lunchtime, controlling all the output, when he made a phone call to his mother.

They were chatting away until his mother said, ' Hold on, Seán. I can't hear you very well. I'll go in and turn down the radio.'

'Stay where you are, Mother,' said his lordship. 'I'll turn it down from here.'

With that, he turned down the output of the entire station by half and continued the conversation. The nation suddenly found *The Kennedys of Castleross* reduced to a whisper. It was only after he hung up that Seán realised what he had done, albeit from the best of intentions.

Ian Corr, another technician, became a close pal. A dry laconic individual with a heart of gold, he was passionate about radio, his father having been an RÉ technician before him. On many an evening, we shared a taxi from the GPO to his house in Ballinteer, where his wife Bernie would supply supper. We talked of 'shoes and ships and sealing wax', of politics, radio and jazz. Ian had written a radio series on the history of jazz, presented by Andy O'Mahony, and he knew his stuff. His testament is in the Sound Library to this day in the valuable collection of rare jazz albums ordered at his behest. Ian also introduced me to Denis Brain's recording of the Mozart Horn Concertos, Jimmy Giuffre's 'Train and the River' and the writings of S.J. Perelman. Ian eventually became a sound operator, a producer and Head of Radio Sport.

Mick Conlan was not easy to impress. An ex-army man, and a rebel at heart, he refused to countenance the Irish versions of names when he had known the original owners by their earlier appellations. Thus, Seán Mac Réamoinn, Proinnsias Ó Conluain and Cathal Ó Gríofa were always openly referred to as Jack Redmond, Frank Conlon and Charlie Griffith. He also had a remarkable talent for causing conflict. Walking down the corridor with me one day, he noticed an engineer of short stature walking in front of us. He roared, 'Hey, Short-Arse!' and disappeared into an office. The engineer turned around to find me, the only other person in the corridor, in a state of some confusion.

John Walsh had come from the Navy and was a stickler for detail. He always wore a black suit, white shirt, black tie and navy gabardine overcoat. He was a bachelor and maintained that his monochrome wardrobe removed the need to make any decisions about his day's outfit. Every year, he went to the January sales in Clerys, pointed to his outfit and said, 'Same again, please.'

Des Coates, Tom Hely, John Penrose, Ted Stack, Ted Berry, Des Morahan, Denis Stephenson and many other technicians became regular colleagues and friends. Gerry Clinton was the oldest member of the technical team, with an irascible demeanour. He could view a cue-sheet setting out the evening's programme announcements and remark aloud, 'Jaysus, there'll be a right cock-up at nine o'clock.' He had spotted a discrepancy, but told no one about it. A typical one, for example, was when a tape label would read 'announcements on tape' and Gerry would see that they were also on the cue-sheet to be read live by the announcer. The listener would then get the unexpected bonus of hearing the announcement in duplicate. Gerry felt that it wasn't his job to cover up for other people's errors.

As the new boy, I drank in the myths and legends like a sponge. The stories about Seán Ó Murchú were part of the folklore of the station, but always told with affection. But my most immediate colleagues were the existing announcers. Una Sheehy had been there for some years and had the most attractive voice of all the woman announcers. A widow, she was the sister of Fergus Linehan and sister-in-law of Rosaleen Linehan and was, as you might imagine, fiercely intelligent and well read. She was also adept at self-deprecation and warned me about a slight anomaly in the design of the Continuity studio: the talkback switch, to communicate with the technician outside the glass, was situated an inch away from the live microphone switch. They had the capacity to be confused, as Una found to her dismay. After a particularly saccharine kiddies' programme, her private comment to the technician went out loud and clear on the air: 'Sweet Jesus,' she said passionately and with great feeling. When the technician explained gently that she had gone out on the air, she sat back and waited for the phone calls. Complaints came there none. Not one. Denis Meehan came up with the theory that people simply didn't believe that they had heard it; that a profanity during a children's programme from such a cultured voice as Una's was simply unimaginable. So, therefore, it couldn't possibly have happened.

In November 1963, Una was on continuity duty during a Sunday afternoon GAA match from Croke Park. She handed over to commentator Micheál O'Hehir and settled back into an armchair, knowing that she had nothing to say for at least two hours. She had no interest in listening to the match, and she dimmed the monitor so that it was just audible. She was engrossed in the Sunday papers when she realised that she could no longer hear the commentary from the outside broadcast. Turning up the monitor, she confirmed that there was indeed a marked lack of Micheál O'Hehir. She opened the microphone and apologised in the usual manner: 'Well, we seem to have lost contact with

Croke Park. We'll resume the commentary as soon as possible; meanwhile here is some music.' As the sound of the Gallowglass Céilí Band was heard throughout the land, the technicians attempted to find the fault on the line. Out of a sense of optimism, perhaps, they had left the channel to Croke Park open.

But it wasn't a fault. What the radio audience knew, but Una didn't, was that the public address system had called for one minute's silence before the game to mark the death of President Kennedy. Everybody was quiet, including O'Hehir, until the radio interrupted the solemnity with a selection of reels. There was an added complication. Many GAA fans brought their transistor radios to the game to follow the commentary as they watched. These radios, held on the shoulders of thousands of spectators, were now filling the stadium with dance music during the minute's silence. Because the channel was still open back at the GPO, the music was now going around in circles— the music on the transistor radios was being picked up by the effects microphones at the ground and being re-broadcast on radio. It was an ear-splitting display of what's known in the trade as 'howlround', sound disappearing up its own fundament. Some sense of decorum was restored eventually, but Una wasn't the better of it for weeks.

Una also took some time to live down her famous announcement on *Hospitals Requests* that became one of the most celebrated indiscretions in radio legend. She was fading a record and happily informed the Irish nation: 'There we must leave Harry Belafonte with his "Hole in the Bucket" and make way for the news.'

Another memorable gaffe occurred in the 1950s when Don Cockburn, an announcer at the time, was reading an item about President Eisenhower (known to all as 'Ike'). It resulted in a spoonerism, an unintended transposition of letters. The story read: 'The president has made an official visit to New Delhi. As he rode through the streets, the crowds shouted "Ike, Ike".' Unfortunately the vowel sounds of the last three words were transposed and the listeners were serenely informed that 'the crowds shited "Ouk, Ouk".' Ignoring the advice that it's sometimes best to leave well enough alone, Don tried to correct the error—'I'm sorry, I'll read that again'—and repeated the mixed vowels even more clearly.

John Skehan was a suave and urbane announcer with a voice that sounded like dark chocolate. He sported a thin moustache and was known by all as 'The Captain', befitting his previous rank as an officer in the Irish Army. He was still in the Army Reserve and spent two weeks every year attached to Military Intelligence ('a contradiction in terms', as he always said). Most of the time, I gathered, was spent in the Officers' Mess, but it afforded John an extra fortnight's holidays, it being a statutory requirement. 'What intelligence work do you actually do?' I asked him once.

'This year,' he said, 'I updated the file on Malta.' Secret meetings, clandestine espionage operations? 'Not quite—I cut out newspaper articles on that island and stuck them in a folder.' What for? 'In case the Irish Government ever declares war on Malta, they need to know their way around.' Valuable work, then.

His military background proved a bonus on the great state occasions, like the funeral of President Seán T. O'Kelly or the reinterrment of the remains of Roger Casement in March 1965. As a commentator, he was familiar with all the panoply and paraphernalia of the military: 'the obsequies, the cortège, the catafalque, the flag officer, the panegyric, the Band of the Curragh Command, the Last Post...' John's knowledge and descriptive powers had the quality of poetry.

John was also familiar to television viewers as an interviewer and presenter on *Broadsheet*, the first teatime magazine programme on Telefís Éireann. He had many stories from those early days, when programmes got on air by the skin of their teeth. The programme came from Studio 3, a small studio with just one interview set, comprising two armchairs and a small coffee table. In the opposite corner was a position for the programme presenter, in this case, Ronnie Walsh. The single interview position meant that there had to be quick transition between interviews, while Ronnie was introducing the next item.

On one occasion, John was assigned to do a live interview with a taxidermist. The complication was that the guest would be arriving late and there would be no opportunity to meet beforehand. They shook hands silently behind the cameras and when the previous interview ended, and Ronnie was introducing the forthcoming item, John and his guest were guided into their seats by the floor manager, Charlie Roberts. They had only thirty seconds to get settled, during which time Charlie had to apply a neck-microphone to the guest by putting a loop around his neck with a mike and cable attached. The introduction was almost finished, but Charlie wasn't. As the camera went live, he dropped to the floor and crawled out of the shot, as John was about to start the interview. Unfortunately, Charlie's foot caught in the cable, tightening around the interviewee's neck. As the guest emitted a startled cry, thinking he was being garrotted, the pressure from behind pulled him back even further, sending his feet into the air and causing him to fall backwards out of his chair. John, seeing his interviewee vanish before his very eyes, covered the occasion with his typical aplomb. When he thought that his guest was finally settled, he started the interview, his wild-eyed guest looking furtively behind him as if anticipating another sneak attack.

'Mr Robinson,' John began, 'you are a taxidermist…'

'No,' he replied, 'I'm a nuclear physicist.'

It was the interviewer's worst nightmare. When I asked John how he coped with the surprise, he replied nonchalantly, 'I just talked to him about nuclear fission, of course.' And he did. And he knew something about it.

Radio announcing equipped its practitioners to handle the unexpected. Announcers also tended to be well read and the knowledge base of the department was extensive, bordering on the esoteric. Maurice O'Doherty, for instance, was a meteorologist and an award-winning amateur actor. Before becoming a radio announcer, he had auditioned for the opportunity of being the first newsreader on Irish television. He was assured that he had been successful, but at the last minute the job went to Charles Mitchel. Lorna Madigan had come in at the same time as Maurice and was a teacher of deaf children. Technicians on the other side of the glass couldn't understand how she could laugh at some of their manly jokes, until they realised that Lorna could lip-read. Mike Murphy had been an actor, trained in the Brendan Smith Academy, and had appeared in the film *The Girl with Green Eyes*, from the book by Edna O'Brien, and had toured with the Gate Theatre. He also produced a couple of sponsored programmes for Brendan Smith Productions, notably with Beryl Fagan and Frank Purcell. Amidst all that talent, I could have felt inadequate, but at least I could explain the Average Clause.

I loved the job, part-time though it was. It also paid better than insurance. The fee for one duty was four guineas (four pounds and four shillings, for our younger listeners) and I was doing five or six duties per week. Back at the ICI, my weekly wage was three pounds and ten shillings, a sum that included one increment. The management had refused to recognise, or negotiate wage increases with, the trade union representing the insurance officials and there had been a number of work-to-rule incidents in response. I was explaining this to my dad on the way home to lunch one day, when he said, 'It's a wonder you wouldn't think of leaving that place.' My immediate response was 'Can I?' My father came from the generation that valued a full-time job for life, with a pension at the end. I didn't think he would recommend dropping a safe job in insurance for the uncertainties of broadcasting but, at least in the short term, the maths were clear. I could make up to five times my insurance salary from continuity alone, while freeing me up to pursue other opportunities.

By the time we reached Kilmacud, the decision was made. After lunch, I told Jimmy Mullarkey that working for the Insurance Corporation of Ireland was a privilege I could no longer afford and I was resigning forthwith. Working out one month's notice was irritating, as much for the company as for me. Whatever interest I had in Fire Endorsements was quickly dissipating and though I still did my work, it was with an increasing sense of tedium.

One morning, two weeks into my notice, I missed the bus and was half an hour late arriving in Dame Street. The assistant manager, Jimmy Edwards, called me in. He said he was aware that I was moving into full-time broadcasting, that they were sorry to lose me, that they all wished me well, but that there was no point in prolonging the agony and I could, if I liked, go now. I thanked him, cleared my desk and left by lunchtime, promising to meet the lads later for a drink. It only dawned on me, while walking down to the GPO, that, technically, even though I had resigned, I had also been fired.

It was early 1966 and I was now a full-time broadcaster, ready and willing to do anything. The most immediate benefit was that I could now do daytime continuity duties and was no longer confined to evenings and weekends. A shift could include some hours on continuity as well as a recording session or two. Denis Meehan didn't differentiate between new recruits and old hands—a trained announcer could be rostered anywhere, any time. Apart from continuity, there were requests for announcers from all the other departments, the Music Department in particular.

There was rarely any advance notice of what a session entailed; all that was on the roster was something like, 'Studio 5, Record 3–6.00 pm, Music Dept'. Usually, this was simply recording linking announcements for a classical concert or recital, but it was not known until the announcer arrived and asked for a script. He or she was expected to be word perfect first time, on both performers' and composers' names. One morning, I arrived for a Music Department booking to find the producer Jane Carty with two pages of script. The Radio Éireann Light Orchestra had entered a European radio competition for arrangements of folk music and James Bolger's 'Three Irish Dance Tunes' had won the prize. Jane wanted to send a copy of the recording to each of the other twelve entrants of the competition. The only slight difficulty was that she wanted to accompany the music with greetings to each country in its native language—and that's where I came in. I was to read three lines of script in twelve languages, which Jane had acquired from the relevant embassies. I could handle French, German and Italian, but was a little rusty on Polish, Serbo-Croat, Danish, Swedish, Norwegian, Hungarian and a few others. A mild panic set in. There was no other announcer around to consult with. I asked Jane if she could give me half an hour to do some preparation, then I'd come back and record within the allotted session time.

I found a phone, rang the control booth of the St Francis Xavier Hall and got the manager of the Radio Éireann Symphony Orchestra. Knowing that the majority of the orchestra was from Europe, I asked him could he bring to the phone a Pole, a Dane, a Swede, a Hungarian and so on. I spelled out the words to each musician, they pronounced them back to me, and I wrote them down phonetically. Half an hour later, as promised, I was back in the studio and delivered myself of the script with some panache. The trick with foreign names, I found, was to say them with a degree of authority. After all, only the person you're naming will know if you're wrong.

Another type of music session is the live recital, where the announcer is sent to an outside location. The Mariners' Church, Dun Laoghaire, and the Chapel in Trinity College were regular venues for recording organ recitals. Equally, I could be sent to the O'Connell Hall, the St Francis Xavier Hall, or the Portobello Studios, then the home of the Radio Éireann Singers—a dozen singers who sang the serious classical repertoire, Irish songs and new choral music. Hans Waldemar Rosen conducted the choir and I would sit at a table in front, supremely conscious that they knew the language better than I did. It did, however, teach me not to be afraid to ask the pronunciation of an unfamiliar word, a habit I continued.

Dermot O'Hara was regularly assigned to supervise music recordings. A regular occurrence was to schedule a Saturday recital in Portobello by a visiting pianist who would be appearing the following night in a concert with the symphony orchestra. Not only would I announce the pieces sitting at my table beside the performer; I also had to turn the pages of the music for him. I had long forgotten my music signatures and signs from Mrs O'Dwyer, so it was a little nerve-racking to stand beside the pianist holding the music of Chopin and watching for oblique nods from the pianist to turn the page. Sometimes the nods were so imperceptible that it wasn't clear if it was a signal or simply the musician being carried away ecstatically on wings of song. All these announcements seemed to start the same way: 'We now come to a recital by the Distinguished Young German Pianist…' On one occasion, we had a DYGP who spoke no English whatsoever and the operator couldn't convey to him that we were about to start the recording. Dermot O'Hara to the rescue: 'Don't worry,' he said. 'I speak German.' He pressed the talkback switch and roared: 'Achtung! Ve are going to record now. Stand by!'

Recording sessions could cover almost anything. Booking descriptions were so vague as to give no warning of what to expect. I had to cover music sessions, record programmes, reading letters on John O'Donovan's popular *Dear Sir or Madam* programme, drama announcements and election results. Occasionally, out of the blue, would come scripts in Irish, which I could read without necessarily understanding fully. I could follow the plot but was sometimes stuck on nouns. I could understand, for example, that Seán had got it from his father, that it was a very valuable object and that he had brought it with him to America, but I couldn't determine whether it was an ashtray or an armchair.

Denis Meehan was always there for advice and convivial chats. I pointed out that, unlike for most jobs, I had never done a formal interview or submitted a curriculum vitae, or even a character reference. 'Not necessary,' Denis responded. 'Remember, I spent six weeks with the candidates on the course, so I could determine their broadcasting skills and potential. I also met them regularly over a drink in the pub, where I could also get an idea of their personality—call it 'character', if you like—so I could determine whether I could leave any of you in charge of the station, that you could act coolly and make the right decisions. And in your case, I was pretty sure you could.'

If Denis was my mentor, he was also Terry Wogan's. Not only was he a great friend to Terry, he also had a strong influence on his broadcasting style. Inspired as he was by the Irish fantasists, Denis would often launch into a Flann O'Brien-style soliloquy on any topic, however esoteric. 'Where do you leave the failure of the Chilean banana crop?' he would ask as he began a stream-of-consciousness discourse on his chosen treatise. 'Isn't it a fright? Of course, the bould Chileans are great men for shinning up the trees to harvest the bendy fruit. Not like the canny Oriental, of course; the inscrutable Chinaman has a natural propensity for harvesting the paddy fields. I knew a Paddy Fields once…', and on it would go into the further recesses of his vivid imagination, often sliding into Latin. Terry would join in, adding more notes, until the two of them were improvising like a pair of jazz musicians, finishing occasionally on a spirited rendition of the 'Tantum Ergo'. It was a delight to hear, if a little confusing for hapless visitors to the Supervisor's Office. Years later, when Terry had joined the BBC, he fantasised happily about the Director-General and Chairman living on the roof of Broadcasting House, and described esoteric staff rituals like the Dance of the Seven BBC Virgins. 'They have it every year,' Terry told his listeners. 'But no one has ever turned up.' He was rebuked in a stiffly worded note from a woman of a certain age: 'There are virgins at the BBC, Mr Wogan, and I'm happy to say that I am one of them.'

The figure of Denis Meehan became a familiar one along the corridor of the GPO: a slightly rotund figure, with an overcoat and briefcase, lugging a fairly portable L2 tape recorder on the way to do another interview for *Who's News?* He lived an almost bohemian life in Ballymun, married to Sylvia with a young family. He later moved to Cornelscourt, but wherever he lived, cars abounded. Some were actually in working order, but were cursed by batteries that went flat. Many a time, having left to go home, he would come back to Continuity looking for a body to help push his car. It became one of the accepted extra-mural duties of the announcing staff. At home, friends were utilised to give a charge to the battery with jump leads. Terry tells of the time when Denis was called into RÉ in an emergency. There was no time to organise a charge-up, so he flagged down a passing car. It was a woman driver. Denis explained that he just needed a good push from her car, to get him going down the hill.

'Certainly,' said the obliging woman.

Denis got into his car, put it in first, foot on the clutch, ready for the push. It was only when he looked in his rear-view mirror that he saw that the woman had reversed a hundred yards up the road, and was now roaring towards him at 30mph. He could only sit, watch and brace himself. The thunderous crash was scarcely noticeable on Denis's wreck, but the woman's car had folded like a matchbox. Denis said that she was very apologetic.

Something of a *bon vivant*, Denis was fond of his food and wine. One Saturday lunchtime, I met him at reception with a guest he had just interviewed. It was the food writer and critic Egon Ronay. 'We are going to lunch,' he said. 'Care to join us?'

He added quietly that he had an impress, RÉ jargon for cash expenses. We went to one of the few good restaurants in the area, The Charcoal Grill, on the second floor of the Carlton Cinema and a favourite with radio people.

'I can recommend the steak, Mr Ronay,' said Denis, 'and the sole on the bone is always good.'

'Well, as I'm in Ireland,' Mr Ronay replied, 'I think I'll have the bacon and cabbage.'

Taken slightly aback at the proletarian choice of the eminent epicure, Denis moved to the wine list.

'The Beaujolais is very good, and the Côtes du Rhône is excellent,' Denis said. 'But perhaps you'd like to choose the wine, Mr Ronay.'

The critic perused the wine list. 'A bottle of the House Red, I think.'

Denis was amazed. 'But the Beaujolais… and the Côtes du Rhône…?'

'Excellent wines, both of them, and if I were sitting by the fire with a good cheese, I'd take the Côtes du Rhône… but for sloshing down bacon and cabbage, always the House Red.'

It's a story I always remember when I hear people being a trifle overstated about wine. Pretentious? Moi? I asked Egon Ronay if he had to judge a restaurant by only one course, what he would choose. He thought for a moment. 'The desserts,' he said. 'Because if they are done well, it's usually a sign that every-thing will be good. Many restaurants fall down on the desserts.' It's a good rule of thumb that still works.

The same restaurant was also the scene of a valuable learning experience. I was on late continuity and, Denis being Late Supervisor, I went with him to have dinner in The Charcoal Grill at half past seven. He had a heavy hand with the wine, but I took only one glass. Denis poured a dash into his mine-strone soup, and into mine for good measure. I refused a second glass, as I had to go back on air. Denis pointed out that as I had nothing to say until ten o'clock, another glass would be well absorbed by then. I took the second glass. It was a Tuesday, the night of the weekly symphony concert and, even though I was due back at nine o'clock, it was the accepted practice that the other announcer, who had plenty of time to prepare the script, would open the concert at 9.01 p.m., directly after the news headlines. I would then close the concert an hour later. As I stood outside the studio, waiting for John Skehan to read the opening announcement to the tape, he rushed out. 'Sorry I can't open the concert,' he said. 'My son has fallen off the roof of the shed and I have to get home immediately.' With that, he was gone.

I sat in the chair, just as the news was ending. I found the script, two and a half pages of the purplest prose that *Groves Dictionary* could supply, adapted slightly by Venetia O'Sullivan in the Music Department. They always began the same way: 'Radio Éireann. We come now to our Symphony Concert, in which the Radio Éireann Symphony Orchestra is conduced by Tibor Paul...' (The Director of Music was a vain man and changed the pronunciation of his name regularly—Teebore Paul, Tibber Powl—and the announcers had to remember what that day's styling was.)

I started to read the script, sight unseen. While reading the first lines on the page, I was also trying to scan the bottom half of the page, to see what lay ahead. Bloody Russians. They were everywhere—Tchaikovsky, Mussorgsky, Rimsky-Korsakov—and I had no idea what was on page two. As I read, the second glass of wine started to take effect. I started to slur, imperceptibly at first, but becoming more conspicuous as I trudged through the turgid script. I slowed down but the slur persisted, particularly on the letter 'S'. I got to page two, scanning down the page as I read the top thereof. There were further Russian obstacles ahead, mainly family names and small villages high in the Caucasus Mountains. This could end in tears. Whilst manoeuvring through contrapuntal melodies and harmonic influences, I decided to quit while I was ahead. 'Apart from all that,' I announced, 'it's a very nice tune.' I gave the signal to cue the tape.

Denis was more bemused than annoyed. I blamed it on the second glass of wine.

'Well, you shouldn't have taken it, should you?' he said.

'But you offered it…'

'Doesn't matter. You should have refused.'

Numerous memos from the Director of Music took great exception to the shorter-than-usual announcement, but Denis batted back on my behalf by quoting Announcer Discretion, the principle that the person on duty had the authority do make any changes he thought meet and seemly. He also suggested that, perhaps, the announcement was too long for the time slot. But I never forgot the lesson: drink after the broadcast, not before.

Some time later, I was sitting in the Continuity studio, waiting to take over from Terry. He had turned on the Rehearse Mode, meaning that the studio was temporarily disconnected and he couldn't hear the output of the station. He was preparing a request programme, listening to records on the two turntables. The technician outside came on the talkback: 'That's it,' he said. The Chamber Music Recital had under-run by ten minutes and Terry hadn't spotted it or been prepared for it. That's the time we would normally say, 'Well, we have some time in hand before the news headlines, so here is some music….' Unfortunatately, both turntables were occupied by The Rolling Stones and The Nashville Teens respectively, not the most appropriate choice to follow the best efforts of the Radio Éireann String Quartet. Terry turned to the clipboard containing all the station announcements: trailers, promotional material, concert advertisements. He read them all, but still had four minutes to fill. He then read the day-sheet, the list of forthcoming programmes that night. Still he was two minutes under. He picked up the only bit of paper left unread: 'Now, before we go to the newsroom in two minutes, you might like to know who will be announcing for you over the next week.' And unabashed, he read the Announcers' Roster. 'On early continuity tomorrow will be Lorna Madigan, while Mike Murphy will be in at lunchtime…', and on he went through the names until he reached the target of the ten o'clock time signal.

We still closed down the station after the morning and lunchtime transmissions, so we were off the air between 10.00 and 1.00 p.m. and between 3.00 and 5.00 p.m. It was an anomaly that Terry, like the rest of the announcers, found slightly ludicrous in the middle of the Swinging Sixties. Signing off after the three o'clock news headlines, he calmly informed Radio Éireann listeners: 'We're closing down now until our Children's Programmes at five o'clock. If, however, you'd like to keep listening, the BBC Light Programme is broadcasting some popular music, which you might enjoy. But be sure to join us again at five. Good afternoon.'

Before we closed down just after three o'clock, we often had to read the List of Declared Runners for a horseracing meeting the following day. The tradition went back to the newspaper strike in the early 1950s, when Radio Éireann also introduced an early-morning news bulletin. The devotees of racing needed to know what was running where.

The list came from the Horseracing Board, or some such, and usually covered six or seven races with, perhaps, fifteen horses in each. There could be over a hundred horses' names, which had to be read clearly at dictation speed so that the punters could write them down. The announcer also had to peruse them ahead of time to check for odd pronunciations (unlike the BBC announcer who insisted on pronouncing the famous Irish horse 'Quare Times' in its Latin form as 'Quar-ay Teem-ays'). The whole list took about ten minutes to read before closedown. The roster ordained that the announcer who was closing down after three o'clock was usually booked for a recording at four o'clock, so he was going nowhere. The continuity technician, on the other hand, finished his shift at three o'clock. One week, the irascible Gerry Clinton was on the same shift for five days. 'Any Gee-Gees?' he asked on Monday afternoon. I confirmed that The Curragh was meeting all week and that there would indeed be a catalogue of contenders to be shared with our listeners. 'Well, hurry up then,' he urged. 'I've a train to catch.' I noticed he had his overcoat and scarf on.

Gerry had been in a foul mood all morning and I decided not to oblige; if I'm staying, I thought, he's staying. I read the List of Runners as slowly as possible, taking huge pauses between each name. Through the glass, I could see Gerry stamping up and down the control room. I proceeded with my slow march, closing the station at a quarter past three, five minutes later than the normal time. Gerry was incandescent.

I, on the other hand, was delighted and enlisted the help of my colleagues to build on the record. The following day, Mike Murphy followed my snail's pace, but added an extra ingredient: he spelt every second horse's name. 'No. 6, Arkle. I'll spell that for you. A-R-K-L-E. That's Arkle.' Mike added another five minutes to the record and Gerry was fit to be tied. The following day, John Skehan made an attempt. He matched Mike's record and then added the *coup de grâce*, 'In case you missed any of those, I'll repeat them for you.' And he read the whole list again. Come Thursday, Terry was on, repeating John's technique and adding, 'Just before we close down, a signpost to some of the programmes you can hear later this evening.' Terry got the closedown as far as half past three. Could the record be matched on Friday?

All our hopes were on Maurice O'Doherty. But before the off, Gerry Clinton came in to tell him, 'You can do what you like, youse whores, and you can stay as long as you like, but I'm leaving. The microphone channel will be open anyway so you can talk away to your heart's content, you lousers.' It was true that the microphone was always on and that the announcer had control of the on/off switch, but Gerry had reckoned without the wiles of Limerick. The continuity microphone was suspended by a cable from the ceiling and as Maurice began to read the list, he set the microphone swinging back and forth like a pendulum, first near, then far away from the sound of his voice. As it swung, Maurice's voice got alternately louder and softer, so that Gerry had to balance the channel to compensate for the variations in sound. Maurice shattered the world record for the List of Declared Runners by closing down the station at twenty-five minutes to four. The whole escapade ended when Gerry put in a claim for half an hour's overtime and Denis told us to lay off.

Another odd facet of public service broadcasting that I had to implement once or twice was also steeped in our equine heritage. If we got a call in Continuity from a veterinary surgeon with an urgent request, and it was outside office hours, we were to call him back to verify it was legitimate and then take the appropriate action at the earliest opportunity: 'Here is a special announcement. A foster mother is required for a foal in Co. Kildare. Please call this number urgently…' We would repeat the announcement slowly in serious tones. I thought it was charming. Most times the baby horse was rescued by a kindly breeder, the announcer sometimes acting as a sort of midwife by answering phone calls from listeners who missed the details and contacting the vet on their behalf.

The scheduled announcer, in the absence of a supervisor, was effectively the duty officer responsible for everything that moved. We also acted as the Press Office, Complaints Department and General Purpose Oracle: all phone calls were put through to the announcer. Occasionally, Mrs Haughey, the switchboard operator, would extend calls to the pub, if you were on a coffee break. Sometimes, the calls were for general information: the capital of the Philippines, the date of the Battle of Clontarf, Elvis Presley's first record on RCA. We were the equivalent of Google or Yahoo.

'You lads in there seem to know everything, so can you tell me the highest mountain in America?' was the usual approach, probably from someone in a pub quiz. Most times, between the announcers and technicians, we could oblige. One regular caller, when he heard me on continuity, was a blind listener. He rang to get the schedule for the forthcoming week's programmes. I had to go through each day meticulously—who is the guest on *Town Hall*

Tonight, what teams are taking part in *Question Time*, who's compering *Morning Melody?*—all taken at a deliberate pace. I don't know how he remembered the details, or how he wrote them down, but it took a long time to cover seven days of programmes.

I don't recall too many complaints, though; maybe our programmes were not offensive or controversial, or perhaps the listeners' sensibilities were not so acute. All complaints were noted and passed on to the Supervisor, who distributed them to relevant departments. The drill was to behave courteously to the listener and not to engage in heated discussion. Sometimes I had to tell the caller that I had to make an announcement and ask would they mind hanging on. This had the satisfying effect of engendering a sense of stupefaction in the listener, as he heard you on his phone and also on his radio. It also calmed him down, somewhat. Maurice O'Doherty, on the other hand, could be relied upon to take issue with the more obdurate callers. He regularly engaged in rigorous debate about the programme in question, often to the point of summarily slamming down the phone on them.

John Skehan gave me a good tip when dealing with phone callers who were overstaying their welcome. 'The trick', he said, 'is to hang up when *you* are talking, not when they are talking. They think there is a fault on the line, as they assume he'd hardly hang up on himself.' It works very well. The response I devised for myself was to tell the complainant that I would be delighted to take a note of their comments, and if they could just give me the serial number of their radio licence, I'd be able to process the complaint immediately. Most times they said they hadn't got it to hand. 'No problem,' I'd reply sweetly. 'Just have a look for it and then ring me back. I'm here for the evening. Thanks for calling. 'Bye now.'

Working in Radio Éireann was the best job in the world, as I had always believed it would be. The training in continuity taught me to be cool in grievous circumstances, to be decisive in uncertain conditions, to be prepared for the unexpected and to be flexible in all situations. It was the perfect bedrock for a career in radio.

∿ SOUNDTRACK ∿

Favourite Irish Tunes—slow airs, poignant songs and some to sing along to.

- ✦ 'Jimmy Mo Mhíle Stór' (arranged by Archie Potter)/RTÉ Concert Orchestra, conducted by Colman Pearce
- ✦ 'Ar Bruach na Carraige Báine'/Séamus Begley and Mary Black
- ✦ 'Moonlight in Mayo'/Frank McCaffrey
- ✦ 'The Ships are Sailing' (selection of reels)/Brian Hughes (tin whistle)
- ✦ 'An Tine Bheo'/Seán Ó Riada
- ✦ 'Táimse im' Choladh'/Iarla Ó Lionáird
- ✦ 'Dancing the Baby' & 'The Lodge Road'/David Curry's Irish Band
- ✦ 'Limerick Lament'/The Chieftains
- ✦ 'The Coolin'/Geraldine O'Grady (violin)
- ✦ 'Teddy O'Neill'/Patricia Cahill
- ✦ 'Cailín na Gruaige Báine'/Aoife Ní Fhearraigh
- ✦ 'Magic Bracelets'/Hothouse Flowers
- ✦ 'Sometimes You Can't Make It On Your Own'/U2
- ✦ 'Easy and Slow'/Jim McCann
- ✦ 'The West's Awake'/Johnny McEvoy
- ✦ 'Cottage by the Lee'/Joe Lynch
- ✦ 'Whistlin' Phil McHugh'/Brendan O'Dowda
- ✦ 'Lay Me Down'/Glen Hansard
- ✦ 'Riverdance'/Bill Whelan
- ✦ 'Spanish Lady'/Maighréad and Tríona Ní Dhomhnaill

Chapter 9 ～

| ANNOUNCER ON DUTY

Donal Stanley held the title of Sponsored Programme Officer in Radio Éireann. Assisted by Billy Wall (who had, in RÉ custom, mutated into Liam De Bhál), he was responsible for allotting airtime to the many programmes presented by the commercial sector and their advertising agencies. I would deal with him later when I entered that world, but my immediate problem was how to get on to *Morning Melody*.

The programme ran from 9.10 to 10.00 every weekday morning and came under the aegis of Donal's department. It rotated among the freelance comperes, of whom I was now one, a body that included stalwarts like Noel Andrews, Larry Gogan, Joe Linnane, Ronnie Walsh, Val Joyce, Bart Bastable and others who had made their name chiefly on sponsored programmes. The panel also included some actors who had a penchant for radio—T.P. McKenna and Pat Layde among them. It was one of the programmes available to the freelance sector and a valuable source of revenue for them.

Donal told me that he would be auditioning soon and he would put my name down on the list of possible comperes. He assembled an impressive list of contenders and, one morning, ran short recording tests, for music presentation as much as for voice quality. I passed and became a new addition to the roster; the only one, to my surprise. On 3 January 1966, I presented the programme with Larry Gogan beside me reading live commercials. The music was in the easy-listening, middle-of-the-road style and was heavy on the orchestral catalogue from such worthies as Nelson Riddle, Lawrence Welk and Herb Alpert, as well as popular singers like Ella Fitzgerald, Petula Clark and Jack Jones. I always made a point of including some current pops—The Beatles, The Spencer Davis Group, Chris Andrews and Del Shannon. With regular access to the Gramophone Library, spending a day picking music was my idea of heaven; they had the Stanley Black and Bert Kaempfert Orchestras in abundance, but they also had a good range of pop, jazz, film music and show tunes, as well as an immense classical catalogue of operas, symphonies, overtures, cantatas, oratorios, tone poems, nocturnes and études. Trained singers were classified under their vocal range—soprano, contralto, tenor, baritone, bass—but I was more interested in the popular singers and groups who were classed, rather snootily, as 'Variety Singers', a category that included everyone from The Dubliners to Barbra Streisand, from The Rolling Stones to Frank Sinatra. Looking for The Clancy Brothers and Tommy Makem one day, I was defeated by the system until the gramophone librarian, Kathleen Evans, told me patiently that they were categorised under 'National Choirs'. Of course. Silly me.

All the *Morning Melody* programmes were scripted and subject to approval by the Sponsored Programmes Office. I still have a script marked 'way above 99 per cent of the listeners', a comment by Billy Wall on a slightly subtle play on words. My defence was that those who got it, got it—those who didn't wouldn't notice it in the first place. The programmes were live and were rehearsed meticulously from 8.00 a.m. by the producer, Petronella O'Flanagan, a formidable woman with a deep voice. She ran the entire programme, timing everything on her stopwatch, while the B&C (balance and control) got a level on each disc, sometimes wincing, in the time-approved RÉ fashion, at the amount of echo or compression on the recording. Only after the rehearsal could the duration of the programme be finally determined and adjustments made.

It seemed to me that the same result could be achieved by doing the maths—adding up the durations of the records and the links—but such an approach would not have spotted the anomalies in Ronnie Walsh's way of choosing a programme. In the Library, he had gone to the FLP Section (Film Music and Light Orchestral), taken out a block of twenty LPs in sequence and typed up a script without the tiresome obligation of actually listening to the tracks. Then, on rehearsal, he introduced the first item: 'Good morning, everyone. To start today, the Monte Carlo Light Orchestra will play a joyful piece called "Fanfare for a Princess".' There followed a fanfare for single trumpet, its suddenness matched only by its brevity: it lasted all of five seconds. Oops. Back to Ronnie: 'That was the delightful "Fanfare for a Princess",' he went on. 'And now that you're well awake, here is Doris Day.'

I presented the programme many times over the coming months. The commercial reader was billed in the credits, from the original concept of passing off the commercials as a social service: 'Bart Bastable with some good music and Larry Gogan with some good news for housewives.' In the beginning, the two alternated, music one day, commercials the other, but the arrangement lapsed and comperes were engaged for one duty or the other, not both. Most of my colleagues, Larry Gogan, Val Joyce, Bart Bastable,

Ronnie Walsh and Noel Andrews, were all well established at this stage: Larry had come from sponsored programmes, Val and Bart were graduates of the Irish Hospitals Sweepstakes Programme and Noel was one of the first to take up compering as a profession, both on radio and also in the theatre, acting as question master at the Theatre Royal. (He told me that he had a standby question in case anyone came near to winning the star prize too early: 'How many sixpenny coins laid on top of each other would it take to reach the height of Nelson's Pillar?' It didn't matter how many the unfortunate contestant guessed— they were always wrong). Ronnie Walsh had come from the theatre, but had also set up Broadcasting and Theatrical Productions Ltd as a production company in the commercial sector, producing *Living with Lynch* as well as numerous sponsored programmes. Between the two hours of rehearsal and broadcast over five days, it was impossible not to strike up a rapport with my new colleagues.

Apart from Joe Linnane, that is. Joe was a legend in Irish broadcasting. He had acted in O'Casey plays in the Abbey Theatre and during the war appeared on BBC Radio as part of the supporting cast of *Meet the Mulligans,* with Jimmy O'Dea. He was one of the first presenters of *Housewives' Choice* on the BBC Light Programme, acted in many British movies and became a household name in Ireland for his cheery, cheeky approach to *Question Time,* which he made his own. He was also a popular rugby commentator for radio, in the days before sports coverage became so solemn, although his extravagant word pictures did not endear him to the more serious aficionados of the game: 'He's heading for the line at a hundred miles an hour and there's ten million Frenchmen hanging on to him.'

Working with Joe on *Morning Melody* was a privilege for me although he appeared less than enchanted by the arrangement. During rehearsal and the live broadcast, he would come into the studio in a marked manner, read his group of five or six live commercials and exit until required again for the next break. I thought this unusual, as all of the others would stay and chat amiably. I mentioned this slight aloofness to Gene Martin, who was the alternate producer. Was it something I'd said? I wondered. No, Gene explained, it was simply that Joe didn't like working with non-professionals. He always took a degree of exception to Cecil Barror, who compered *The Bird's Programme,* one of the afternoon sponsored programmes. Cecil worked in the ESB in Fleet Street, Dublin, and during his lunchtime, two or three times a week, had a bite in a local café and strolled down to the GPO to present the live quarter-hour programme, before ambling back to the day job.

Joe thought that if you wanted to be a broadcaster, you should have the courage of your convictions and do it as a profession, not as a hobby or a sideline. And Joe thought that I was an insurance official, moonlighting as a compere. Hence the distance. I explained to Gene that I was a complete full-time professional since I had left the ICI four months before. Gene must have brought up the subject in conversation with Joe, because the next morning he was sweetness and light, chatting away happily and, moreover, staying in the studio for the entire programme. We went for coffee afterwards and became the best of friends for the remainder of his career.

There was something unsullied, almost magical, about presenting the first live music programme of the day. Even as I played the music, I began to appreciate that I had the ear of the nation, that anyone listening to the radio that morning was probably tuned to me. I could imagine, in my mind's eye, the music emanating from radio sets in kitchens all over the country, in villages and towns, cities and suburbs. I hoped they liked what was offered. In fact, working from the GPO, I was able to see the audience in real life. I discovered a practical version of audience reaction as Dubliners gave instant comment on programmes outside the door in Henry Street. 'Merciful hour,' they would cry. 'Where did you get that bleedin' record from? Did someone throw it out, or what?' One thing about Dubliners: they kept your feet on the ground. The Moore Street Ladies, dealers in fish, fruits and vegetables, were not shy either in voicing their comments. My colleague, Bill O'Donovan, overheard one of them discussing Jackie Kennedy's recent marriage to Aristotle Onassis. 'I wouldn't have him', she said, 'if his arse was encrusted with diamonds.' Joe Linnane often told the story of coming in on a Saturday afternoon to do a programme in his gardening clothes—not dirty, just worn. Looking into Arnotts window, he heard two of the dealers talking about him behind his back. 'It is, I'm telling you.'

'No, it couldn't be,' said the other.

'I'm sure of it. It is Joe Linnane.' A pause. 'Jaysus, wouldn't ya give him a penny?'

Terry Wogan, by now a familiar face from television, had a similar experience with two Dublin denizens in Davy Byrne's pub. The two ladies of nighttown joined the company to talk to Terry about his work. Terry was, as always, exceedingly polite and charming, even though he was with others. Eventually, the girls got up to leave, Terry wished them well and as they reached the door, one of them turned around and in a loud voice addressed the entire pub: 'Would you look at him? Terry Wogan. Thinks he's fuckin' wonderful.'

As a freelance, I continued to present the children's record programme at a quarter past five, for which I had suggested a slightly catchier name change, *Five into Fifteen*, and I had been back with my original contact, Róisín

Lorigan, who offered me the chance to present *Ireland's Top Ten*. Broadcast on Mondays at a quarter to seven, this was the most listened-to pop music programme on Radio Éireann. In fact, for many years, it had been the only pop programme on the air, but by now had been joined by *Pop Call* and *The Seventeen Club*. As a barometer of Irish musical tastes, the Irish pop charts of 1966 reflected the big international hits as well as the continuing popularity of the Irish showbands, with Manfred Mann, The Beatles and The Kinks sitting cheek by jowl with Dickie Rock, Joe Dolan and the Royal Showband. Increasingly, Irish records were achieving the coveted No. 1 slot; there were eighteen that year, compared with only seven international. A new trend was also emerging, as folk groups and soloists plumbed the catalogue of Irish and faux-traditional songs to usher in an era known as 'The Ballad Boom'. The Ludlows and The Johnstons were first, and that year also marked the debut of a solo singer whose longevity can be attributed to a fine voice, musicianship and rapport with an audience. Johnny McEvoy was in GPO reception, he later told me, on 14 November 1966, wondering if his first single was going to squeeze into the Top Ten. The chart was a closely guarded secret until airtime, but I gave him the thumbs up and he got the impression that the news was good. A couple of hours later, he heard me announce that he was No. 1 with 'Muirsheen Durkin'. The Ballad Boom can be explained, to some extent, by the nationalistic feelings generated by the extensive celebrations of the 1916 Rising at Easter that year. But it was not the only boom that year.

As a freelance, I was increasingly presenting more record programmes, but I was also working on continuity. On Tuesday, 8 March 1966, I was scheduled for early continuity. The ritual was always the same. Up at six, breakfast while listening to the BBC Light Programme, taxi calls at seven, arrive at the GPO before half past seven. It was a bright crisp morning and, as usual, the streets were deserted and clean. As the taxi came across O'Connell Bridge, there was a distinct change to the streetscape. The top half of Nelson's Pillar was missing and was lying in the street below. All that remained was a stump. Nelson's head was nowhere to be seen. Round the decay of that colossal wreck, gardaí and soldiers were looking officious. They stopped the taxi at O'Connell Bridge and refused to let me through. I persuaded an inspector that I was the duty announcer on Radio Éireann and explained that, if I weren't let through, the station wouldn't open. Chunks had fallen off the roof of the GPO into the top of Henry Street, but otherwise the building looked intact. There were few people about, apart from officials; I wondered why, but, of course, how could anyone have heard about it until the radio went on the air? I got through and went to the Continuity studio. Charles Mitchel was the early newsreader in Montrose. I was tempted to steal his thunder by saying, 'From a Nelson Pillar-less GPO, over to the newsroom', but I resisted and let Charles announce the news that Ireland's brave patriots had also blown up parts of the GPO as a sign of their discontent. It made as much sense as Catholics blowing up the Vatican or Muslims blowing up Mecca. Fortunately, no one was killed in the explosion.

The stump of the Pillar was removed a couple of days later by the army, causing more damage to the surrounding area than the original explosion, and, as a side effect, giving The Dubliners their first hit record with 'Nelson's Farewell'. The monument was much missed by their fellow citizens and I was glad that, unlike most other Dubs, I had actually climbed the thing.

One month later, security was tight at the GPO as the fiftieth anniversary of the Easter Rising was formally commemorated. For the first time, Radio Éireann issued security passes to enable staff to access the GPO, a practice that continues to this day.

I was on duty on Saturday morning and John Skehan was on the soporific late Sunday evening shift. John suffered from 'the sleeping sickness' and was prone to bouts of narcolepsy, slipping into the occasional catnap. He even managed to go asleep while reading the news: he handed over to John Ross for the five-minute Topical Talk after the bulletin and slipped into a pleasant snooze while it was being delivered. John Ross soldiered on, despite intermittent snores from across the table, and by kicking his shins, managed to awaken his colleague in time for him to say, 'That was John Ross.'

So, John Skehan was in relaxed mood that Easter Sunday evening, knowing that if he did nod off while reading the papers, the technician would wake him by the simple expedient of momentarily cutting his monitor. John was woken by silence, not noise.

Suddenly, the door of the Continuity studio opened and in walked a character straight out of Central Casting: a trilby hat pulled over his eyes and a white raincoat, with a suspicious bulge under his left armpit. 'Garda Special Branch,' he said, and showed his credentials to John. He seemed upset. 'What can I do for you?' asked John politely.

'I'll tell you what you can do for me,' said the officer through gritted teeth. 'I've been doing a security check on the GPO. I came in off Henry Street, gave no identification to the four gardaí and six soldiers guarding the entrance, just asked them where the live radio studios are. They sent me up in the lift to the third floor. At the reception desk, there were more gardaí and soldiers and I asked your own security man where was the live studio. "End of the corridor," he said. I came in to your technical people and asked where was the studio that was always live and could over-ride any programme. They sent me in here, no questions asked. So, I have passed through three separate check-points, without being asked for any credentials, my identification never challenged or checked. So, here's what you can do for me, mister. You can answer this question: what if I was an IRA member and marched in here and pulled a gun on you and demanded to address the Irish Nation? What would you do?'

John calmly looked him in the eye. 'I'd stand aside and show you how to work the place.' John was used to dealing with such overbearing people in the army. 'I may have been willing at one time to die for Old Érin,' he continued suavely, 'but I'm certainly not willing to die for Radio Éireann.' The Special Branch officer left, a chastened man.

The Irish Army had peacekeeping troops in Cyprus at the time and Radio Éireann started a request programme to send greetings from the troops to their loved ones at home. Along with other announcers, it fell to me occasionally to present *Cyprus Requests* and John's army experience proved invaluable. 'Remember, the men always try to send coded messages that would bypass the officers, so you've got to look out for certain phrases,' he warned, 'particularly those personal messages addressed to their wives or girlfriends.' Really? Secret Codes? 'Absolutely,' he said, naming two phrases that I had been happily reading out for weeks: 'You won't feel it until Christmas' and 'It won't be long until September.'

Sometime in the early summer of 1966, I left Radio Éireann to go for lunch, while Valerie McGovern took over on continuity. By the time I returned an hour later, the name of the station had changed. Valerie was preceding the sponsored programme announcements with a new Station Identification—'Radio Telefís Éireann'. And so, RTÉ was born—and Valerie was the first to say it.

It wasn't the only thing to change. Denis Meehan called me into his office and said that there was a permanent announcer job vacancy and that I should go for it. He'd like me to get it, he said, but there were a few official procedures to get over. RTÉ had to advertise all vacancies publicly, so there would be a formal job description circulated to which I should reply. 'You would then have to do another training course,' he said, 'before we could consider appointing you.' I looked at him, dumbfounded. 'If, on the other hand,' he continued, 'you had holidays arranged to coincide with the course, there's not much we could do about it, as long as you're here for the final audition.' He looked at me meaningfully. I got the message.

The job advertisement was issued and I was pleased to note that, for the first time, they had lowered the minimum age to 20, which I now was. Apart from the usual pleasant voice and ability with languages, Denis had couched one requirement with Jesuitical precision—'the ability to read aloud in Irish'. I could do that, anyway.

The training course started as I ended a stint on *Morning Melody* and on 9 September left to go on holidays with my pal from the control room, Des Coates. He had been taking German lessons, so to the Fatherland we went, stopping off to stay with Des's brother in London on the way. It was my first time abroad. Swinging London was all we had heard about it and Carnaby Street and Soho lived up to expectations. Then, by boat to Ostende and down the Rhine we went by steamer from Cologne to Munich, stopping off at towns along the way. We hit Munich in time for the Oktoberfest, managing to consume large quantities of beer and sausages and still remain remarkably sober (it's the pure water, you know).

Being radio buffs, we went to see Radio Free Europe's studios in Munich, having been given an introduction by journalist and writer Breandán Ó hEithir, who used to work there. I was surprised to hear it, as I'd always pegged him as leaning towards the left. RFE was a CIA operation to combat the Red Menace with the Good Ol' Red, White and Blue. We then hired a Volkswagen Beetle and set off south for Austria. I was driving and between the left-hand drive and the confusing roundabouts, we found ourselves steaming east towards Paris, without any chance of parole, because the Autobahn had no turn-offs. *Ich bin einbahnstrasse.* We corrected eventually, and reached Innsbruck in time to miss our hotel booking completely. Throughout Austria and Germany, Des was able to do most of the communication, although I found I could get by quite easily on 'Zwei Bier, bitte' and 'Haben Sie Zimmer frei?' On 19 September we were in Salzburg and checked into an old hotel at random. It was dark and slightly scary, but the room keys were magnificent: big iron implements with the room numbers forming the handle of the key itself. The ancient receptionist handed us a room key in the shape of 21. Appropriate, really. It was the night of my twenty-first birthday.

Back in RTÉ, I did the final audition for permanent announcer and on 17 October 1966 was offered the job, 'subject to the Broadcasting Authority Acts and the enclosed Conditions of Service', at the minimum salary of £1,152 per annum. Denis suggested that, bearing in mind my experience to date, I should seek to enter at a higher rate on the scale and, eventually, the Personnel Department agreed to start me at £1,292 per annum. It doesn't seem a lot, but it was considered good at the time (my father, as a department manager, wouldn't have been making much more), and £26 per week was certainly an improvement on the £3.10.0 I had been paid in the ICI, just one year earlier.

Following a medical examination, I formally took up the appointment on 2 December.

Now that I was on staff, my continuing stint on *Ireland's Top Ten* caused a few raised eyebrows, as that programme was considered to be within the ambit of the freelance comperes. There had always been a rivalry between the freelances and the staff, as much to do with departmental influence as with talent. Freelances tended to be employed by Light Music Department, Sponsored Programmes Office and Features Department and were perceived to do the lighter end of the programme spectrum, while announcers tended to do the more formal work. In fairness, though, management was always conscious of the need to have an 'open door' policy to people who depended on short-term contracts. It was, after all, the way I had entered. Nonetheless, in his department, Denis encouraged announcers to expand their range, and many of the staff had long been free-lancing in radio and television. Terry Wogan and John Skehan were television regulars and Denis himself presented *The World This Week* and the Irish quiz *Ceist* on television, as well as his radio interviews on *Who's News?* So it was that on one weekend, I presented *Céilí House* on Saturday night, the live Symphony Concert from the Gaiety Theatre on Sunday night and *Ireland's Top Ten* on Monday night. No other station in the world, I believe, offered that assortment of programmes or that range of presentation experience. At the time, though, I thought nothing of it. It was just the way the schedule fell.

Being a staff announcer was not much different from being a relief announcer, with one exception: I was now allowed to present *Hospitals Requests*, the most famous radio programme in Ireland, broadcast every Wednesday afternoon from one o'clock to half past two, with a break for the news at half past one. I prepared it in the same way as all my colleagues, by going through each of the hundreds of cards received from listeners and segregating them into two piles. One pile contained requests for specific records, those tunes that get requested over and over, the chestnuts, the hardy annuals—and they were many: 'The Chorus of the Hebrew Slaves', 'Bring Flowers of the Rarest', the duet from 'The Pearl Fishers', the serenade from 'The Fair Maid of Perth', 'The Nuns' Chorus' (not a pious refrain, but the girls looking for a man), and yards of John McCormack, Bridie Gallagher and 'any céilí record', which usually resulted in the Laictín Naofa Céilí Band getting another unlikely spin. The incongruity about request programmes is that most people have a small musical repertoire; some know only one or two songs. They tend to request what they heard on last week's programme.

The other pile of cards comprised requests for 'any nice record', and those were highly prized by announcers, because we could now validly play our own choice of record, particularly current pop records, for the Doctors, Nurses and Staff of Portiuncula Hospital, the Best Mother in the World, and to wish an ailing patient a speedy recovery from his sister. Sometimes, we got it wrong though, as John Skehan pointed out to me when I played 'Gin House Blues' by Amen Corner for an eighty-year-old geriatric patient in Ballinasloe. No one complained, but Terry Wogan later caused some havoc by playing, sight unseen, so to speak, a track from The Clancy Brothers new album called 'Isn't it Grand, Boys'. A jolly little ditty, he thought, to cheer up the sick and shadowing on a wet Wednesday afternoon. Unfortunately, the lyric went on to roar lustily 'Isn't it Grand, Boys… to be bloody well dead.'

I arrived in Continuity at two o'clock that day to relieve Maurice O'Doherty. 'The you-know-what has hit the fan,' he said. 'I've been on the phone for the last forty minutes taking complaints and apologising. Your turn now.' For the next hour, I fielded complaints from the public who were incensed by the unfeeling nature of the track and wanted some redress. Again, in the absence of a press office, all calls came to the announcer on duty. I tried my Radio Licence subterfuge a few times, but it didn't stem the flow of under-standable indignation. Terry was contrite, if only for a day. Some weeks later, he was away for a while and asked me, as a favour, to prepare his programme. I organised all the cards, put them in neat piles, typed up a running order and left them for him. I had managed to include every one of the hardy annuals (as listed above), as well as a few more frighteners: Elvis Presley's 'Old Shep' (a song about a dead dog), 'Ebony Eyes' by the Everly Brothers (about a plane crash), and the deathless 'Terry' (a significant work of art by Twinkle in which the eponymous hero is killed in a bike crash). Terry had no choice but to play most of them, as there were no other records supplied, but he flipped 'Ebony Eyes' to its more acceptable other side, 'Walk Right Back'.

On another day, the disc operator played the wrong side of a record by accident, and Terry had the privilege of introducing 'Gentle Mother' by Big Tom and the Mighty Mainliners to an unsuspecting Irish public. The same band, incidentally, acquired a devoted following in the New York salons, impressing the Hippies and Gentle People with its psychedelic name, which, in Sixties culture, was a synonym for intravenous drug takers. The band played New York regularly, particularly during Lent when no dancing was allowed in Ireland. The band would fly to America, but Big Tom refused to get onto an aeroplane and went over the long way, via the *Queen Elizabeth*.

'We're losing fortunes of money,' said his manager, John McCormack, hoping that financial hardship might change Tom's mind. 'It takes two weeks for you to sail there and back. The lads are back by plane, but we're off the road for a fortnight waiting for you. Would you not at least try the aeroplane?'

Tom's reply contained the wisdom of the ages and the sagacity of the Northerner. 'No,' he said. 'I can swim a bit... but I can fly fuck all.'

The 6.20 wasn't a plane or a train, it was the scheduled time for public announcments, advertisements from the Civil Service Commission ('applications are invited for the positions of Meteorologists, Poultry Instructresses and Forestry Workers, Grade 2...'), station announcements and a programme signpost. It could easily have been done from Continuity, but because it could be over five minutes long, it was deemed to be a programme, rather than a fill-in. It came from Studio 5 and followed the *Nuacht–Chaint*, a topical talk in Irish. The announcer had to wait in the control room while the speaker read his or her talk. There was one regular contributor whom the announcers dreaded: an Irish writer who had a personal hygiene problem. Even though the studio had a window overlooking the internal buildings of the GPO, there was no time to air the studio. As the continuity announcer downstairs closed the talk, I would nip in while she removed her ample frame. If I occasionally sounded nasal, it was because I was sometimes unable to resist the temptation to hold my nose while reading my bundle of scripts:

'The 1966/67 series of Subscription Concerts continues in the Gaiety Theatre, Dublin on Sunday...'—a sentence that looks harmless on paper but is deadly when said aloud. It's full of S's. Moreover, I found I couldn't say 'subscription' easily. I slid over the word, in the same way as some Dubliners pronounce Phibsboro as 'Fizzboro'. The next evening, it came up again and despite a supreme effort to slow down and say it clearly, the same result ensued. I was now getting paranoid about the word. I even dropped the script behind the cupboard in Continuity, but a fresh one arrived from the Music Department, marked 'Urgent—Don't Forget'. I had to rewrite the entire piece to avoid the offending words, 'The current series of Concerts with a contributory admission price, continues at the Gaiety....' Not in the least felicitous, but sayable. To this day, I have developed such a mental block, that I still can't say 'subscription'. I can say it quite happily in social surroundings, but not in front of a microphone. Odd, that.

Seán Mac Réamoinn, he of the unique gravelly voice, was a regular on the *Nuacht-Chaint* and one evening I watched in admiration as, with no script, he proceeded to talk fluently about the new Bórd Fáilte brochure launched that lunchtime, occasionally consulting a cigarette pack of twenty Players on which he'd written a few names. He ended on time, to the second. Seán was one of the scriptwriters, having graduated from collecting traditional music with the Mobile Unit and acting as Regional Officer in the Cork studios. In answer to an enquiry about his health, he famously replied that he felt 'like a Census form—broken down by age, sex and religion'. He was also responsible for a major policy change in Irish radio, which had huge economic repercussions. One morning, he sought to cash a salary cheque in Brady's Pub, directly across the road from the Henry Street entrance. It had been the Radio local pub for years and Seán was one of its most regular customers, but he was incensed when Old Mister Brady told him that he wasn't going to cash his cheque. He repeated the old saw: 'We have an arrangement with the Bank of Ireland. They won't serve drinks and we won't cash cheques.' Seán left with some ceremony, taking the other radio regulars with him. By lunchtime the word about cheque-cashing had spread and, by five o'clock that day, the entire radio station had decamped to Madigan's of Moore Street, official purveyors of drink to RTÉ, who even opened a branch in Donnybrook when we moved out to Montrose.

Seán's colleagues in the Scriptwriters' Department were versatile pro-gramme makers, turning out features, documentaries, music programmes and talks: Norris Davidson, Proinnsias Ó Conluain, P.P. Maguire and Ciarán MacMathúna, a kindly and courtly man. My colleague and friend Mike Murphy was greatly taken by Ciarán's intimate radio style. 'Listen to him,' he'd say. 'He sounds like he's talking to each listener personally.' Mike began to emulate Ciarán's approach on request programmes, talking directly to the listener in a friendly, casual style. It was one of radio's most misunderstood anomalies; even though there are thousands of people listening, they are listening in ones. Radio listening was no longer a communal exercise, so it made sense to speak to them as individuals, avoiding the trap of addressing the audience in the plural—'some of you', 'all of you', 'if any of you' and so on. It helps to picture the audience, not as a huge crowd in Croke Park being addressed over a loudspeaker system, but as a single, smart person in his or her kitchen or car.

As the two youngest announcers, Mike Murphy and I hit it off immedi-ately. We spared our modest salaries by trying, where possible, not to spend too much on drink. This happy state was achieved by engaging in Hotel Crawls. We would go to the Gresham Hotel, a hundred yards from the GPO in O'Connell Street, look at the Function Board in the lobby and decide which reception to attend. 'ICA Craftswoman of the Year' would do just fine; we would go to the reception and sign in as being from RTÉ, helped by Mike's face start-ing to be familiar from occasional television spots. We'd then be plied with drink and food until we made our departure. The trick was not to stay too long, or we could be subject to too much scrutiny, like where would the coverage be appearing, or when might they hear a mention on the radio. After a while, back we went to the lobby to pick another reception—'Esso Pump Attendant of the Year', perhaps—and spent some time there getting the low-down on the innovations in the petrol delivery system and its pitfalls. We found that when our eyes started to glaze from boredom, rather than from drink, it was time to go. One evening, we moved across the street to the Catholic Commercial Club (from whom RTÉ rented the O'Connell Hall) to demand drink. They, in turn, demanded that we join the club. We did and were paid-up members for a year, entitling us to all manner of delights—snooker, sandwiches and sodalities. When offered a renewal of our member-ship, we declined gracefully. We had been delighted long enough.

One night, I decided that Mike had taken more drink than was necessary and persuaded him not to drive home. But we were out of funds and he had no money for a taxi, so he insisted that he'd have to drive because he was on early continuity in the morning. 'No, I'll drive you home,' said I, 'and pick you up in the morning at seven.' This I did. Much taken by the neighbourly deed, he tried to repay the favour many years after, but that's for later.

Apart from Mike, I was good friends with my other radio colleagues, John Skehan, Maurice O'Doherty, John Keogh, Pat Kenny, Ruth Buchanan, Lorna Madigan and the inestimable Larry Gogan, one of the most pleasant and gen-erous people you could meet and a thorough professional to his fingertips. My oldest friend in radio was Jimmy Wogan. He had started in the Eamonn Andrews Studios in 40 Henry Street as a disc-operator and had even record-ed a big pop hit 'Wimoweh' by Carl Denver in 1962 in the radio studio. A northsider, the first I'd met, he married a French girl, Liz Guillaume, and was one of the few radio people whom I regularly saw socially. He eventually became Head of Sound in RTÉ Radio, retired early to France but always comes back for the football matches. An all-round good egg, a snappy dresser and a fair judge of vodka.

Outside broadcasting, in the social scene, there was a Gang of Four: Dermot Herbert, Andy Maher, Peter Williams and me. I was the common link between all. Dermot was from my ICI days and was now one of my partners in Marquis Productions, Andy was from The Barn and Canoe Club days and had studied with me for the Bank Exam, and Peter, who worked in the Bank of Ireland, was a bass player and a brother of the late Paul Williams of The Greenbeats. We were great friends, went away on holiday weekends and started a Saturday practice that went on for years. We would gather in the Stillorgan Shopping Centre around five o'clock, pay a visit to Frewen and Aylward, Gentleman's Outfitters, to buy shirts, and repair to the bar. Home then for dinner and we would foregather later with respective girlfriends in the Dubliner Bar in Jurys Hotel. The crowd would invariably expand as we met more friends, and there could be anything up to thirty people in the company by closing time. Next, on to Elizabeth's, one of the first nightclubs on the Leeson Street strip, run by Maurice Boland. We might be there until dawn, arguing who would spend twenty pounds—no, I have it, put your money away—on a bottle of Green Label White Wine, which, we were convinced, was distributed by Dockrells Builders Suppliers and was best opened in a well-ventilated room. Eddie Shanahan was the DJ and the night wasn't deemed a success unless we stayed for rashers and eggs cooked by the club manager, Paddy Warren.

Sunday was spent having a few pints in the afternoon, usually somewhere in the Dublin Mountains, and then it was down to Peter's house for tea. His gracious mother, Eve, was always welcoming, whether it was one or three extra guests. His father, Roy, who was still mourning his other son, would respond to my requests to read from a book by Patrick Campbell, which I had given him in the hope of distracting him. He enjoyed one essay so much, 'Awash in Toffee-'n'-Choc', that he would read it to us every Sunday at the tea table. It was wonderful to see the tears rolling down his cheeks as he read the tale of Paddy Campbell's visit to the cinema: 'I took in Brigitte Bardot the other evening and eight and sixpence worth of mixed confectionery, with the result that I had to send a pair of slacks and a pullover to the cleaner's.' Frank Kelly, who lived up the road in Monkstown, told me earlier that the cry of anguish from Roy when he heard the news of Paul's death in 1967 could be heard all over the area. It was a car accident outside Limerick that killed Paul and injured Keith Donald and Eddie, another band member. I drove Peter to Limerick to collect Paul's remains and followed the hearse back to Dublin.

As the radio service started to expand, Ciarán MacMathúna found himself billeted in VHI House, Talbot Street, along with the Music Department. He was told that Mary, one of the secretaries, was leaving and that he'd be welcome to join them that evening for the farewell party in Mooney's. Ciarán finished his work and thought he'd drop in to the reception on his way home. He went to the pub, asked where the going-away party was happening and was directed to the upstairs lounge. It was crowded to capacity. He took the drink he was offered and started to mingle. He didn't recognise anyone, but he put this down to the fact that he hadn't worked with the Music Department for long. They were a very friendly crowd anyway, and thank you, he would have another pint. The hours passed and only when the speeches started did Ciarán realise that something was wrong. 'Is this Mooney's?' he asked. 'No, it's Madigan's,' came the reply. 'Who is leaving?' he persisted. 'Tom is leaving Clerys after fifteen years' service; that's him over there.' Ciarán introduced himself. The speeches started and, catching the mood of the moment, Ciarán made an eloquent speech that was much regarded. As the tributes to the departee became more heartfelt and tearful—'Tom was one of a kind, they broke the mould when they made Tom, there'll be a hole in our heart where Tom used to be, we'll never forget Tom, life will not be the same, we are all completely heartbroken and desolate'—Ciarán asked one of Tom's tearful colleagues, 'Where is he going, anyway? England? America? Australia?'

'No. Arnotts.'

The upstairs lounge of Madigan's in Moore Street became more like an RTÉ club than a regular pub. Watched over by Niall Fleming and Des Winters, it was the meeting place for the colourful breed of experts and eccentrics with connections to the radio station. What I loved about it was its democratic demeanour. No attention was paid to rank or office. Poets talked with pop stars, peasants talked with producers. You might see Séamus Heaney talking to Larry Gogan, Ben Kiely talking to Luke Kelly.

One of the regulars was Con Gleeson. A rough diamond, he owned some of the lock-ups around Moore Street where the women stored their stalls overnight. He could be seen regularly hauling crates of vegetables around the street on a cart. Smelling strongly of fish, he could often be heard giving his views on current events, famously commenting on a notorious murder case when Shan Mohangi was acquitted of the murder of Hazel Mullen: 'Terrible thing, terrible thing. If that happened in any other country in the world, he'd be fucked in the Liffey.'

Con's brother, he told us, worked 'for the ESB in Nevada'. I saw Con one morning come to the upstairs lounge. Of the ten stools at the bar, only one was occupied and that was by the august figure of Roibeárd Ó Faracháin, writer, poet, man of letters and Controller of Programmes, RTÉ Radio. He sensed Con before he saw him and bristled slightly as, ignoring all the other stools that were free, Con sat beside the radio boss and pointed to a story in his newspaper about a painting selling for a million pounds.

'I'll tell you what, Mister O'Farracan, we're both in the wrong job.'

Mr Ó Faracháin's response was not recorded.

∾ SOUNDTRACK ∾

Any Requests?
Song titles and lyrics are sometimes confusing to listeners. What would you play if these were requested (as they were)?

Please Play....
1. 'The Girl with Colitis Goes By'
2. 'Ireland's Industry'
3. 'My Heart and Eye'
4. 'Pot o' Nails'
5. 'You Are The One'
6. 'Nine Stone Cowboy'
7. 'You Feed Me Breakfast'
8. 'The Ants are My Friend'

Answers...
1. 'Lucy in the Sky with Diamonds' ('The Girl with Kaleidoscope Eyes')
2. 'Islands in the Stream'
3. 'My Heart and I'
4. 'Chopin's Polanaise'
5. 'Night and Day'
6. 'Rhinestone Cowboy'
7. 'You Leave Me Breathless'
8. The answer my friend, is... 'Blowing in the Wind'

Chapter 10 ⌒

| OUT AND ABOUT

One summer's evening in Madigan's, we were all enclosed in the upstairs lounge. Outside it was sunny and warm. Inside, it was smoky and smelly.

'Isn't this disgraceful?' said Benny Slevin, an honorary member of the cabal, as he worked in the Department of Posts and Telegraphs in the GPO. 'Sitting in a pub on a glorious summer's evening, when we should be out in the fresh air.'

'Doing what?' came the response of the crowd.

'Anything,' said Benny. 'Walking, swimming, playing pitch and putt... anything.'

'There's a good pitch and putt course in Tallaght,' said one helpful comrade.

So it was decided. We would all meet the following Monday evening at the course in Tallaght for an evening of getting a small ball into an even smaller hole. Kick-off was eight o'clock.

On the following Tuesday, we again had foregathered in the Upper Room, when Benny entered.

'Where were you, you shower of lousers? Eamonn Timoney was the only one to turn up. Only two of us.'

We muttered regrets and excuses. Had to steep the peas. Had to sandpaper the car...

'I have nonetheless done a report on the game, as if you had turned up. I shall now proceed to read it into the record.'

Benny then read a witty report on the non-event, describing in detail the actions of the non-players and capturing with great drollness the personality traits and foibles of Mike Murphy, Terry Wogan, Ian Corr, Fintan Ryan, Eamonn O'Connor, Des Coates, Des Morahan, Eamonn Timoney and me, amongst others. It was decided that the group should be formalised and officers appointed: Secretary, Treasurer, Religious Adviser, Public Relations Officer, Director of Retreats. Benny had already decided on the name, and so

I found myself elected first President of The Stay-At-Home Pitch and Putt Society. Its rules were manifold, but the key regulation had all the simplicity of genius: if you turned up to play, you were disqualified.

The finest legal brains available to us soon found a solution to the dilemma. We could play 'under the auspices of the Society' as long as we didn't purport to play 'in the guise of the Society'. This Solomon-like ruling enabled us to run events like the D-Day Tournament (The DDT, as it became known, or The Insecticide Two-Ball) on 6 June at Stepaside. Handicaps were decided in advance, prizes were acquired and players were despatched in twos to tackle the treacherous nine holes on the side of a gentle slope in the Co. Dublin village. Speeches were made with due solemnity in the bar afterwards, culminating in the highlight of the evening: the awarding of the Captain's Prize, a foot-high plastic Buddha acquired from Hector Grey's. In the SAHPAPS, as in RTÉ, every expense was spared.

The Society grew in numbers and reputation, its fixtures often figuring in sports bulletins on RTÉ Radio. Later, we decided that a formal dinner should be held at the end of the year and a private dining room was booked in the Aisling Hotel, near Kingsbridge Station. Dress was formal and the function was For Gentlemen Only, or as Benny called it, 'Soirée sans Broads'. Donal Stanley was invited to be Guest of Honour and to read a paper on 'Peace in Our Time'. The Society's Annual Awards were also announced. The Showbiz Award went to Har and The Escorts, a new band from the Provinces, whose first record was also their last; the Irishman of the Year Award was unanimously bestowed upon the hero who tried to hijack an Aer Lingus transatlantic flight with a plastic knife and fork.

One of the founding members of the Society was Eamonn Timoney, a senior Balance and Control Officer who worked mainly with the RTÉ Symphony Orchestra. He could be found in Madigan's at the end of the working day, resting from his labours of balancing the finer niceties of Berlioz, Tchaikovsky and company in the Gaiety Theatre. 'Very difficult pieces this week,' he said once. 'Can't get the orchestra to do what I want.' As it happened, I was scheduled to announce the concert that week, my first time doing so live from the venue. 'Come up early,' said Eamonn, 'and I'll show you the lash-up.' The next Sunday, I met Eamonn in the control box high up in the upper circle.

His mixing desk utilised only two channels for two microphones—one was for the announcer and the other, for the entire orchestra, was hanging by a cable from the roof of the theatre. Some lash-up, I thought. The announcer's position was backstage right, in the wings, beside the stage manager's position. There was a stool, a lip-ribbon microphone and an amber cue light.

At eight, the cue light went on and I read the opening announcement, timing it to coincide with the entry of the leader and the conductor on stage. The orchestra launched into the first work by Berlioz. As the applause died, I started into a half-page introduction to the second work. To my horror, I saw the leader and the conductor leave the stage and the orchestra began to chat amongst themselves (I could swear I could even see one of them knitting). Then three stagehands appeared from the opposite wings of the stage and started to roll on a grand piano, taking infinite care with their task and showing themselves to be in no particular hurry. It then dawned on me: the next piece was a Tchaikovsky piano concerto with a Distinguished Young German Pianist. I had now introduced the piece, but there was no sign of anyone willing to perform it. I had run out of script and I was live on air, alone and isolated, with nothing to say. I went back to the Berlioz script and sort of read it backwards, noting how enjoyable it had been, how the different movements had lived up to their promise and how lucky the people of Cork were to have the concert repeated for them the following night in the Opera House.

Still no sign of the concert resuming. Leaning out from my dark cubbyhole, I put my head around the corner of the curtain to see the auditorium. Patrons were talking away, some had gone to the bar, but the house lights were on and I could see the audience. Feeling a little like Richard Dimbleby, I heard myself saying 'What a wonderful old theatre the Gaiety is, famous for its pantomimes and stage shows and, of course, for many years, the home of the late Jimmy O'Dea, who died only recently, the same day, incidentally, that The Rolling Stones played another famous Dublin venue, the Adelphi Cinema.' I was now down to dictation speed as I described the plasterwork and the light fittings. 'These concerts have been the highlight of the Dublin musical calendar for many years, and I can see many of Dublin's musical cognoscenti among tonight's audience. I can see the Minister for Industry and Commerce and his party, captains of industry and members of the diplomatic community… but, of course, music is for everyone, the great and the good, young and old, those of the highest birth and the humblest circumstances… and let me just remind you about Tchaikovsky's piano concerto, which I've told you about already…' At last, to my left, I saw the conductor and leader, standing querulously beside me, and I motioned them on stage. 'The leader of the orchestra and the conductor are now back on stage, as we welcome the Distinguished Young German Pianist….'

'What kept you?' I asked the conductor after the concert.

'We were waiting for you to finish talking,' he replied.

The main event in radio in 1967 was the extension of broadcasting hours to fill the morning and afternoon gaps in the schedule. It was advertised as

'Round the Clock Radio'. Donal Stanley asked me to produce some promotional trailers and I gave some fast and zippy spots to advertise the wonders of having a radio service that actually provided a service. It was the first time that RTÉ had used pre-recorded trailers, a practice now commonplace. One of the benefits to the announcing staff was that we gained a new programme, *Rogha na mBan* (The Choice of Women), every morning at ten o'clock. It was a housewives' request programme, whose signature tune was 'Red Roses for a Blue Lady' by Bert Kaemphert, chosen by Denis as a floral bouquet for the oppressed housewife. It was staffed by the announcers, who took turns to both present and produce the programme: I produced Mike Murphy, Mike produced Terry Wogan, Terry produced me, Maurice O'Doherty produced Una Sheehy and so on. Lorna Madigan took on *Rogha na nÓg* on Saturday mornings for the kiddies.

That same year, we began broadcasting live request programmes from the RDS Horse Show in Ballsbridge. The announcers carried the brunt of it but shared the burden with the freelance comperes. It was the first time that the listeners could actually see a live programme being done. It answered the question: what do they do in between the records? Not a lot, was the answer in plain sight. We sat there looking slightly embarrassed, shuffling requests, re-arranging bits of paper and smiling benignly at our listeners outside the glass. They in turn looked back at us, slack-jawed and vacant, as if inspecting a fish that might have gone off. We had an information desk promoting the VHF service and I overheard a harried engineer trying to explain to a customer that Plan B wouldn't qualify him for a new radio set and that, maybe, he might be confusing us with the VHI. Terry Wogan and Joe Linnane struck up an instant rapport and made a very funny on-air duo. Joe was in the studio and Terry was out in the grounds with the roving microphone. He was talking to a group of schoolchildren who told him they were on a day off because they had done their Religious Knowledge examination that morning. 'Bet you can't tell them the Fourth Commandment, Terry,' Joe chipped in. Terry was flummoxed but recovered with, 'Now back to Joe Linnane for a time-check in Irish.'

Back on continuity, the programmes rolled on. After *Rogha*, there was a quarter-hour magazine programme, a recorded music programme and a short story, until *Music at Midday*. More magazine-style programmes, plays and features followed the afternoon sponsored programmes. One programme I particularly liked doing was *The UpBeat Show*, a music programme featuring the RTÉ Light Orchestra conducted by Noel Kelehan, going out live at 4.30 p.m. I've always liked working with musicians, and no stereo system can beat the sound of a full orchestra, particularly when the announcer's position is right beside the conductor. Róisín Lorigan booked me regularly on bank holidays for *Out and About*, a three-hour afternoon programme, based on linking outside broadcasts with music. There could be a golf game, a cycle race and up to three other mobile units—Terry Wogan at the Zoo, Larry Gogan at Castletown House, Noel Andrews at Tramore Beach, for instance, talking to the customers and sending greetings to their friends. It was a fast-paced programme and I was the studio anchorman. I suspect I was chosen as much for my perceived talent for being cool under pressure, as for my ability to introduce pop records succinctly. The key to being cool, incidentally, is to be prepared. When I introduced, say, Jimmy Magee in Bratislava, I did so on the understanding that he probably wasn't there, or the line would break down, or he couldn't hear the cue. So, I had something ready—a record, a request, a story—so that I wouldn't be caught out. I assumed the worst, and when I did hear Jimmy Magee coming through loud and clear, I was pleasantly surprised. It was the continuity training: Denis always told us that if mistakes happen, we should get out of them by being honest. Apologise and move on. The only mortal sin in broadcasting, he maintained, is to embarrass the listeners. If they are cringing at home, mortified at your error and horrified at your inability to get out of it, you have lost the battle—and the war.

Another of Denis's innovations to help maintain standards was the Refresher Course. Every few weeks or so, he would roster a few hours with each announcer to work on possible problems. The location for these sessions, in the case of Mike and Terry, was usually the first tee at Woodbrook. In the case of Maurice and me (we didn't play golf), it could be the Trocadero Restaurant. 'Everything okay?' he would enquire. 'Absolutely,' I'd reply. 'I heard you doing the Recital the other night,' he would continue. 'It was fine, but you could afford to use your lower register a bit more. Now, what are we eating…?' That was a refresher course. He was aware that announcers could get stale and he tried to head it off.

Murphy's Law dictates that if something can go wrong, it will. In radio, a sub-section of the law states that the wrong record will always be played after a momentous event. There are many examples, but let me tell you mine. I was presenting *Rogha na mBan* on Thursday, 6 June 1968. There was no talkback into my headphones, so the producer couldn't talk to me while the microphone was live. In the middle of a request, something caught my eye through the glass. It was a piece of paper held up to the window. It said: 'News Flash. Don Cockburn.' It was a scary moment. Was it World War III? I handed over to Don without delay. The news was that Senator Robert Kennedy had been shot, perhaps fatally, in Los Angeles. More news as we get it, meanwhile back to Brendan. I thought it would be invidious to continue with lists of greetings, so I decided to go straight to the next record. It turned out to be 'The Lights Went Out in Massachusetts' by the Bee Gees. Thinking that a song about the senator's birthplace was singularly inappropriate, I jumped down to a safer song, communicating with Charlie Clegg, the disc operator, by saying with heavy emphasis, 'Moving on from Number 6 on our list to Number 7 on our list….' I could see his annoyance, turning to bewilderment, turning to relief, as he saw what we had avoided.

The following Saturday night, 8 June, I was on late continuity and also acting as Station Supervisor. RTÉ had arranged coverage of the funeral by reporter Mike Burns, who was in New York. The coverage was due to start at eight o'clock, but I was to present a half-hour filler programme beforehand, starting at half past seven. The first problem was that we couldn't make contact with Mike Burns by telephone. I kept playing music. We got through to Mike around nine o'clock. He was watching television in his hotel room and commentating by telephone. The second problem was that the entire funeral was running hours behind time. The coffin was on a train travelling from Los Angeles to Arlington Cemetery in Washington, a long journey made slower by the thousands of people who lined the route at stations and all along the tracks. The family had asked that the train travel at a serene pace to allow the spectators to pay their respects. I continued to play music, conscious that, although we were mourning a figure much beloved in Ireland, he was still only the Junior Senator from New York, albeit a presidential candidate. (He had not the status of the President of Ireland or An Taoiseach, the music for both of whose funeral broadcasts had already been chosen, and was kept in two boxes in Continuity marked Project X and Project Y.) I had, therefore, to be somewhat circumspect in my music choice, avoiding full dirges and laments but aiming for sedate and moderately paced classical, Irish and orchestral music. 'The Dead March' in Saul was eschewed, but Dvorak's New World Symphony came into its own, particularly the slow movement, 'Going Home'. The music choice was academic anyway, because the library was long since closed, and I had to rely on what I'd brought down for my filler programme and whatever else was in the studio.

The Deputy Director-General, John Irvine, rang in before midnight to compliment the coverage and to pass his good wishes to all the staff. I thanked him, but pointed out that all the staff consisted of two—the technician, John Walsh, and me. Even Mrs Haughey, the operator on the switchboard, was leaving after his call, breaking contact with the outside world. A decent man, Mr

Irvine arranged for the Gresham Hotel to send over coffee and sandwiches to us.

Still the music played, with occasional updates from Mike Burns. (I handed over to him 'in America', a ubiquitous phrase to suggest he was straddling the continent, rather than watching a television set in his New York hotel room.) It was a strange, almost ethereal, feeling, sitting in that studio, wondering if I was the only person in the country who was awake. Around three in the morning, more substantial information was forthcoming, as the cortege reached Washington and the ceremonials began. Mike did half-hour bursts, and then handed back to me for more music. And so it went on, until dawn started to break over a tranquil and deserted Dublin City. Through the window, I could see the light hitting Moore Street, clean and empty on a Sunday morning. Mike finished around half past six and handed back to me for the last time. It didn't seem sensible to close down the station then, only to open again in an hour's time, so I decided to keep going until Una Sheehy relieved me at half past seven. Only then did I realise that I had been on the air for twelve hours continuously. It was, I was later told, the longest-ever radio broadcast by an individual. It has been beaten subsequently by disc-jockey marathons and novelty talk-ins, but for a time I held the World Record.

The Director of News passed on a letter from a Mrs W.M. Glynn of Waterford: 'We were greatly impressed by the presentation of "Brendan" (other name unknown) of the very difficult and prolonged fill-in period on Saturday night.'

Complimentary letters are more rare than you might think and are always highly valued. The Controller of Programmes, Roibeárd Ó Faracháin, also wrote:

> With cordial agreement of the Director-General I wish to thank you (and of course your other colleagues) for the very special effort you and they made on the occasion of the funeral of the late Senator Robert F. Kennedy.
>
> The enthusiasm and efficiency with which you completed the broadcast are very much appreciated and as a token of this appreciation the Director-General has approved the payment to you of a gratuity of £10.
>
> I am happy to enclose a cheque for that amount.

I was touched by the gesture. It mightn't seem very much now but, in 1968, you could have a good night out on ten pounds.

I enjoyed doing continuity, despite the occasional schoolmarm appearances of Brigid Kilfeather, who insisted we kept the studio tidy and wished 'announcers wouldn't wear their beach clothes when announcing', a reference to my summer slacks and short-sleeved shirts. She had a propensity for correcting her wards, even at a party in her flat on Fitzwilliam Square: someone asked the name of the classical tune that Allan Sherman had utilised for his comedy hit, 'Hello Muddah, Hello Faddah'. I happened to know the answer. 'It's "Dance of the Hours" by Ponchielli,' I said, pronouncing the 'ch' as in 'chief'. Brigid caught it in a flash. 'Pon-key-elli,' she said and insisted I repeat it. 'Go on, say it, Pon-key-elli.' I declined. Maurice discovered that Brigid abhorred bad language and if ever she came in to upbraid him, he would use his saltiest vocabulary to hasten her departure.

In fact, it was the morning after one of Brigid's parties, which itself was after the RTÉ Christmas party, that I arrived to open the station at half past seven. Feeling less than perky, I was setting up the gramophone when I noticed that I seemed to be alone. There was no technician at the Continuity desk, none in the control and no technical supervisor. As the clock ticked towards opening time, I thought I should act. Having watched my technical colleagues like Ian Corr, Des Coates and Seán McCasey over the years, I had a rough idea of what to do. I dialled up the Athlone transmitter and put in the 'pads', the connections to the Dublin transmitter, putting the station on the air. I started 'O'Donnell Abú', lined up the sponsored programmes on the two tape machines and, manning the Continuity desk, made contact with Charles Mitchel, the newsreader. I explained that when I gave him a red light, he should open the station as well as read the news, because I couldn't announce and operate the desk at the same time. When he finished, he should remain silent and when I got the interval music rolling in the studio, I would come out and close his microphone. During the three minutes of music, I briefed him on the three sponsored programmes coming up, which he was to announce when I gave him a red light. In this convoluted manner, we got as far as the nine o'clock news. I was lining up the next live programme when one technician, then a second one, arrived. Their supervisor, Joe L'Estrange, arrived shortly afterwards. No words were said, apart from a muttered, embarrassed 'thank you'. The technical log showed no discrepancies, nor did the announcer's log.

As far as anyone else was concerned, it had been a normal day. But from then on, I was regarded as a sort of Honorary Technician, welcome to sit in the control room and free to use the gas stove and kettle in the Technical restroom at the far end of the long corridor.

There were other less severe methods to lighten the hours on continuity. Mike Murphy and I sometimes did shared announcements, to see if anyone would spot it. We would sit together at the microphone and take turns reading every second word: Radio/Telefís/Éireann/the/time/is/two/o'/clock/

and/here/is/*The/Bird's/Programme/*. Nobody ever noticed. Another whimsy was to re-name the tunes when playing Irish dance music, so that they told a story: 'That selection of tunes was—"The Maid Behind the Bar", "Father Pat's Fancy" and "Haste to the Wedding".'

I liked giving even more exotic names to orchestras who specialised in interval music: Frank Chacksfield and his Singing Strings playing 'Moon Over Naples', were announced as Frank Chacksfield with His Satin Banjos and Velvet Mandolins playing 'Midnight in Drimnagh'. No one said a word. It sounded plausible.

The Radio Éireann Players continued to be known as 'The Rep', the double meaning still valid for the versatile repertory company, even though the station had changed its name. The *Sunday Play* continued to be the highlight of their week, as well as serials, short plays and readings. They were a talented bunch and characters in their own right. When P.P. Maguire was appointed Head of Drama, they became known as 'The Cast of Loves Maguire'. Their key producers were John Stephenson, Dan Treston and Séamus Breathnach, whose famous cry to them was, 'Would ye cut out the actin' and get on with the play!' Having announced dozen of plays, I knew most of them and their names are as a Roll of Honour in radio drama: Ginette Waddell, Celia Salkeld, Neasa Ní Annracháin, Florence Lynch, Daphne Carroll, Conor Farrington, Brendan Cauldwell, Jim Norton, Breandán Ó Dúill, Peter Dix, Séamus Forde, Vincent Bradley, Lionel Day, Brian O'Higgins (for many years the voice of Santa Claus), George Greene, Thomas Studley, Niall Toibín. Watching them at work and listening to their performances subsequently on air, I could usually work out who was playing whom. The exceptions were Tom Studley and Niall Toibín. Tom was the consummate radio actor, whose chameleon qualities were never better utilised than when an actor became ill during a live performance and Tom took on his part, as well as his own. As the two characters had many scenes together, Tom had to play against himself. This was not just impersonation: he caught not only the voice of the other, but also his dramatic persona, ensuring that Tom's performance matched the others actor's original interpretation of the role. It was a *tour de force* that has gone down in the annals.

Niall Toibín was the other actor who was hard to identify. A powerful and passionate performer, he could play a range of roles, the comedies of Wilde, the dramas of O'Casey, the tragedies of John B. Keane, as well as all the classical parts. One morning, early on, I was announcing a play in which he played the lead. The last scene was an intense soliloquy in which Niall's character had to bare his soul. The producer told me to slip into the studio because the play was ending on Niall's agonised speech and, after a pause, I had to be ready to read the cast list. As I crept slowly and silently towards the microphone, my foot trod on a floorboard. It was a floorboard that everyone knew about, and avoided, because it was loose. But I, being new, didn't know. It made a noise like a creaking door in a horror movie, long and lingering, ruining Niall's dramatic finale. He flung down the script in a rage, stamped his foot and called down the curses of his ancestors upon the young pup who had ruined his moment. Somewhat traumatised, I muttered an apology. If the ground had opened up then and there and swallowed me, I would have lived happily ever after. The producer restored peace. Niall picked up a few pages back and I did the announcement when he had left the studio. A few days later, Niall sought me out to apologise. It was a good lesson, though: performers have to concentrate on their work; outside distractions are not welcome and can have serious consequences.

Dates stick in my mind from those days in the Continuity studio. The eight o'clock news on 22 November 1967 carrying the death of my friend, Paul Williams of The Greenbeats, in a car accident; Sunday, 24 March 1968, reorganising programmes after Don Cockburn came on with the news-flash that an Aer Lingus Viscount had 'come down' near Tusker Rock; Monday, 21 April 1969, deferring programmes while waiting for a possible announcement of the resignation of Terence O'Neill as Prime Minister of Northern Ireland.

The O'Neill story had a sequel. I finished duty at five o'clock and had arranged to meet Mike Murphy for a drink on the way home. We met in the Merrion Inn, down the road from the TV studios in Montrose. Mike was now reading sport results on television, so he had to nip up to the studios for the six o'clock bulletin. He came back in high good form.

'You'll never believe what happened. I was sitting in the News studio with Charles Mitchel coming up to six o'clock. He was giving out yards about a new newsreader who had been hired particularly to, at long last, give Charles a break at weekends. He then had the nerve to tell the newsroom that he was only free on weekday nights. Charles was not at all pleased. I then pointed out to him that they were running film of O'Neill's resignation on the monitor. "Not at all, dear boy, that's only a rehearsal," said Charles. "They're only timing the clip. Anyway, this newsreader chap...."'

That's what was happening in the studio. But this is what the nation saw and heard.

O'Neill: 'And therefore, I have reached the decision that I must resign as Prime Minister of Northern Ireland.'

Cut to Charles: 'It's ridiculous. The least he could do is work the weekends.'

In early 1968, Terry Wogan had also resigned to present *Late Night Extra*, on BBC Radio. He had appeared in the famous photograph of the first line-up of BBC Radio 1 DJs in 1967 and now it was time to make a commitment. The Director-General of RTÉ had asked, with some justification, why their Senior Radio Announcer was working for another station, particularly as he was blazoned across all the papers. It was a point, I suspect, that Denis had to concede, notwithstanding his aim to expand opportunities for his staff. Terry was doing only the Wednesday edition of *Late Night Extra*, but it was going out as a shared transmission on BBC Radio 1 and 2. He was already presenting *Terry Awhile* on RTÉ Radio, commuting between London and Dublin. A side-effect of his major career development was the demise of the poker school that met regularly, on a rotating basis, in each player's house; it included Terry, Ian Corr, Des Morahan, Des Coates, me and other stragglers. Good fun, and good company, but I was no threat; I could never remember the sequence of the winning hands.

Then, on 26 January 1969, we lost Denis Meehan. He died in St Vincent's Hospital, after a long and courageous battle with cancer. Roibeárd Ó Faracháin paid tribute to him:

> Above all things, he was a delightful companion, humourous, sunny-natured, felicitous in conversation, a man whose presence gave out a soft glow of kindliness. One welcomed his company as a favour, as more than a pleasure. And yet in his broadcasting work there was unmistakable authority, not asserted often in speech but investing him as part of his personal distinction of mind and character.

Denis was only forty-four when he died. There was a pall over the station on the day of his funeral. I missed him sorely. He was, to my mind, the embodiment of Irish radio and its contract with the listener: witty, learned, mischievous, and underpinning everything with a profound sense of integrity. Whatever I learned about broadcasting over the following years was built on the foundation of his wisdom and insight.

∿ SOUNDTRACK ∿

The Rolling Stone **Top Twenty Albums of All Time**

1. Sgt Pepper's Lonely Hearts Club Band/The Beatles
2. Pet Sounds/The Beach Boys
3. Revolver/The Beatles
4. Highway 61 Revisited/Bob Dylan
5. Rubber Soul/The Beatles
6. What's Going On/Marvin Gaye
7. Exile on Main Street/The Rolling Stones
8. London Calling/The Clash
9. Blonde on Blonde/Bob Dylan
10. The White Album/The Beatles
11. The Sun Sessions/Elvis Presley
12. Kind of Blue/Miles Davis
13. Velvet Underground and Nico/Velvet Underground
14. Abbey Road/The Beatles
15. Are You Experienced?/Jimi Hendrix Experience
16. Blood on the Tracks/Bob Dylan
17. Nevermind/Nirvana
18. Born to Run/Bruce Springsteen
19. Astral Weeks/Van Morrison
20. Thriller/Michael Jackson

Chapter 11 ~

THE NEXT PROGRAMME IS SPONSORED BY...

'They send in things. And we play a record for them?' he asked. 'That's right,' I said. 'We'd write the script and take care of the objects. I'll be the producer and all you would have to do is act as compere. We're calling it *Surprise Package*.'

'And it's for Urney Chocolates…?' he asked.

'That's right. You used to do it before—Dantro, Mystery Man from Mars and all that….'

'All right. Sounds like it's not a bad idea. I'll do it.'

'Thanks, Gay, I'll get back to you. The fee is twelve pounds.'

'Okay. Thank you.'

I put the phone down and breathed a sigh of relief. It was 1965 and I was in the hall of my parents' house on Lower Kilmacud Road. I was nineteen years of age and I had just asked Gay Byrne to present a sponsored programme for Urney Chocolates. At the time, the irony of hiring Gay three years after asking for his autograph at the first *Late Late Show* was lost on me. I was just glad that he had responded to my nervous overture and had agreed to do it. It was the beginning of a separate broadcasting career in the commercial sector, running parallel with my work in RTÉ as an announcer and compere.

It grew out of Harry Thuillier asking me to write scripts for the Murray Rent-a-Car sponsored programme. That led to writing the Urney Chocolates programme for Harry, when he presented and produced it in a half-hour slot at eleven o'clock on Saturday nights. I had asked my pal in the Insurance Corporation, Dermot Herbert, to help with the writing chores. Serendipitously, Dermot had a school friend, Peter Blake, who was now an accounts executive in O'Keefe's Advertising. We all got on well together and when Peter was setting up a sponsored programme for Plus Washing Powder, he asked me to present it and Harry Thuillier to produce it. It was recorded in

ACT Studios with Colin Morrison as disc operator and (I think) Bill Somerville-Large on the desk. The programme had the slipperiest of formats: it was called *The Plus Factor*, showcasing performers who had that mysterious Extra Something. Like many sponsored programmes of the time, it was the thinnest of threads on which to hang five records, but it was my first commercial programme.

Whatever the plus factors of the product, prolonged existence was not one of them; both powder and programme vanished down the plughole after six months.

Sponsored programmes had been the backbone of the morning, afternoon and late-night transmissions on Radio Éireann. For a client, they were an effective means of promoting a product or service, but they had a more subtle effect as well. Many of them became radio institutions and had the effect of making listeners feel positive about their product. Because commercials were limited to ninety seconds per quarter hour, their softer sell and friendlier approach made them enjoyable listening and an integral part of the aural landscape. On RTÉ programmes that occasionally invite archive choices from guests or listeners, invariably the top requests are excerpts from sponsored programmes—Frankie Byrne, Leo Maguire, Monica Carr, Denis Brennan, Maura Laverty. Some advertising agencies had their own radio departments (Niall Boden ran one of them), while others sub-contracted out to production companies and studios.

The long-running Irish Hospitals Sweepstakes programme was unique, in that it was both the client and the production company, recording its nightly programme in its studio in the Gate Lodge of its Ballsbridge headquarters, modestly dubbed 'the largest office building in the world'. (Val Joyce, incidentally, beat Gay Byrne to the post as studio operator in The Sweeps, at first recording the compering team of Ian Priestly-Mitchell and Bart Bastable, later becoming one of them and generating his life-long interest in horses.) Apart from ACT Studios in Upper Mount Street, the main commercial studios were those of Peter Hunt on St Stephen's Green, Bill Stapleton on Merrion Row and the Eamonn Andrews Studios, originally over a shop in Henry Street and latterly in the Television Club, Harcourt Street, Dublin, 'the home of with-it dancing'.

Sponsored programmes tended to change hands when a new advertising manager was appointed in a commercial firm, a new advertising agency was contracted, or a new account executive took over from a colleague. So it was with the Urney Programme. Peter Blake asked Dermot and me to come up with an idea to pitch to his new client that would be different from anything on the air. The *Surprise Package* was Dermot's idea, I recall, but we both saw the comic possibilities for a programme that was not just different but bizarre in the extreme. It invited listeners to send in an object to us and we would match it with a record. The senders of the five objects we used would receive a hamper of delicious confectionery and the winner of the Most Unusual Object Award got extra succulent goodies on top of that. The Managing Director of Urney liked the idea, but it depended on getting Gay Byrne to present it; hence the importance of my phone call. The MD also pointed out kindly that Cadbury, his arch business rival for the sweet tooth of the nation, had a 'Surprise' chocolate bar on the market and asked could we please find an alternative title.

And so, at a quarter past two on Saturday afternoons, the audience was subjected to the Urney *Mystery Parcel*. The signature was the same one we had used on Harry Thuillier's earlier version: 'Minuet Mash' by Les Reed, which was the same tune as my mother's masterpiece, 'In an Eighteenth-Century Drawing Room'. The incongruous tune, not to say the programme itself, seemed to match the weird streak in the Irish psyche. Listeners caught on to it immediately and sent in a range of objects that were odd, uncanny, creepy and, in some cases, just plain unhygienic. We got locks of hair, toenail clippings, foreign coins, old tools, strange toys, bits of cars and packages that were soft to the touch and malodorous to the nose (we didn't open those ones). I managed to match a tune to each, most of them mercifully forgotten, but etched in the brain somehow are a ram's horn which prompted 'I'll Never Find Another Ewe', a tiny mouth-organ which couldn't be played very well, until Gay suggested that 'Blowing in the Wind' was the way to go about it, and a dried piece of plaice which provoked 'Somewhere' from *West Side Story* (think about it). I wrote the scripts in a comedy style that suited Gay, recalling that he had done comic pieces on the Sunday Night Concert circuit for years and was well able to handle a gag in a deadpan fashion. Sometimes, when the pun was so offensive, the script instruction to Gay was to 'cry and fade out'. He took the crying device elsewhere, but I must own up to having caused it. Sorry about that.

To formalise our production efforts, Marquis Productions Ltd was formed to produce radio and sound programmes. There was no particular reason for the name, other than that we wanted something grand and slightly regal. It was pronounced as spelt, not 'mar-key' in the French fashion. Dermot Herbert, Peter Blake and I were the directors and we took premises on the top floor of Bective House, Dawson Street, Dublin 2. Dermot, although still in Insurance as a loss adjuster, made a superb business manager; Peter was in advertising and became a *de facto* promotions manager, on the lookout for new business; and I was the creative and production department. We hired Candy as a secretary, who became adept at opening suspicious packages for the Urney Programme.

To record the programmes, we used the newly opened Avondale Studios in Lower Dominick Street, part of the building occupied by EMI Records. I was familiar with it from my first TV commercial voice-over when Willie Styles, producing for Arks Advertising, asked me to read 'There are just two words to remember about tipped cigarettes—Gold Leaf'. The studio was owned and operated by Ciarán Breathnach, who, with his dynamic junior helper, Patrick Gibbons, had come from Stapleton Studios. They brought with them a programme guaranteed to pay the rent for many years afterwards: *The Kennedys of Castleross*, the drama serial sponsored by Fry-Cadbury and produced by Willie Styles. Marquis Productions used Avondale because we wanted a studio not associated with another production company—Eamonn Andrews Studios and ACT were the friendly opposition—but, because we started around the same time, we constantly had to counter the rumour that we had a financial interest in the studio.

The Urney Programme was a roaring success and made our name. More programmes came our way. By popular agreement, one programme in particular changed the way pop shows were done in Ireland. The *Yardley Top Choice*, again presented by Gay, was an energetic, pacy programme that stood out amongst the other morning sponsored programmes for liver-fluke cures, porridge oats and hair tonic. It went out at 8.15 a.m. and it was loud, starting on a staccato signature tune that left gaps for Gay's introduction. I then squeezed in the Top Five record choices from listeners' postal votes, one oldie, two new releases, two commercials and one beauty talk from Yardley's bouffanted Beauty Consultant, named (I think) Paula Healy. Using a slight echo on Gay's voice and pushing the sound levels to the maximum, it jumped out of the radio at the listeners. It is fondly remembered to this day, Dave Fanning quoting it as the only programme worth listening to when he was a teenager, and John Clarke, later Head of RTÉ 2FM, reminding me that he wrote in to Marquis Productions enquiring about the signature tune. It was 'Hell Raisers' by the Syd Dale Orchestra and John purloined it to use as his own radio theme ever since.

In 1967, RTÉ announced that it would offer half-hour sponsored programme slots on a Wednesday, at 8.30 a.m., 1.00 p.m. and 1.45 p.m., *Hospitals Requests* having moved to a midday slot in the new dispensation of extended programming. We produced two of them. The morning programme was sponsored by Aer Lingus and was a kind of radio travelogue presented by

Noel McCaul. Ted Bonner contributed a 'Faraway Places' slot, drawing on his years of travel anecdotes, and Aer Lingus staff in the far-flung empire of the National Airline would send occasional biased reports. It was bound together with music and a novel feature I had to negotiate with Donal Stanley. One of the key reasons why people listened to the radio in the mornings, I reckoned, was for accurate time-checks. These came on the quarter-hour, and even if you missed the continuity announcement, you could always tell the time from the signature tunes of the changing sponsored programmes. With a half-hour programme, there was no such obvious junction and my fear was that people would not listen if they were not going to get the accurate time. The solution was simple. In recording the programme, I made sure that there was an instrumental piece of about three minutes at the halfway point of the programme. This allowed the continuity technician to fade the tape and the announcer to give a live time-check over it. It was the only programme I ever heard that, in its introductory menu, listed 'news, previews of holiday destinations, reviews of historic sites, music... and an accurate time check'.

The other programme was *The World of Entertainment,* sponsored by The Irish Permanent Building Society and broadcast at 1.00 p.m. on Wednesdays. It was the first popular arts show on RTÉ Radio, encompassing film, music, theatre, and celebrity guests. I offered the compering seat to the irrepressible Joe Linnane, not only for his presenting and interviewing skills, but also for his knowledge of show business.

The resident film reviewer was a journalist friend of mine, Seán Carberry, and there was a Guest DJ spot, where other comperes contributed a seven-minute piece. They covered a range of personalities, from Gearóid Ó Tighernaigh (famous from *Ceol do Pháistí* on Sunday evening radio and, in the day job, Secretary to the Minister for Justice), to Johnny Moran of Radios Luxembourg and Caroline. I recall writing a piece for Gay, where he introduced pop records in the classical style, intoning solemnly, 'We come now to a recital of modern music from The Rolling Stones String and Percussion Ensemble, with Michael Jagger, tenor.' As one of the guest DJs on the programme, Terry Wogan took the opportunity to announce his resignation from the staff of RTÉ, prompting Joe Linnane to respond to his old sparring partner with, 'There you go, taking the bread out of the mouths of our starving children, as if there weren't enough freelancers around the place....' I got the impression that Joe was not being entirely flippant.

We had promised Star Guests to the sponsors, and celebrity interviews had to be arranged every week. Many came directly to the studio in Lower Dominick Street to be interviewed by Joe. Local artists were happy to oblige, for the most part, but some international celebrities also climbed to the second floor of the old house. The singer Tom Paxton comes to mind in particular. He established an instant rapport with Joe and sang his biggest hit, 'The Last Thing on My Mind'. He was so impressed by the recording quality achieved by Patrick Gibbons that he took a copy home with him and, I believe, issued it commercially.

Joe had a wonderful knack of connecting quickly with people and finding an interesting way into the conversation. It was evident in an interview he did with Tom Jones in April 1967, who was then launching 'Funny Familiar Forgotten Feelings'. Tom Jones was not at all used to interviews and had not yet acquired the testosterone-filled confidence he developed later. He was quite shy, really, but Joe produced a friendly and engaging interview. Likewise with Hughie Green, in Ireland auditioning for his TV talent show, *Opportunity Knocks*. They had never met, but Hughie knew Joe from his days on BBC Radio and his film roles. The interview was almost a comedy double-act and it was a delight to hear two pros at the peak of their performance.

Joe didn't like the inconvenience of going out with a portable tape recorder and recording guest interviews. We set up the interviews for him, but most stars were available only at night, usually after their performance, and that meant late nights backstage in a theatre, waiting for the interview. Joe would much rather be at home with his wife and family, but with some stars, Joe needed little prompting. Louis Armstrong was a case in point. He played the Adelphi Cinema, Dublin, and we arranged access for Joe to record an interview. His opening gambit, intended to show his appreciation of Louis's natural gift for trumpet playing, left the interviewee somewhat nonplussed: 'Tell me, Louis, do you practise much? Because to hear you out there tonight, you'd think you never practised in your life.' The interview proceeded, somewhat stonily, and it was hard to know whether Louis was naturally monosyllabic or just couldn't be bothered talking to some Irish cat who had insulted him.

We eventually settled on a separate fee to compensate Joe Linnane for expenses in travelling to outside interviews. I think it was prompted by an interview in Dublin Airport. With our contacts in the Aer Lingus press office, we were occasionally privy to celebrity arrivals. We heard that The Rolling Stones' manager, Andrew Oldham, was due in Ireland the following day and Joe was despatched to capture him on tape.

He was waiting in the VIP lounge when his quarry disembarked. A helpful press assistant pointed him out to Joe.

'Welcome to Ireland, Mr Oldham,' Joe said breezily, pressing his microphone into Andrew's face.

'Fuck off,' said Mr Oldham.

Joe thought quickly.

'Thank you so much, Mr Oldham. And with those words, the first words issued in Ireland by The Rolling Stones' manager, Mr Andrew Oldham, this is Joe Linnane, live at Dublin Airport, returning you to the studio.'

Joe reported afterwards that Mr Oldham blanched satisfactorily at the subterfuge and, for all his technical prowess in the recording studio, never realised that Joe's microphone led to a tape recorder and not to a live transmission.

More subterfuges were employed to capture celebrity interviews for the programme. Dermot and I regularly went to London, each equipped with a portable recorder. Dermot went to film sets and interviewed the cast and crew of *Up the Junction,* directed by ex-Telefís Éireann producer Peter Collinson and starring Suzy Kendall and Dennis Waterman, and also talked to Christopher Lee, then filming the Hammer Horror, *The Devil Rides Out.* I stayed around Shaftsbury Avenue and interviewed theatre stars like Evelyn Laye (who sounded exactly like Dame Celia Molestrangler, the overacting actress from the Charles and Fiona sketches on BBC Radio's *Round the Horne*) and Nicholas Parsons, who in response to a 'How did you start in this business?' line of enquiry, took the microphone from my hand and told me his life story in gruesome detail for half an hour, or whenever the tape ran out, whichever was the sooner. A fascinating conversationalist, as long as the fascinating topic was him.

These interview questions would be re-voiced by Joe Linnane back in Avondale, with Patrick matching the background sound and microphone quality so perfectly that no one ever spotted that Joe never left his front room. What wasn't used for the *World of Entertainmen*t turned up as part of a London Theatre Feature on the Aer Lingus programme. I did a long interview with singer Tommy Steele in his dressing room that turned out so well that I kept it for myself and made it into *A Handful of Songs,* a half-hour musical feature for Róisín Lorigan.

Those recording sessions with Joe Linnane were the most enjoyable of the week and whenever I hear Procol Harum's 'Whiter Shade of Pale', I can recall its first airplay in Ireland, with Joe sitting in Avondale in May 1967 and opining that, for his money, it would turn out to be the best pop record of the year. He was right, too. Gay Byrne has always credited Eamonn Andrews as his most important influence, but, to my ears, Joe Linnane was the model for Gay's cheeky, charismatic approach. Joe was the first of the personality broadcasters, the first to bring an irreverent approach to Irish radio.

Marquis Productions gained a fourth director when Gay formally joined the enterprise, pooling his programmes with ours. The first phone-call programme came out of Avondale, as Patrick lashed up a system of putting callers directly on air as they talked to Gay. Albright and Wilson were the first sponsors and the National Dairy Council continued the format as *The NDC Family Show*. It was aimed at housewives and, because the programmes were recorded, we had to ring the listener, rather than the other way around. We recorded all Gay's programmes on a Monday morning, one after the other, with one eye on the ticking clock. Each programme was allotted a maximum of one hour for recording and editing; anything over that meant that we paid double in studio fees. With compere fees and music copyright fees to pay, going over time in studio could negate the profit margin on some programmes.

It was good training, though. I prepared as much as I could in advance, timing the links and music and preparing the edits on paper. Most programmes were recorded 'as live', without a break. The phone call programmes couldn't be prepared in advance, though, and relied completely on the quality of the phone conversation. Gay would ask them for their music choice and we prided ourselves on getting the record out before the caller hung up. Avondale had a large library, I also brought along some heavily requested tunes and, *in extremis*, we could nip downstairs to Tony Hanna in EMI for a loan of the disc.

One Monday morning, we were having no luck whatever in raising suitable prospects for phone calls. Everyone we called was either out or the line was engaged. We were running out of studio time. I had an idea. Tony Gaynor, a producer in Light Music Department in RTÉ, would occasionally lapse into old Dublinese, bemoaning the weather, the Government, the lack of decent films, the price of the pint, the jungle music the kids listened to and other topics of concern. These flights of fancy caused some mirth in the pub and I suspected they might be corralled for radio use. I rang him in RTÉ, told him our problem with the lack of phone calls and set up the scene. He was a plumber doing some work in a house and he had answered the phone because the Lady of the House was out shopping. He would talk to Gay and ad-lib through whatever topic came up. What was his name, Tony wanted to know. The answer came from somewhere in the back of my head. 'Your name is Malachy Scully.'

The phone call was successfully made and Malachy rambled on about the Eurovision Song Contest, complaining that half the entrants couldn't sing in English, that there was a Mrs Grey in their pub who would knock that crowd into a cocked hat, not to mind Crooked Paddy, who sang Jim Reeves songs with a bit of a limp, because of the way he held his mouth, and if that foreign crowd could learn decent songs like 'I Know a Millionaire', something we could all join in with, those kinds of songs, the world would be a better place. It was a minor *tour de force* on Tony's part and Gay almost expired trying to control his laughter and appear interested. We rang Malachy 'by accident' many times later and he discoursed on the EEC and his reaction to Ireland's forthcoming membership, suggesting that we flood Ringsend to make it the Venice of Ireland and that somebody start a new business by breeding snails for consumption by the canny foreigner.

'How would that work?' asked Gay.

'We just collect a load of snails—boy and girl snails—and keep them together in the same place for as long as possible.'

'In what sort of a place?' Gay persisted.

'How do I know, Gay? Some sort of a snail house.'

'And what do you call a snail house?' said Gay, pushing his luck.

'I don't know what they call them out in Howth, Gay, but where I live we call them shells.'

As we produced more and more sponsored programmes, Avondale Studios became a sort of home from home. I was there a couple of days a week and ran into a rich cast of characters. The agricultural sector provided Peter Murphy, Jim Norton and his sister, Mary Norton (better known as Monica Carr); Barbara McCaughey and Des Nealon, the voices behind the *Fruitfield Information Desk*; and the entire cast of *The Kennedys of Castleross* came in once a week to record two or three episodes per session. There were several sub-plots to the serial. First, Mrs Kennedy, played by Marie Kean, had to be in every episode. That meant that Willie Styles and Ciarán Breathnach had occasionally to go to London with a tape machine when Marie was on a film location or appearing in a play. They would record her lines in isolation for dozens of future episodes and bring them back to add the other actors. Marie became so good at it that she could time her pauses, leaving just the right space for her colleagues to fit in their lines exactly, allowing the scene to be run non-stop. The other sub-plot was to do with budget: to keep costs under control, there could be only five actors per episode. This resulted in a sort of echo effect over the five scenes of the episode. Mrs Kennedy would talk to Brian, then Brian would tell Christy what his mother had said to him, Christy would meet Joan, who was surprised at what Mrs Kennedy said, Joan would confront Mrs Kennedy about what she said, and finally, Mrs Kennedy would explain to Peadar that she had been taken up wrongly, that it wasn't like that at all and that she was going to ring Jim Lonergan to make sure. Jim, being the sixth character, was on the other end of a phone and his voice was not heard.

Another of the Wednesday half-hour sponsored programmes was *Miscellany*, originated by Willie Styles and introduced by Ronnie Walsh. A regular parade of speakers came to Avondale—Stephen Rynne, John Ryan,

Benedict Kiely—to contribute talks, short radio essays and poems, interspersed with impeccably chosen classical music. When, eventually, Fry-Cadbury ceased its sponsorship of *The Kennedys*, the programme moved down the street to the GPO and Willie went with it, also taking the Miscellany programme. *Sunday Miscellany* became one of the jewels of RTÉ Radio and is oft quoted as the epitome of public service broadcasting. It is sometimes conveniently forgotten that it was originally a commercial programme, sponsored by, of all supporters of the arts, Shell Oil.

There was always a touchy relationship between the in-house 'station programmes' and their counterparts in the commercial sector. It was an affiliation that was necessary for funding the station as well as promoting Irish business interests, but it was viewed, in Albert Reynolds's words about coalition government, as 'a temporary little arrangement'. Indeed, the sensitive delineation between public service broadcasting and commercial advertising has dogged RTÉ from the beginning. The 'dual funding' argument was always thrown at the broadcaster by newspaper interests; as if they weren't equally dual-funded through both cover price and advertising. In practical terms, I had a foot in both camps. My commercial interests were known to RTÉ, particularly as I dealt regularly with Donal Stanley and Billy Wall in the Sponsored Programmes Office. But as I had been producing sponsored programmes before I became a staff announcer, there was no objection made, as long as I didn't appear on any sponsored programmes or read any commercials. We were permitted to do station programmes, and I still occasionally presented *Ireland's Top Ten*, but to have the Voice of the Station on a commercial programme was too much to bear. I had the greatest difficulty in persuading Brigid Kilfeather that the winner of the 'Search for a DJ' competition on the *Imco Show* was not me and that there really was a person called Ashley Pringle.

Terry Wogan's resignation from the staff of RTÉ freed him from the ban on compering sponsored programmes. His first one was for Oliver Barry's music management organisation, International Artists. Marquis Productions was asked to produce it. We called it *Take it from Terry*, a half-hour show promoting the attractions of Oliver's army of artists: The Freshmen, Seán Dunphy and the Hoedowners, the Capitol Showband and The Wolfetones. I decided to go for a very fast show, along the style of a Radio Caroline programme. The bands' dance dates in ballrooms now disappeared—Roseland Moate, the Top Hat, Dun Laoghaire, the Crystal Ballroom—were delivered over Scott Walker singing 'Land of a Thousand Dances'. I made up jingles from records by the Kirby Stone Four (who had that American Jingle sound) and introduced pre-recorded one-liners from comedy records by *Rowan and Martin's Laugh In* and *The Stan Freberg Show*. Many became famous: 'Now, if you aren't chicken, turn up your volume knobs all the way!' and 'Let's run up the flag and see if anyone salutes' and 'Shall we dance?'—'Sorry, I'm a little stiff from bowling'— 'I don't care where you're from, let's dance.'

At first, I scripted the programme for Terry. Then, as he relaxed into it and found his 'DJ voice', so to speak, I encouraged him to ad-lib his way through it, supplying him only with a running order of discs and one-liners. He would cue us to spin the record, so we in the control room would follow him. We then reversed the process and spun the discs and one-liners whenever we wanted, meaning that Terry had to follow us. Aided by a little compression and echo on the voice, he managed to speak faultlessly over the introductions to records, ending just before the vocal started. There was an element of catharsis about it as he shed the manacles of Senior Announcer and became an entertaining popular broadcaster who was funny, iconoclastic and, more often than not, outrageous. Despite Terry's send-up of some of the artists, we had a string of hit records: 'Two Loves' and 'The Lonely Woods of Upton' by Seán Dunphy, 'Slievenamon' by The Wolfetones and 'Go Granny Go' by The Freshmen. When pop shows were few and far between on Irish radio, *Take it from Terry* sounded most unlike an RTÉ late-night programme, not suitable for those of a nervous disposition.

Terry was still commuting to London for *Late Night Extra* on BBC Radios 1 and 2 and the occasional appearance on television. Still, he wanted something more permanent, possibly during the hours of daylight, the most listened-to broadcasting hours always being between 7 a.m. and 7 p.m. To persuade Mark White, his BBC mentor, that he was capable of a more prestigious slot and could adapt to the pop-oriented daytime format, he sent him a copy of *Take it from Terry*. Mark offered him Jimmy Young's morning slot while its incumbent was on a month's holiday. Its success led to Terry being offered the afternoon slot on BBC Radios 1 and 2 and, at the end of 1969, he packed his bags and left for good. I was delighted to have played a small part in the Wogan success story, in recompense for all the help he had given me.

As it happened, I wasn't very far behind him. In October 1968, I had written to Derek Mills, producer of the *Dave Cash Show* on BBC Radio 1. He suggested that I send a tape, so I recorded a half-hour programme in Avondale and sent it to him. He replied in a courteous letter that he liked it, that he had no openings himself, but that, if I liked, he would pass it to some colleagues. Then, at the end of January, I got a phone call in Continuity from Brian

Willey, who introduced himself as the Executive Producer of *Roundabout*, the teatime show on BBC Radio 2. He had heard the tape, felt that my style was suitable and asked would I be interested in compering the programme in March. Absolutely. No doubt. Delighted. Thank you for thinking of me. Very thoughtful.

I didn't realise, until I looked back at the dates, that the BBC rang me two days after Denis Meehan's funeral. I suspect that there was more a sense of novelty rather than burning ambition behind my application to the BBC, but perhaps I wanted to see what other avenues were available. Michael Carroll had taken over as Head of Presentation, after a brief interregnum when Liam Devalley acted as Department Head. He was an engineer and it cannot be said that the announcing staff greeted his appointment with universal acclamation. I had to ask permission to work for the BBC, which was granted in typical RTÉ fashion—as long as I took annual leave.

I arrived at the Aeolian Hall, New Bond Street, London on Monday, 24 March 1969, having booked into my slightly faded lodgings in the Irish Club the previous night. The Aeolian housed a large BBC studio for music recordings, as well as offices for *Roundabout* and other programmes that used live bands, orchestras and groups. Brian Willey was an outgoing friendly type who introduced me to his production assistant. Then, the three us hopped into a taxi for the short ride up to Broadcasting House, the assistant clutching a large box containing records, tapes and scripts. By 2.30 p.m., we were ensconced in Studio B6, deep in the bowels of BH, as it was known. I was handed a running order. It was seventeen pages long, with three music items (including copyright details) typed on each foolscap page, with large spaces in between for the compere to write links or notes. Each space had a timing on it, indicating that the link should be fifteen or thirty or forty seconds; it didn't give any clue as to what you should say, as long as you said it in fifteen seconds.

The music pieces were largely drawn from recordings made by the BBC Orchestras and other specially recorded ensembles—Chico Arnez and His Cubana Brass, the Ronnie Aldrich Continental Group, the Derek Cox Quartet with Sheila Southern and dozens more. Commercial gramophone records were in the minority, due to 'needle time' restrictions imposed by the Musicians' Union: Radio 1 ate up most of the quota, so Radio 2 had to stretch out its programmes with 'house recordings' by real musicians.

The exception was a 'Feature Record', chosen to make a specific point—the birthday of the singer, or an important anniversary. Apart from the music, there were items drawn from the 'Talks Bank', short ninety-second spoken pieces by regular contributors on subjects ranging from Rose Pruning and Paris Parking to Silver Hallmarks and What's New in Clubland. They were usually recorded, but sometimes live. On that first day, I had to interview Helen Shapiro about her new single. She seemed surprised to be asked the obvious question, 'Where did you get to?' because she had not been heard of for six years. I think she thought it was none of my business, but it was the question on everybody's mind, in my view. The interview went well after that.

At 4.32, the familiar signature tune, 'The Windows of Paris', rang out over Britain and I was on the air to introduce my first record on the BBC, 'The Kerry Dance' by the Dennis Walton Orchestra. Nice thought, Brian. My continuity training came into its own, as I had to do split-second links to allow for an opt-out for the shipping forecast and traffic reports. Production and writing expertise were taken for granted too. I had to present an anniversary tribute to the pianist Billy Mayerl (his widow sent me a note saying that I spoke as if I had known him), and on the third day, that most British of BBC bandleaders, Billy Cotton, died. Working only from newspaper clippings, I had to write a tribute to him in the hour before the programme and present it live. The irony was not lost on me: here was an Irishman eulogising a British National Institution, as well as an employee of RTÉ extolling the father of the Controller of BBC Television.

The BBC production method was efficient, sometimes to the point of excess. Nothing was left to chance. It was different from the more freewheeling methods back in Ireland and I think they were somewhat surprised that I ad-libbed the programme, jotting down only key words to remind me where I was going. It worked, anyway, and there were no glitches and only positive feedback. One BBC contrivance that we could borrow successfully in RTÉ was known as 'The Doomsday Disc'. It was permanently set up in readiness for a disaster on a news bulletin and was designed to be amorphous, antiseptic and devoid of any negative connotations whatever. Ours was 'Catch the Wind' by the Mantovani Orchestra, which was as bland and inoffensive as you could get, unless the Queen Mother was blown aloft with her umbrella, coming to rest on top of the Cenotaph.

The other producers during the week were Frances Line (later to become Controller of BBC Radio 2), Charles Clark-Maxwell (who looked exactly as you'd imagine), and Bev Phillips, an agreeable and friendly young man with whom I got on well. He produced music recording sessions as well as the live programme. He introduced me to a peculiarly London phenomenon, the drinking club, to Turkish restaurants and also to a young man in a corridor in the Aeolian Hall: 'May I introduce the current compere of *Roundabout*, Brendan Balfe,' Bev said.

I shook hands with a dark young man with a bandana around his head. He appeared shy and withdrawn. 'How do you do,' I said.

'This is Jimi Hendrix,' said Bev.

'Nice to meet you,' said Jimi. Then he was gone...

Back in Dublin, Brian Willey rang me a few weeks later. He was very impressed with my stint on the programme. They had decided to narrow the roster of presenters down to four, who would rotate every week: they were Pete Murray, Kenneth Kendall, Brian Matthew—and me. That was the plan agreed with the team. Unfortunately, since then, the Controller had told them that *Roundabout* was being discontinued completely, to make way for a new approach. We're very sorry, but there you are—nothing we can do about it.

Back in Dublin, Terry's leaving seemed to have had a domino effect. Brigid had gone to television as Head of Presentation and Maurice O'Doherty had become a full-time newsreader, permanently based in Montrose. One night, he told me, his colleague Andy O'Mahony came to him to ask for a favour. He was scheduled to read the 6.30 radio news but had to meet a friend at the airport and would be very much obliged if Maurice could do the duty for him. He would, of course, return the favour at the first opportunity. Maurice, always an obliging chap, explained that he couldn't. He was scheduled to read the six o'clock television news and that wasn't due to end until 6.28. He would never make the dash between the TV studio and the radio studio in different parts of the building in time. Andy persisted. There was talk about how disappointed his friend would be, not to be on the receiving end of an Irish Welcome.

Maurice eventually agreed. He went through the TV bulletin 'like a scalded snot', as he put it, coming out two minutes early and utterly discommoding Presentation, who had to fill the gap. He dashed down the corridors, into the newsroom, and grabbed the script from the sub-editor. A minute to go. He went into the radio studio and quickly scanned the copy for strange names and exotic places. Nothing too unusual. As the pips of the time signal went out, he took a deep breath. As the red light came on, Maurice looked down and read the first words he saw on the top of the page: 'Here is the news read by Andy O'Mahony.' There was a deathly silence, as he considered how he could possibly correct it. He decided that anything he said would only make matters worse, so, unabashed, he continued with the bulletin.

Some time later, Maurice handed over to Brendan Keenan, sitting opposite him for a report on the heiress Patty Hearst, who seemed to have joined the gang that had kidnapped her. As Brendan read his report, Maurice leaned back, unaware that one of the casters was missing from the back of the swivel chair. He fell over with a thump and landed on his back, feet in the air. The Special Branch detective, stationed outside the studio, was convinced that the studio was being infiltrated by subversive elements and also came in. The whole debacle was recorded for posterity and the attempt by Brendan Keenan to continue without suffocating from laughter is a joy to listen to.

Ruth Buchanan joined the announcers in November 1968, along with Treasa Davison. I was supervising Treasa one evening when the Technical Supervisor told me that there had been a breakdown on the Dublin transmitter. It was standard practice to make an apology when service had been restored, so I went to Continuity to tell Treasa to do so at the next break. She made the announcement, but ascribed the wrong wavelength to the Dublin transmitter, saying that the breakdown had been on 530 metres, which was the Athlone transmitter. Now, engineers are notoriously sensitive about their areas of influence and, within seconds, the Engineer-in-Charge in Athlone rang me in some anguish. He demanded redress for the foul calumny committed against his transmitter, his staff and his professional reputation. This injustice had to be corrected immediately, he insisted. I refused, saying that I had no intention of asking the announcer to apologise for the previous apology. He was incensed and demanded to go over my head. Sorry, there is nowhere else to go, I told him; as Station Supervisor, my decision was final. There were memos flying between Athlone and Dublin for weeks afterwards, but the law laid down by Denis Meehan was still honoured. The Supervisor had the wheel.

But engineers can be tamed. The next intake of trainee announcers included a long-haired blond engineer with glasses. His face was unknown, but his legs became famous in the movies as part of the cinema advertisement for Dingos, 'jeans to step out of line in'. Unlike Elvis, who was shot from the waist up, Pat Kenny was shot from the waist down, gyrating groovily in mauve jeans like a true hipster. He was assigned to shadow me in Continuity as part of the training course. He sat in the chair behind me as I announced the lunchtime sponsored programmes. Just before an announcement was due, I got up to leave the studio.

'Hold on—who will make the announcement?' Pat asked.

'You will.'

And so, out of sheer necessity, the Kenny tones were heard throughout the land for the first time. He was appointed as an announcer shortly after, the second member of his family to appear regularly on radio; his brother, Paul Kenny, was an erstwhile compere of *Ireland's Top Ten*.

There was another surprise appointment in RTÉ when Donncha Ó Dúlaing was promoted from the Cork studios to become Head of Features.

He asked me to present a new programme on Saturday mornings, modelled on the *Out and About* format I'd been doing for a couple of years with Róisín Lorigan. I was to act as studio anchorman and interviewer, linking outside broadcasts from around the country. It was to be called *Away for the Day*. I agreed to do it and went to see Michael Carroll, whom I suspect had already been briefed by Donncha. He gave me permission to do it, on the basis that announcers could undertake one freelance programme each. Then, out of the blue, the Assistant Controller, Micheál Ó hAodha refused permission.

I made two quick visits down the corridor. First, to Donal Stanley to enquire if I could be put on the Commercial Reading panel. He said that I would be, at the first opportunity. Then to Kevin Roche to see could I be added to the roster for *Pop Call*. Again the answer was in the affirmative; moreover, Kevin was starting a new series with the Jim Doherty Quartet and was looking for a compere. I could have that, if I wanted.

Having established that there was a safety net in place before actually jumping, I went back to the Supervisor's Office and wrote a formal letter to Michael Carroll, thanking him for his efforts to enlarge the bailiwick of the announcers. It continued:

It appears, though, that being an experienced professional broadcaster on the staff of a Broadcasting Station is, in itself, a deterrent to that person broadcasting.

Accordingly, I hereby resign as staff radio announcer with effect one month from Wednesday 21st May 1969.

Mike Murphy took up a collection for my going-away present. When I heard about it, I was touched, but determined not to have a formal valediction. After all, I didn't intend going very far. The funds collected were turned into wine and we had a small, but long, gathering in Michael Carroll's office. Una Sheehy presented me with the BBC Handbook for 1926, Mike Murphy did his famous 'Who Killed Big Julie?' routine and, for the first time in history, John Skehan sang.

～ *SOUNDTRACK* ～

Selling Slogans
These catch phrases were burned into our brains through constant repetition from sponsored programmes.

- 'The Magic of Mystic is yours for the asking.'
  THE MYSTIC NYLONS SPONSORED PROGRAMME

- 'Bird's Custard and Bird's Jelly-de-Luxe. After all, you do want the best, don't you?'
  THE BIRD'S PROGRAMME

- 'It's easy to keep on saving, once you make a start.'
  EDDIE GOLDEN ON *THE POST OFFICE SAVINGS PROGRAMME*

- 'The problems we're discussing today may not be yours, but they could be someday.'
  FRANKIE BYRNE ON *THE JACOB'S PROGRAMME*

- 'Jellies, jams and marmalades—made by particular people, for particular people.'
  NIALL BODEN ON *THE CHIVERS PROGRAMME*

- 'If you feel like singing, do sing an Irish song.'
  LEO MAGUIRE ON *THE WALTON'S PROGRAMME*

- 'Put your money in a good mattress.'
  THE ODEAREST OLD LADY

- 'Remember—makes no difference where you are, you can wish upon a star.'
  IAN PRIESTLY-MITCHELL ON *THE IRISH HOSPITALS SWEEPSTAKES PROGRAMME*

- 'Yardley—the top choice in perfumes and cosmetics.'
  GAY BYRNE ON *THE YARDLEY PROGRAMME*

- 'A-cleaning and a-pressing and a-dyeing for you.'
  THE FIRST IRISH ADVERTISING JINGLE ON *THE IMCO SHOW*

- 'Buy now.'
  NIALL BODEN SIGNING OFF *THE DONNELLY'S PROGRAMME*

Chapter 12 ～

| ON THE STAGE

'Get Away' by Georgie Fame was the signature tune I picked to launch *Away for the Day* on Saturday, 14 June 1969 between 11.35 a.m. and 12.59 p.m. The eighty-four-minute programme was considered a long stint by the standards of the radio in the 1960s. I was the studio linkman and Maurice O'Doherty was on the road with an Outside Broadcast Unit, aided by Blánaid Irvine, as they visited festivals, events and field days all over Ireland, talking to the customers and organisers and, generally, trying to convey a sound picture of an Irish summer. My friend from the announcer's course, Brian Reynolds, who had moved into production, was riding shotgun. There was no shortage of events to cover; every village in Ireland had a festival, sometimes hung on the slimmest of ideas. Many were really excuses for bar extensions and marquee dancing. In fact, Maurice was particularly tickled one week to be asked to open the Castlegregory Onion Festival.

Up in Studios 3 and 4, I was to link the reports, play music, read event guides and interview visiting studio guests. The studio producer, in his English nomenclature, was Paddy O'Neill. Compared to the BBC, it was more casually prepared and I wouldn't know whom Paddy had lined up for interview until the morning of the programme. His occasional propensity for meeting people in pubs on a Friday night and offering them a slot on the following morning was no bad thing; it added to the informality of the programme, but it did sometimes have unfortunate consequences.

One morning, we lost contact with the unit in Achill Island and Maurice was silenced mid-sentence. It was ten minutes to twelve. I took over and introduced a record, but simultaneously there was a short circuit on the disc-operator's console, resulting in the loss of the turntables and also the cartridge machine for playing commercials. Back to Brendan. All I had left was notices of two events and as I was reading them, I saw Paddy through the glass with someone I'd never seen before. He came on talkback into my headphones: 'I'm sending him in now.' With nine minutes to fill, as I was talking, a man came into the studio and sat at the desk opposite me. Paddy was smiling in at me with the satisfied look of someone who had averted a disaster. The microphone was still live, so I had to start the interview without the benefit of the most basic information—who was he and why was he here? He, a friendly sort, seemed to assume that I had been briefed. The interview with this complete stranger went something like this:

BB: So, on to our next studio guest. A busy weekend ahead then?

Stranger: Absolutely. Looking forward to a great turnout.

BB: How many are you expecting?

Stranger: Well, over the two days, about six hundred.

BB: Where are they coming from?

Stranger: All over the country, with a few coming from Belfast.

BB: Where in particular? What type of people?

Stranger: Well, we have lots of regulars who show at the major exhibitions. Many of them would have been at the Chelsea Show earlier this week.

BB: What are you calling your show? Has it got a particular emphasis?

Stranger: No, just a general flower show. For the amateur as well as the professional.

BB: And what about the general visitor, who would just like to have a look at some nice flowers and have a pleasant afternoon out—what's the best route?

Stranger: Turn right at Leixlip village and follow the signs.

BB: And what will the signs say?

Stranger: Leixlip Flower Show, of course.

BB: And the admission price?

Stranger: Well, it's ten shilling per car or three shillings a head.

BB: Today and tomorrow, I presume. What are the main events this afternoon?

And so it went on, talking about flowers, seeds, advice to gardeners, what to wear at the show, until I got to twenty seconds to twelve and felt that I could wrap up the interview:

BB: A fascinating topic, flowers, and thank you so much for telling us about the Leixlip Flower Show, this afternoon and tomorrow, ten bob per car, it's well-signposted, so just follow the signs. And may I wish you and your hard-working committee every success. The time now is twelve o'clock.'

The red light went out. I shook the guest's hand and thanked him for coming in. I never got his name. (I wouldn't be surprised if I have mistaken the venue as well; I could barely remember my own name afterwards.) Paddy O'Neill thought that the interview had gone very well.

Away for the Day ran for the entire summer and, as I was now a freelance again, I was open to all offers. The series promised by Kevin Roche turned out to be *Downtown Dance Date*, a half-hour late-night programme with the Jim Doherty Quartet, featuring singer Des Smyth. Jim was Kevin Roche's nephew, classifying him forever as 'The Man from Uncle', but nepotism had nothing to do with it. Jim was a superb musician, as well as being one of the wittiest men in the business. I never met them during the series, because they recorded in the O'Connell Hall and I wrote and recorded the links at an editing session with producer Tony Gaynor. The script was certainly irreverent, in the approved manner of dealing with musicians: 'Des Smyth is currently appearing in An Old Blue Suit at the bus shelter in Raheny,' or 'The Jim Doherty Appreciation Society will be holding its Annual General Meeting next Tuesday in the phone box on Burgh Quay.' The percussionist, John Wadham, was particularly taken by 'The Jim Doherty Quartet—three musicians and a drummer'.

Another programme to keep the wolf from the door was *Pop Call,* one of the most popular programmes on RTÉ Radio and the first live pop request programme on the air. At first, the Gramophone Library was kept open to access the records but eventually it dawned on everyone that, as the Top Twenty Records were consistently the ones being requested, a small library of about fifty records would do the job, consisting of chart hits and new releases. Most people, anyway, were more interested in sending greetings, and hearing their name on the radio, than in picking a specific tune. But like John Skehan's coded army messages, we were stung once or twice by spurious dedications: 'Congratulations to Mary Maguire on her engagement to John Murphy' later turned out to be a slanderous coupling of a lady of Easy Virtue with the local young curate. From then on *Pop Call* did not mark engagements or weddings.

Róisín Lorigan eventually decided to rotate *Pop Call* between Larry Gogan, Val Joyce, Noel Andrews and me. The new arrangement meant that we were on every fourth week, which prompted a form of paranoia amongst us. Sitting in the pub on a Wednesday evening, I would have a sudden panic attack and would relax only when I had rung Continuity to check who was scheduled on the day-sheet. It was only a matter of time before the inevitable happened. It had all started when Val Joyce asked Róisín if he could go out of sequence as he had an engagement. Róisín told me of this and asked would I mind doing the programme the following Wednesday. Unfortunately, she met Larry later in the day and also asked him. Then, the following day, running into Noel, she remembered that she was missing a compere and asked Noel to do it. The result, as you've guessed, was that all three of us turned up to do the programme. We did a three-handed opening and then, as Larry had been first to arrive, Noel and I left him to finish the programme and repaired to Madigan's. There was method in appearing at the opening: we had all been booked, we had all turned up, we had all gone on the air, we all had to be paid. Róisín arranged payments promptly, saying, 'Just don't tell Kevin about it.'

You might imagine that Kevin would have spotted the irregularity on the air, it having been heard nationwide, but it ain't necessarily so. One day in 1975, a disc operator, Jimmy McEvoy, told me that he had been down in the printed archives looking up some old RTÉ Guides and he noticed that Pop Call would be ten years old on the following Wednesday. I was on that week and, seeing a promotional opportunity, I extracted the original log of the records played in 1965 and asked Val Joyce, the original compere, to come in and mark the tenth anniversary. I also arranged for a newspaper photographer to come in as we re-created the original programme, complete with its old signature tune, 'Cotton Candy' by Al Hirt. The following morning, there was a photo in the paper of the two of us under the heading 'DJs Celebrate Pop Call's Birthday'. Thursday is always the day for the Editorial Board to meet. They saw the photo, prompting the general cry, 'My God, is that shaggin' thing still on the air? I thought we got rid of it years ago.' And there and then, that day, Pop Call bit the dust. The tenth anniversary edition was also its last, proving that, in RTÉ at least, it doesn't help to draw attention to oneself.

Kevin Roche instituted a new breed of broadcaster in the late 1960s: the staff presenter. They were comperes who would be on a long-term contract and would present a range of programmes, as bidden, for a yearly salary. Mike Murphy (now also resigned from staff) was asked, as was I, but we felt that it would be too constricting. We had both just left staff positions and were in no hurry to return. The contracts went to Joe Linnane, Noel Andrews and Valerie McGovern. Joe did two days of the teatime show, Music on the Move, while Gay did three; Noel did a country music programme and a Saturday after-noon show, while Valerie took over Morning Call, a programme that I had loved doing when it was rotated among some of the announcers.

Before these new arrangements came into place, Noel was moving off Saturday Spin, the morning pop show he had shared for many years with Larry Gogan. Larry has often recounted how his circumstances changed, in a series of five phone calls over five days from Róisín:

Monday: 'Larry, I want you to do the whole programme yourself. It's fifty minutes, mind you. Will you be able to handle it?' (No problem, says Larry.)

Tuesday: 'Larry, would you mind if a young man came in to watch you on Saturday? You probably know him—John McColgan, a vision mixer in tele-vision, he used to be DJ in the RTÉ Club.' (He's very welcome, says Larry.)

Wednesday: 'Larry, you know the New Releases spot that Noel used to do. I've asked John McColgan to do that spot on Saturday.'(That's fine, says Larry.)

Thursday: 'Larry, remember I asked John McColgan to do the New Releases. Well, I've asked him to do the Album Reviews as well'. (Glad to hear it, says Larry.)

Friday: 'Larry, you're not doing the programme at all. John McColgan is doing the whole thing.' (I'm sure he'll be very good, says Larry.)

Then in 1970, a whole new raft of pop shows took to the air on wings of song, as Tony Gaynor wrote a jingle that we recorded in Avondale with John Keogh and The Greenbeats. Musicologists may later catalogue it as being an early version of Rap. It went after this fashion:

Larry:	Hi there, Popsters, Larry Gogan here
	I've a new show on Thursdays which will bring you cheer:
	Charts and new releases, hits from overseas.
Brendan:	Dis is marvellous, really, Larry.
Larry:	*Discs-a-Gogan*, Mister B.
Chorus:	It's on RTÉ, RTÉ,
	Remember it's the radio and not TV
	If the new sounds in pop are what you crave
	We're on VHF and Medium Wave.
Brendan:	Well, the best sounds on Monday, I have no doubt
	Is when I do my thing and let it all hang out
	Showbands and the beat groups and the new LPs.
Larry:	On the wireless, is it, Brendan?
Brendan:	*On the Balfe Beat*, Mister G.

The two new pop shows were welcome additions to the radio schedule and were designed to be complementary. On Monday evenings, *On the Balfe Beat* would concentrate on albums, progressive rock, beat groups, and some chart hits. Larry's *Discs-a-Gogan* was more chart-orientated and carried the new Top Twenty. It's interesting that RTÉ still couldn't bring itself to call a programme directly after a person, like *The Larry Gogan Show*; it had to be a play on words, like *Terry Awhile*. The cult of the anti-personality was still prevalent, as Terry Wogan always believed. He came home one Christmas and agreed to present an early morning programme on St Stephen's Day. He was aghast at the title: *The Terry Wogan Early Early Show*, 'which you'll notice spells "The TWEE Show",' as he pointed out to his listeners.

Both shows were in prime slots, running from 6.45 p.m., directly after the main evening news, until 8.00 p.m. Because they were still viewed as being extraordinarily long slots (a whole seventy-five minutes), each programme had extra features. Larry had Val Joyce and Ken Stewart to cover new releases and American Billboard hits, while I had Pat Ingoldsby covering heavy rock and Donall Corvin covering news and gossip from the music scene. Donall had arrived from Belfast with Sam Smyth and was a witty and acerbic commentator. He wrote for *Spotlight Magazine* and, simply by hanging around Madigan's, was hired for radio. His pieces for my programme were not entirely unaided by chemistry, but I was a fan of his free-form style and of the man himself. He died early, in tragic circumstances.

Musically, the singer/songwriters and the supergroups dominated the early 1970s. On my programme, Joni Mitchell, James Taylor, Carole King, Simon and Garfunkel and John Lennon rubbed noses with Led Zeppelin, the Moody Blues, Pink Floyd, Black Sabbath and Deep Purple. There were precious few Irish acts to include, apart from Van Morrison and Rory Gallagher, but one group did catch my ear. I had come across them in Avondale when they recorded some demo tracks with Paddy Gibbons, so when their Decca album arrived one evening just before the programme, I wanted to include a track. Because I hadn't time to listen to the album, I chose a familiar title, 'Whiskey in the Jar', to see how it sounded. I played it again the next week, and the week after, and then included it in my top picks of the year, until eventually, following listener reaction, Decca records released it as a single. It became Thin Lizzy's first hit and one of the band's signature songs.

John Keogh, in a fortuitous manifestation of the cyclical nature of radio, produced *On the Balfe Beat*. I had hired him as a musician in The Barn; now he was my producer. Then, the roles were reversed again as he asked me to produce his new album, made in the Eamonn Andrews Studios in the Television Club. The studio was really the ballroom, with screens around the musicians when recording, to dampen the echo. On Monday nights though, The TV Club was the centre of Irish show business, as under the benevolent eye of the manager, Seán Sharkey, showband members, singers, managers, agents, disc jockeys and producers met to gossip and to drink some of the vilest concoctions a non-alcoholic licence could produce, a taste somewhere between cough mixture and Babycham. It was still the height of the showband era, but its bloom was beginning to fade as the 1970s progressed.

I knew many of the singers and musicians in the business. I had even been to Larry Cunningham's wedding in Longford. At least, I was there the night before for the pre-wedding party, having driven down with Paddy Gibbons as a passenger. The next morning, Paddy was feeling less than perky and decided that he had been poisoned and wanted to go home. I drove him home and missed the wedding completely. But the thought was there. Now being available to compere sponsored programmes, one of my first was for Release Records. Some of the records, by Larry Cunningham, Dermot O'Brien and Ray Lynam, were well produced, but great efforts were made to avoid playing Dermot Hegarty, whose 'Twenty-One Years' was the stuff of nightmares. Jimmy Magee reminded me that Dermot was, like Jimmy himself, a director of the record company and had enquired mildly how the programme for which he was paying wasn't playing his records. I got the hint and made some room.

Tending to take people on face value, I didn't realise that one particular individual was indulging in nefarious activities in Madigan's. For the purposes of the story, I'll call him John. He was on the peripheries of the showband world, often turning out to play football with singers and journalists. A plausible fellow, he was good company and would often join the old-time throng in the upstairs lounge. He had set himself as a sort of freelance promotions man and would take on particular contracts to promote a particular record, occasionally asking me and my colleagues to give it a spin. My standard answer was that, if it were any good, it would get spun anyway. One lunchtime, I went into Madigan's to see John talking to someone at the back of the lounge. He joined me at the bar and I bought him a pint. He asked me if I had got a copy of a particular record. I said I had and that it was, in fact, on the following morning's programme. Great stuff, said John, because that's the band manager down there and he'll be delighted. I turned and waved at the man at the back. John went back to join him. All so friendly, all so innocent: only in Ireland would the disc jockey buy the promotions man a drink, rather than the other way around.

That evening, a colleague who also knew John came to me. He was there at lunchtime and told me that there was another side to this episode. He happened to have been sitting near John and had overheard the conversation with his contact, after he had left me. John had told him that he had persuaded me to play the record the following day, but that I had wanted £100 to do it. It was well worth it, he said, because one airplay would make the band. (The profits in record sales were incidental; the real value of being played on air was to increase the band's booking fee for dances.) The money was handed over and went straight into John's pocket. When I heard about the scam, I was angry and made sure that, whatever happened, the record in question would not be a part of my programme. The ending was a form of poetic justice. When the band manager heard not a whisper of the record that he thought he had paid to have played, he rang the Release Records directly after my programme to complain and demand his money back. 'What money?' they asked, and the whole plot was exposed. It wasn't the first time that John had pulled the trick, but it was certainly the last.

Marquis Productions continued to attract more clients, based on our increasing reputation for innovative and well-produced programmes. I presented a few in the Eamonn Andrews Studios and some in Avondale, for food companies, sewing machine firms and for Danfay Distributors, the Irish firm co-founded by Danny Keany that had the agency for Yamaha bikes and musical instruments. I had to write and produce commercials for guitars, trumpets, drums, motorbikes, lawnmowers, pianos and outboard motors. Danny told me about the Yamaha Song Contest coming up in Tokyo and thought that Ireland should have an entry. The problem was that the closing date was only a few weeks away and we would not have time to organise a song contest with heats and finals. I thought that the only solution was to commission an original song and send it over. I contacted John Dardis of Trend Studio and asked had he come across an original composer in the pop field who might have a few songs ready. John had the perfect candidate, a young man from Limerick who was showing promise. He contacted him, he sent up some sample tapes to me, I picked one and sent it out as Ireland's entry in the Yamaha Song Contest in Tokyo. It did well but didn't win the prize. No matter, he succeeded subsequently on the international stage and Bill Whelan and I became good friends.

A television rental company sponsored the commercial programme that had most impact. The programme recognised the incongruity of advertising television sets on radio. So was born *The Berney Mastervision Television Spectacular*. I presented it as a television programme, with phrases like 'as you can see' and 'have a look at this from Monty Python'. It contained news and gossip from TV magazines, which eventually degenerated into spoof news. The competitions became sillier by the week and comedy records gave way to original comedy pieces I wrote for myself, as there was no budget to hire scriptwriters. With Paddy Gibbons as operator, we double-tracked my voice, so I could talk to myself. I had a facility for impersonating a small but select band of RTÉ people—Ciarán MacMathúna, Leo Maguire, and a plethora of Northern reporters, at that time taking over the radio and TV newsrooms. I also did a mean Eamonn Andrews, catching his voice rhythm by pausing in all the wrong places. I wrote a send-up of *The Search for the Nile* TV series as a send-up of Irish television called 'The Search for Montrose, City of the

The Godfather Photograph, taken at my sister Jacinta's wedding. Peter Williams, Theodore Karellas, Dermot Herbert, BB, Costas Mavrikis (my brother-in-law) and Andy Maher.

With Larry Gogan and Mike Murphy recording *Beat the Band* with the RTÉ Concert Orchestra in the O'Connell Hall, March 1974.

RTÉ

In character as a barman, in John McColgan's TV version of a sketch from the comedy LP, *Balfe, Bothered and Bewildered.*

An artistic pose, suitable for framing.

Myself and
Eileen.

Family portrait.

John McColgan, Eileen Balfe and Mike Murphy at a Balmar reception in Jury's Hotel, 1983.

BB in the sparkling new Studio 2 in the Radio Centre, Donnybrook. *RTÉ*

BB with Director of Radio, Michael Carroll, and Eamonn Andrews, after recording Eamonn's contribution to *A Day by the Wireless*, his last programme for RTÉ in December 1986.

On stage at Kilmainham, 1988: Kathy Nugent, BB, Helen Jordan.

Johnny Devlin responds to the toast at his surprise 90th birthday party.

Two old pals: Jimmy Wogan and one of my
successors on *Céilí House*, Breandán Ó Dúill.

The lovely tenor voice that
epitomised Radio Éireann,
Liam Devalley.

Joan, Jacinta and me.

Eileen pays her respects to John Lennon at Strawberry Fields, Central Park, NYC.

Bro and Sis: John and Ellie in NYC, 2007.

If you stick at it, you'll make it to Broadway! Old pals on the Great White Way: John McColgan, Shay Healy, Mike Murphy, Tina and Joe O'Donnell, Ted Dolan, Gay Byrne and BB.

Gods', and narrated it in true Biggles style, with lots of English pluck, faithful native bearers and devilled kidneys for breakfast. Adding spoof commercials to the mix, as well as the occasional dramatic monologue, made it a somewhat loud quarter-hour on Tuesday afternoons.

The client, whom I never met, left me alone. As long as people were listening, he was happy. I even recorded a television commercial in one of the branches, but when I chased my fee, the company went bankrupt, virtually overnight (really). However, two opportunities came out of it.

Rosaleen Linehan, actress and comedienne, happened by one day in 1972 as we were wrapping up and heard some of our efforts. A few weeks later, her husband and scriptwriter, Fergus Linehan, phoned me. He was preparing a late-night satirical revue for Jonathan's Restaurant on Grafton Street, starring Rosaleen and Frank Kelly. The problem was that both she and Frank were appearing in separate plays around Dublin and couldn't reach Jonathan's until half past ten at the earliest. As an incentive for the diners to come early, something had to happen on stage around nine o'clock. Fergus suggested that, having heard me doing my comedy bits on the *Berney Mastervision*, I might be the incentive. I would do a solo spot and then when the other two arrived, make up a threesome. I had never done anything like it before, apart from compering an occasional concert, but I immediately agreed. I didn't think I was being reckless; it was just that I was always attracted by an element of danger.

For my solo spot, not having done one before, I thought I'd try to utilise my radio experience on stage. I made up a tape of suitable items, to include spoof commercials, a backing track for Cliff Richard's 'Congratulations' to which I added new words as a Eurovision send-up, music for talking over, a few monologues and a running telephone quiz, where I pre-recorded one side of a conversation and added the other side live on stage. I asked Paddy Gibbons to equip a tape recorder with a hand switch, so I could start and stop it exactly on cue. The show was called *Gulliver*, in tribute to Jonathan Swift, and there was a full house on opening night and the tape sequences worked perfectly, the hit of the night being the orgasmic 'Je t'aime' performed by me as a slightly overheated announcer closing down the station in Irish.

The small stage was halfway down the long narrow room and when Rosaleen and Frank arrived, we sat on stools and performed the main part of the revue, lasting about an hour, with Maisie McDowell, and later Peter O'Brien, at the piano. I sang a song about 'Máirín De Burca, the Darling of Érin', 'The Bonny Boy', adjusted to address the problem of unmarried mothers going to England and 'I Suppose', a secular-religious song for those who thought 'I Believe' too committed.

I was also the straight man in sketches and we interspersed the sketches with fake commercials, recorded with the cast. Rosaleen was her usual effervescent self and Frank did a deadly impression of Maurice O'Doherty in the news section. It was a wonderful device: the satire was as up-to-date as the nine o'clock news that evening. Fergus would come in with a story and Frank would read it directly from a script, no rehearsal necessary. It was a format since used by NBC's *Saturday Night Live*.

It ran for months, with changes of script and cast, as *Gulliver* developed into an Irish version of *That Was the Week That Was*. Fergus Linehan's deft touch with scripts demonstrated an important element of satire that I never forgot: it has to be funny, as well as topical. Everything else is just vituperation.

The revue was so successful that the manager, Enda, proposed that we do extra performances on Sunday nights. The cast was against it; nobody went out on Sunday nights. Maybe, Enda replied, it was because there was nothing to go to. We agreed to do a Sunday night. When it came about, the cast outnumbered the audience by a factor of two to one. They were an engaged couple who seemed to be having an argument. They looked like they had wandered in by mistake. Seeing it as our sacred duty to spread sunshine and laughter wherever we went, we decided to do the show anyway; it would be an opportunity to rehearse the new scripts. We bounced on stage, beaming like a demented *Tops of the Town* cast, and, with our pianist, ran the show even louder and bigger than with a full house. The couple didn't know where to look. Frozen in bewilderment, they couldn't talk and they couldn't leave. Not only was a trio of brazen performers roaring at them, they were also getting over-attentive table service as the head waiter and all his staff focused exclusively on them. We took pity on them eventually. 'We can do this for another hour,' we said from the stage, 'or we can buy you a drink and call it quits.' They settled gratefully for the second option. We had a little party at their table and our audience went home happy. There was no more talk of Sunday nights.

Shay Healy joined the cast for a few weeks, then Chris Curran, who brought down the house with his impression of de Valera, and Dearbhla Molloy replaced Rosaleen for a while. Then Frank had to leave, and so had I; and there was nobody available to do the all-important Maurice O'Doherty impression. As we were all racking our brains for a replacement, I had, if I may say so, a small brainwave: 'Why don't we ask Maurice O'Doherty?' The response was downbeat, at first. 'He'd never do it. It's outside his range.' Maurice was an award-winning amateur actor, I pointed out, and well able to do it. I rang him. He joined the cast. He was an excellent addition, proving himself a versatile performer and happy to send himself up gently. He went on to become President of the Irish Actors' Equity Association.

The next unexpected move came from Brian Molloy of Hawk/Lunar Records. Brian was one of the most pleasant and straightforward men in the business. His record labels carried showband stars and ballad singers like Johnny McEvoy. Based on the success of the *Berney Mastervision* programme and, I suppose, my stint in Jonathan's, Brian suggested that I should do a comedy album for him. Falling back on my 'keep-going-'til-you-hear-breaking-glass' philosophy, I said I'd be delighted. I then set to wonder what on earth it would contain. I pulled together some material I'd written with Tony Gaynor for radio shows and wrote some new stuff. There was a priest's sermon focused entirely on acquiring money; a heartfelt appeal for Help the Needy, which turned out to benefit the speaker and no one else; a commentary on a Royal Visit, where nothing is happening (prompted by my Symphony Concert experience); a fake piano lesson called 'Parliamo Pianoforte'; a send-up of the 'Desiderata' monologue; recruitment commercials for exciting careers in the Special Branch and as Traffic Wardens; and a 'This is Your Life' on myself, where, through the wonders of sound recording, I played Eamonn Andrews, all the guests and myself.

The musical numbers were recorded in Trend Studios with (who else?) John Keogh and The Greenbeats, masquerading as the Band and Choir of the St Barnabus Martyr and Confessor Men's Sodality. *Balfe, Bothered and Bewildered* was released early in 1975, making it the first original comedy LP ever to be issued in Ireland. It sold out its first run (which doesn't mean much, unless you know how many they ran), and it became a sort of collector's item, highly prized by aficionados of the fine arts and a byword among the cognoscenti whenever the conversation turned to megalomania. John McColgan, by now a television director, turned the 'This is Your Life' piece into a highly complicated television sketch for a teatime show presented by Cathal O'Shannon. Again, I played all the characters in a production sequence so complex that it formed part of the TV Producer Training Course for years afterwards. All credit to John.

The first notable comedy production for RTÉ, the station, was for a radio competition run in Monaco called The Prix Jean Antoine. Kevin Roche asked me if I had any ideas for an entry and I suggested taking a simple song and arranging it in different styles, linked by suitable announcements. The tune was 'Three Blind Mice' and, over a rushed week, Róisín Lorigan recorded a céilí band version with Dermot O'Brien, a blues adaptation with Colm Wilkinson, a jazz reading with Jim Doherty, a classical piano rendition with

Michael Casey (Ludwig Van Beetroot's 'Rodent Trio'), a choral edition by the
RTÉ Singers, a street busker interpretation by Frank Kelly on violin, a Hawaiian
guitar performance by Basil Hendricks and a symphonic adaptation by the RTÉ
Symphony Orchestra. In between, to parody various styles of presentation, I
told the story of the three sightless animals and their eventual demise, in the
manner of a newsreader, a northern preacher, a concert announcer, a pop disc
jockey, a travelogue narrator—and an ancient Irish *seanchaí*:

> Come all ye loyal heroes, and listen to my song
> Of three myopic mouses and their tails no longer long,
> Of the lovely tenant farmer's wife who drove them from her hearth.
> Just because you're snaggin' turnips, doesn't mean you aren't smart.

The script was hurriedly translated into French, given the title *Variations on a
Nursery Song* and, with the tape under their arm, Kevin Roche, Róisín Lorigan
and Liam Devalley (ex-announcer and now Assistant Head of Light Music)
set off for Monte Carlo. Róisín called the following Sunday evening to tell me
that we had won. The same trio, incidentally, were regulars on the competition
circuit of the European Broadcasting Union, and before Larry Gogan took it
over, Liam was the preferred radio commentator for the Eurovision Song
Contest. One of his radio commentaries has gone down in legend.

For reasons unclear, Liam's schedule didn't allow him to be there for the
dress rehearsal of the show. Róisín told him that she would watch the rehearsal,
take notes and pass on any comments that might add extra colour to the
commentary. (The commentator's workload is one of the hardest jobs at the
Song Contest, incidentally: he has to research all the singers, performers, composers and conductors from twenty-five overloaded press kits, one from each
country, check the pronunciations and make sense of the song lyrics.) Liam
did his usual splendid job on the main body to the Song Contest but when all
the songs had been sung, and the interval act was introduced, he realised that
Róisín had neglected to brief him adequately on an important element of this
performance: it was a mime act.

As acrobats, performance artists and folk dancers pranced about in total
silence, Liam had to commentate manfully on what was unfolding before his
eyes: 'He's now lifting his right leg and catching the flowers on his head, while
the two girls in rabbit costumes pour water onto the head of the clown, who has
now drawn what looks like the shape of an elephant on the wishing well, or is
it the Troll's House…I wish you could just see this…It's very funny…' The old
maxim that the pictures are better on radio was severely tested that evening.

Liam Devalley had been an announcer for years and, to me, epitomised the sound of Radio Éireann. He was also a singer, who recorded songs like 'The Lucan Dairy' for Waltons ('the lovely tenor voice of Liam Devalley', as Leo Maguire invariably announced him). I was introducing *Overseas Requests* one evening and read further down a card than I had intended, to where I inadvertently mentioned the singer requested: 'Mary says she is a big fan of Liam Devalley and would like to hear any of his beautiful songs. (Pause) Here's Louis Armstrong.' It was an accident, your honour, honest.

Liam fell foul of technician Mick Conlon one day, when Liam was Acting Supervisor after Denis's death, and it was also related to a European commentary. There was a soccer match scheduled at 7.30 p.m. from Reykjavik, with commentary by Philip Green. The commentary would be routed on landline from Iceland, via Oslo, Amsterdam and London to Dublin. At four o'clock that day, the British Post Office told us that the cable between Iceland and Oslo was broken and wouldn't be repaired until the following day at the earliest.

As I was due to take over from Liam at 7.30, I proposed that I prepare a fill-in programme, as the match was not going to materialise. Liam would hear none of it. They always said things like that to cover themselves, he said confidently, but the technical chaps always came up trumps in the end. I prepared a standby sequence, just in case. The control-room technician, Mick Conlon, told us again at five o'clock that the line was definitely down and there was no possibility of any coverage. Optimism is an admirable quality, but not that night. At 7.30, Liam announced the match, regardless: 'Soccer. Over now to Philip Green in Reykjavik.' Mick looked in at him disbelievingly through the glass. 'Open the channel, please,' said Liam. 'I'll tell you what,' said Mick on talkback. 'I'll open the feckin' window and you'll have a better chance of hearing him.'

My stint in Jonathan's, the issue of my comedy LP, and, I suppose, the success of *Variations on a Nursery Song* led to more on-stage activity. I was bemused by it, regarding it very much as a sideline to my real job, which was radio presentation and production. In late 1976, Oliver Barry introduced me to a friend of his, Pádraig Hassett, who had just taken a lease on a historical building in the heart of the Liberties. The Tailors' Hall had been built in 1706 and was the last surviving Guild Hall in Dublin. Pádraig had renovated it to include a lounge, a dining suite and a large function hall. They wanted to put on 'fashionable musical evenings', as had been done three centuries before, and they wanted me to do them. Taking the term at its loosest, I devised a one-man show, based largely on the repertoire assembled for the LP and using backing tracks, one-sided dialogue and commercials on tape, operated by a foot switch. Leaving room to update the scripts and gratefully accepting some scripts from Fergus Linehan, I added some songs and, to accompany me, brought in a small band, billed as the Billy Whelan International Modern Dance Orchestra, a slightly embellished trio comprising Bill on keyboards, Des Moore on guitar and John Drummond on bass. Later, with the addition of drummer Desi Reynolds, they became known as Stacc and were highly rated wherever teenies bopped. Anne Marie Mooney, known as Lola, had provided backing vocals for my album and she joined Bill and the band in the second half for some classy singing.

The stage was at the end of the large high hall, an open rostrum with no wings, posing the problem of how to get onto the stage effectively. Inspired by the recent spate of power failures, a solution emerged: I prepared a half-hour of background music, which was started by a waiter on a cue from me, and it played softly as the diners knocked back the last of their Irish stew. With thirty seconds of the tape to go, we suddenly turned off all the lights in the hall, producing a complete black-out while, in a spoof of the current Guinness Advertisement, Grieg's Piano Concerto filled the hall followed by the tag: 'This Thirty Seconds of Darkness...was brought to you by the ESB.' During the black-out, Bill, the band and I slipped through the hall and onto the stage; when the lights returned, we appeared to have manifested ourselves supernaturally.

Balfe at Large Late Show opened in mid-October 1976, just in time to get some satirical mileage out of Minister Patrick Donegan's disparaging remarks about President Ó Dálaigh, prompting his resignation. It ran on Thursday, Friday and Saturday nights and was well received, at least not prompting the kind of review presaged by its initials.

A couple of years later, Stacc was being managed by Noel Pearson. Bill Whelan told me that Noel was mounting a new stage show based on the songs of Cole Porter, compiled and written by Fergus Linehan and Jim Doherty. It was loosely based on the *Side by Side by Sondheim* format, incorporating a company of singers with the scenes linked by a narrator. Gay Byrne had already acted as narrator in the Sondheim show in 1977, followed by Maurice O'Doherty in a hotel version, and Bill had suggested me for the narrator role in the Porter show. I had already compered a Tony Kenny Show for Noel at the Gaiety Theatre, but, strangely, had never stood on the stage; all my introductions were done from a box in the auditorium, stage right. Noel had opened out the theatrical profession in the 1970s, by taking musicians who came from the showband world or folk music and putting them on stage in formal productions. He had done it notably with *Jesus Christ Superstar* and

Joseph and the Amazing Technicolor Dreamcoat. Noel was probably sceptical about my musical prowess, but I suspect that Bill convinced him that, if not actually a singer, I could at least hold a tune, after a fashion, kind of.

Soon after I met him, Noel offered me the part of the narrator in *Playin' Porter*, to open in the Cork Opera House and then transfer to the Gaiety. Tony Kenny and Rosaleen Linehan were the main leads, with Loreto O'Connor, Nicola Kerr, Des Smyth and Emma Angeline Butler making up the cast. I was the narrator, Jim Doherty the Music Director and the whole show was choreographed and staged by Eleanor Fazan, a distinguished director from London. She was famous for staging *Oh, What a Lovely War* and worked as choreographer on most major British films since the 1960s, including *The Ruling Class, Savage Messiah* and *Oh, Lucky Man*, right up to *Mrs Henderson Presents*. A gentle and self-effacing lady, she was married to Stanley Myers, the musician who had written 'Cavatina' for the film *The Deerhunter*.

It was the first time I had undergone a formal theatrical rehearsal and the process fascinated me. The first weeks were spent learning the music in a room in Noel Pearson's office in Harcourt Street. It was there that I realised that I was not just the narrator; I was also part of the performing company. Jim Doherty had included me in many of the scenes and all of the company numbers, so I had to learn harmony lines and ensemble singing. Then we hit the floor of the TV Club with Eleanor Fazan, to block out the show and learn the moves. As is the custom, the set was marked out in white tape on the floor to represent the amount of space available. I was intrigued by references to 'stage right' and 'stage left', but once I realised that they were directions from the performers' perspective, the penny dropped.

From the musical rehearsals, I was familiar with the songs but now I had to remember the moves, as well as the script of the narration. I had no capacity to memorise even the simplest dance steps, but Eleanor said, 'If I can teach Peter O'Toole to dance, I can teach you.' It was a close-run thing, but I managed to learn the big ensemble numbers that became the showstoppers: 'Another Opening, Another Show', 'Blow Gabriel Blow' and 'Anything Goes'. The big Cole Porter numbers such as, 'Begin the Beguine', 'At Long Last Love', 'I've Got you Under My Skin', 'Night and Day', 'Every Time We Say Goodbye', were sung as solos by the excellent cast of real singers. I did, however, get a solo song of my own, 'Be Like a Bluebird', not one of Mr Porter's best, but I'm sure Tony Bennett had no sleepless nights as a result of my vocal attributes. Apart from her choreographic contributions, Eleanor found comedy business with some of the lighter songs that complemented Fergus Linehan's witty script.

Playin' Porter opened for a week's run in the Cork Opera House on 10 April 1978, prior to its opening in the Gaiety Theatre, Dublin. The all-white set looked like something out of a Fred Astaire film, with a broad staircase for glamorous entrances and a full eighteen-piece big band on stage, conducted by Earl Gill. The costumes were sophisticated and stylish and it got a huge ovation from the Cork audience. I was delighted that an old friend from Mount Merrion, Maeve Flanagan, came back stage to see me. Over the run, many of Cork's theatrical leading lights came in to see the show and, following Tony Kenny's warning, I listened out to see if their complimentary comments were adjusted as the night, and the drink, went on. 'Very professional,' they said. 'A really lovely show.' Ten minutes later, 'Now, my wife didn't enjoy it as much as I did. She thought some of the girls were out of tune, but I'm sure no one would notice.' Half an hour later came the *coup de grace*: 'We were going to do something like that ourselves last Christmas, but we didn't bother. We thought it would be way over their heads.'

We did a preview performance on *The Late Late Show* and the show opened a week later in the Gaiety. By now familiar with the script, the songs and the moves, I found it an enjoyable experience. I was fascinated by the traditions and practices of the theatre: never whistle in a dressing room, never mention the name of the Scottish Play, never wear a watch on stage, always walk around the entire stage before the curtain goes up, so that you 'own the stage'. But after six weeks or so, I was looking forward to its ending. The difference between radio and theatre is that one is built on informal ad-libs, never to be heard again; the other is based on a highly structured format that is repeated every night. In theatre, you can't change the lines because, apart from the fact that the author doesn't like it, your words could also be a lighting cue or a signal for someone's entrance. You therefore have to learn to ignore the nagging little voice: 'but you said that last night.'

Maureen Potter came in one night and we got on very well together. As she sipped her regular whisky and milk in the Green Room, she told me about the Thursday night audience. 'It's always the worst night of the week. The audience doesn't get the jokes, or they're restless, or refuse to be entertained. It's the same every week, whether it's a play, a pantomime or a musical. By the law of averages, there will always be some people who have no sense of humour, some will have had bad news that day, some never really liked you anyway and were brought by someone else, others might be sick, some are worried about the mortgage, and many are just generally a bit slow on the uptake. But the mystery is: why do they all decide to come on a Thursday night?'

Tony Kenny, Des Smyth and I became fast friends during the run of the Cole Porter show. Tony had come from the pop world of the Sands Showband (before that, The Vampires, one of the groups on the roster in The Barn, if memory serves) to make a spectacular success of his roles in *Joseph* and *Superstar*. The latter musical prompted Maureen Potter to remark that evening in the Green Room that 'I could never get used to seeing Judas getting a bigger ovation than Jesus.' Des Smyth also came through the showband world with the College Men, but was more steeped in the tradition of the song stylists like Frank Sinatra, Nat King Cole and Bing Crosby.

Des came to me a few months after the show ended to pitch an idea: Bing Crosby had died the previous year and, so far, nobody had done anything on him. Prompted by the success of *Playin' Porter*, he thought we could do a show about Bing, drawing from the huge catalogue of songs he sang. Des had already lined up a friend of his, Tony Barry, who combined journalism with music management, to back it financially. Des wanted to know if I would write the show. I said yes. Would I appear? 'Possibly,' I said. 'But let me get back to you.' I wasn't convinced I wanted to do another theatrical run, and even I wanted to see a script first.

As I trawled through the Crosby catalogue of songs and films and reading as much about him as I could, it was obvious that he was the inventor of the popular singing style known as 'crooning'. It came from his appreciation of the microphone and how to use this new-fangled contraption. He had been something of a shouter during his days with the Paul Whiteman Orchestra, but when the electric microphone came in, he appreciated its possibilities for singing a song in a conversational style. 'Louis Armstrong plays a trumpet,' he said. 'But I play a microphone.' Identifying the secret of singing to the microphone as if it were an individual listener, rather than a crowded hall, his first success, not surprisingly, was on radio in 1931, commissioning 'Where the Blue of the Night Meets the Gold of the Day' as his theme song. By the mid-1950s, he had become the most familiar voice in the world, with well over 300 international hits out of a total catalogue of 3,000 recordings over his lifetime. Adding in his film career, his appearances with Bob Hope and other stars, his television shows and his interest in sport, it was obvious that here was a singer *par excellence*, who was also a fine actor and an accomplished light comedian. Of himself, he said modestly that he was just 'an average guy who could carry a tune'.

There was more than enough for a stage show. Apart from Des Smyth, we now added to the cast with Anne Bushnell, Pat Reilly and Rita Madigan. I came up with a list of songs, breaking them into sets and medleys to form big production numbers: Hollywood songs, South American songs, Irish songs, drinking songs, sporting songs. These were interspersed with key solo songs for Des, as well as songs for the girls, either as solos or trios as The Andrews Sisters. I was the narrator, much more informal than in the Porter show, and took on some comedy songs and duets that Bing had sung with others. Ursula Doyle, another stalwart of the Variety stage, came in to direct and Chris Keneavy was the Music Director. I unearthed a Dean Martin song called 'If I Could Sing Like Bing', which formed the basis for Des to teach me how to croon. Des didn't try for a Crosby impersonation, but captured the style and vocal range superbly. Well dressed and staged, fast moving and good humoured, *Sing a Little Bing* opened in the Eblana Theatre on St Stephen's Night, 1978. It was a cold and snowy evening, so after the audience joined in on 'White Christmas', I was able to tell them that they could stop now, because their dreaming had worked. There was a poignant ending when, as Des sang the last notes of 'That's What Life is All About', Bing's voice filled the darkened theatre, as if from heaven, saying:

I really want to thank everybody here. I love you all, I love those days, I wish they could come back. Those were the times that we all enjoyed so much. Thank you, thank you very much.

The clip came from his acceptance of a radio award years before, but it caused many a damp eye in the theatre. The show ran for many weeks in the Eblana, became the Christmas Night Show on RTÉ 2 Television the following year and was revived successfully a few years later in The Braemor Rooms, Churchtown, Co. Dublin. But the most unexpected performance came about at the behest of Ann Wold, who ran a travel company out of New York specialising in Incentive and Corporate Travel, organising large groups and conferences, sometimes taking them to Ireland. She was friendly with an Irish man, Tony Graham, who was working on the technical side of the show. She saw the Crosby production and asked us to do a shortened version for some of her groups in Jurys Hotel and Dromoland Castle. We were rhapsodically received, prompting Ann to book us for a more exotic location.

'Puerto Rico, Spain?' I asked.

'No, Puerto Rico, the Caribbean,' Tony Graham said on the phone, late one New Year's Eve.

'For how long?' I enquired, not sure if he was entirely sober.

'One night only. St Valentine's Day. And you'll have to cut the show to forty minutes. They have a very small attention span, the Americans. You'll be there for ten days.'

It was the best of surprises. We flew, via New York, to Puerto Rico with full board in a five star hotel, all expenses paid and a fee for performing, as an added bonus. Chris Keneavy arranged for a local 'pick-up' band and took them in rehearsal. It was an extraordinary thing to hear local musicians, who had never heard of Ireland, blowing their way through the arrangements for 'Dear Old Donegal' and 'Two Shillelagh O'Sullivan' at a frantic pace, while Chris tried to explain the difference between a reel and a jig, without benefit of the vernacular. We had a few days to get the show ready, rehearsed a few hours every morning and spent the rest of the time eating, drinking and dozing by the pool.

Our audience was doing much the same, with the addition of golf. They were the medics of the radiology department at Cornell University and they were being spoilt. They signed up for a tax-deductible conference on radiology in Puerto Rico over ten days, attended one mass meeting where a paper on future developments was read, and they all went back on the golf course, accompanied by a drinks cart to alleviate the considerable pressure of having to decide what to have for lunch on the beach.

On St Valentine's Night, we performed the show, all forty minutes of it, to a rapturous reception. The next morning, I was coming down in the elevator with Des Smyth when one of the senior radiologists who had been at the show got in. He recognised us from the night before and complimented us on a fine piece of work. Then, looking directly at me (and not at Des), he said, 'I just want you to know that you are one of the best singers I've ever heard in my life. Congratulations.' He got out. I went in to breakfast, highly chuffed. Des didn't speak to me for the rest of the day.

The next chapter in my theatrical career was opened when Anne Bushnell asked me to write a one-woman show on Judy Garland, to follow her successful Edith Piaf show.

I used much the same technique as in the Crosby show and arranged the show into different scenes. Utilising her 'Born in a Trunk' number as a running motif, there was a large wicker basket on stage to contain Anne's minimal costume changes—hats and scarves, mainly. The opening number was 'Quiet Please, There's a Lady on Stage', written by Peter Allen as a tribute to his mother-in-law Judy Garland. Anne would sing that as herself, dressed in a white trench coat, after which she would drop the coat into the basket and become Judy for the rest of the night. At the end of the show, which ran for about ninety minutes, she would reverse the process, don the trench coat and walk off. 'The thing to remember, Anne, is that you stay as Judy all through the show,' I said. 'No talking. I'll tell the story. You be Judy.'

The first performance was at Milltown Golf Club before a capacity Saturday-night audience of members, in mid-December. I was acting as narrator and the show was going well, with Anne in fine form. We got to a scene incorporating the songs from *Meet Me in St Louis*. In the film, the family was going to lose its home and Judy sang 'Have Yourself a Merry Little Christmas' to cheer up her little sister. I set up the scene and Anne sang a heart-rending version of the song. A magic spell of nostalgia and wistfulness was created through music. Before I could catch the mood and continue with my next link, I heard Anne saying, 'Have yourself a merry little Christmas? Jesus, I haven't even made me puddins yet.' After that, it was very hard to maintain the illusion of a sad and heartbroken Judy in the depths of despair.

I viewed these theatrical excursions every now and then as a novelty, a change from my broadcasting work. I still welcomed a challenge and an opportunity to learn more, as well as having more than one string to my bow. They were also a welcome additional source of income. I produced a series of shows for Muriel Quinn who ran the Braemor Rooms in Churchtown. Cabaret was peaking in the mid-1980s and needed, in my view, a new look. In both the Braemor Rooms and its north-side counterpart, Clontarf Castle, cabaret shows were simply a solo performer, with a comic to start the night and get the star on and off. I'd worked with Twink on television and when she came to me in early 1986 to put together a Rock 'n' Roll show for the Braemor Rooms, I pulled out from the mental filing cabinet an idea I'd been considering for some time. It was to compile a show by taking authentic Rock 'n' Roll and golden oldie tunes and, putting them into a sequence, to tell a story. If the story could be told without dialogue, so much the better.

Inspired by memories of American-style summer days in Blackrock Baths, I set it in a Soda Fountain in Hollyville USA, with jukebox, high counter, stools, and lots of Coke signs. The main characters were Tammy, played by Twink, a 'sweet old-fashioned girl' who had a crush on the local greaseball, Johnny Rocco, played by Fran Dempsey. In the middle was the original soda jerk, Bobby, played by Joe Conlon, trying to get back into Tammy's favour. There were lots of songs to cover the plot about Tammy, Johnny and Bobby and it ran for ninety minutes of energetic nostalgia, aided by a four-piece vocal group, Harmony Suite, sax-player Jerry O'Connor and three female dancers. And not a word was spoken; the entire plot was contained in the song lyrics. The cast had severe reservations about the plot line; they thought they had signed up for a straightforward, concert-style cabaret show and were a little nonplussed to see a Brechtian mini-opera unfolding. It opened on

17 February 1986. The applause and ovations on the first night made them realise that they had a hit on their hands. It came back a few months later and I then wrote *Tammy 'n' Johnny Part 2*. It was the beginning of a string of productions I put together for the Braemor Rooms, starting a trend that moved away from a straight cabaret to what became known as a 'Produced Show'. Many years after, it was satisfying to see a storyline format being used in compilation shows like *Mamma Mia!*, but none, as far as I'm aware, managed to do it entirely in the operatic manner, without dialogue. As the cast wrote in their card at the end of the run, 'We said it couldn't be done— and it was.'

I was back on the Gaiety stage that same year with Twink and Fran Dempsey in a production I wrote and narrated called *Starflight 50*, celebrating the golden anniversary of the national airline, Aer Lingus. I found myself working with the company's Musical Society and rehearsals seemed to last most of the summer. I realised that amateur performers love the process of rehearsal and the social life around it, repairing to each other's houses afterwards, ready to do the entire second act of *My Fair Lady* at the drop of a hat.

Later that year, I put together another show with an entirely different premise. *A Royal Occasion* celebrated the glory days of Irish variety, emanating from a radio series I'd just done. It brought back to the stage some of the survivors of a world of entertainment now almost vanished, as Chris Casey, Bridie Gallagher and Johnny Butler shared a bill with acts like Blue Champagne, Pat and Jean, Vera Morgan and Arthur Murphy, who was also compere. But the top attractions were Seán Mooney singing his hit songs 'If We Only Had Old Ireland Over Here' and 'Are you there, Moriarity', and Cecil Nash who, at the age of eighty-four, topped the bill and brought the house down with his monologue about Time. When Seán Mooney joined him for 'The Gendarmes' Duet', they were almost knocked over by the waves of affection from the audience. In thanking the audience, Cecil reminded us,

That the man who came from Nazareth and walked by Galilee
Has saved a special spot above…for Old Pros like me.

I think he's right. I have come to admire and respect performers, people who go on and do it, who can do their best work when they don't feel like it. I have always felt most at home among musicians, artists, presenters, actors, comperes, announcers, writers and those with a creative streak who take the risk of putting themselves and their work before an audience. In touching our lives and our spirits, they make the world a friendlier place.

∿ SOUNDTRACK ∿

Favourite Classical Pieces—If you don't know them, check them out.

1. Sibelius: Symphony No. 2
2. Litolff: Scherzo from Concerto Symphonique No. 4 in D
3. Brahms: Symphony No. 3
4. Mozart: Four Horn Concertos (Denis Brain recordings)
5. Donizetti: Sextet from *Lucia di Lammermoor*
6. Bizet: L'Arlesienne Suite No. 2
7. Beethoven: Symphony No. 6 ('The Pastoral')
8. Bizet: Au fond du temple saint (duet from *The Pearl Fishers*)
9. Chopin: Waltz No. 7 in C Sharp Minor
10. Handel: I Know That My Redeemer Liveth (from *Messiah*)
11. Mozart: Sonata No. 4 for Organ and Strings
12. Dvořák: Symphony No. 5 in E Minor ('From the New World')
13. Handel: Harp Concerto in B Flat Major
14. Rodrigo: Concierto de Aranjuez
15. Mendelssohn: Symphony No. 4 ('The Italian')
16. Godard: Angels Guard Thee (Berceuse de Jocelyn)/Kenneth McKellar
17. Borodin: Polovtsian Dances from *Prince Igor*
18. Vivaldi: Gloria
19. Puccini: O Mio Babbino Caro from *Gianni Schicchi*
20. J. S. Bach: Chorale: 'O Haupt voll Blut und Wunder' from *St Matthew Passion*

Chapter 13 ~

| MOVING HOUSE

It looked like I was back in Insurance. The Open Plan decreed by the architect looked more like an administrative centre than a radio station. The proliferation of palm trees and rubber plants did not disguise the arid setting on the main floor. In fact, they were the first Radio Centre redundancy when the accountants discovered that they were on hire at a cost of £50 per plant, per month, and they had to go. No harm, either; it was beginning to resemble something like *Bridge Over The River Kwai* set in an Ikea showroom. The eleven new studios were downstairs, to avoid traffic noises, they said, but also handy in the event of an irate listener launching a nuclear attack. Some people have a remarkable capacity for indignation.

It was satisfying to see radio getting some resources at last. All studios were equipped with top-of-the-range Rupert Neve sound desks. There was a large studio for the RTÉ Concert Orchestra, a drama suite, a band studio, two presentation suites and six all-purpose studios for music programmes, talks and features. The Gramophone Library acquired a position overlooking an atrium, with a coffee bar on the opposite side. Only the presentation suites could see daylight in the atrium.

It was a far cry from Henry Street, with its long corridor and the omnipresent smell of cabbage from the GPO canteen. The greatest difference between the two locations was the lack of a visible audience. In Henry Street, instant audience reaction was an everyday occurrence; shopkeepers, barmen, dealers and passers-by were not reluctant to give an immediate and pointed response to a programme you'd just finished. Even though RTÉ Radio was the national station, it had the inherent feel of a local station as well. That was probably as much to do with its rabbit-warren design as its people. It had a welcoming atmosphere for all sorts of artists, performers, writers, poets and boulevardiers who might be dropping off an article to one of the national newspapers, recording a talk, practising a piano recital or waiting for Groome's Hotel to open so that they could get a late drink.

The Radio Centre started broadcasting on 24 September 1973. Ireland had joined the EEC on January of that year and, in February, another significant milestone was the beginning of *The Gay Byrne Hour* (You will notice that RTÉ couldn't yet bring itself round to calling it a 'show'). It started from Kevin Roche's plan to let Gay 'have his head', so to speak. Billy Wall was the producer and it came from Studio 12 in the GPO. It started as a conventional magazine programme, with a Mystery Sound Competition, a Where Are They Now? slot to find missing friends, vox pop recordings from the streets of Dublin and lots of music. One morning, out of the blue, Gay read a letter from an unmarried mother looking for accommodation for herself and her child. The response was immediate, with phone calls and, later, letters offering help of all kinds. That one letter primed the pump, so to speak, and turned what could have been a fairly predictable morning magazine programme into a National Listening Event. Over the twenty-five years or so of the programme, it covered the light and the serious, the flippant and the fatal, as Gay and his audience accepted that life really is composed of Tragedy Tomorrow, Comedy Tonight. On both radio and television, he innately realised that the opposite of Entertainment is not Seriousness; its opposite is Boredom. If it doesn't entertain, engage, or connect, it doesn't work.

The vacancy created by Gay on *Music on the Move* meant that the programme began to rotate among the freelancers and, with other programmes like *Soon After Noon* and commercial reading, I was kept busy enough, as well as filling in for Gay when he took holidays. The phasing out of sponsored programmes began around 1974, with just the 2.00 to 3.00 p.m. slot remaining, as station programmes took over the airtime.

But not everyone was luxuriating in the verdant grasslands of Montrose, one-time home of Guglielmo Marconi. Even though the Radio Centre was on the air, Continuity and the control room were still in Henry Street, along with certain other programmes, necessitating a shuttle service between the two venues. Continuity was there until the very end, like the captain on a sinking ship. Then came The Mouse That Roared, the rodent interrupting Treasa Davison as he brazenly walked across the Henry Street Continuity desk as she was making a live announcement. No one else ever saw it, but actresses like Treasa are more perceptive than most and she used its appearance to hasten the final move to Montrose. There was one more final apparition, in the naked form of a current affairs presenter streaking down the long corridor in a personal ritual of leave-taking.

The Radio Centre became completely autonomous on Tuesday 9 November 1976. On the previous evening, the duty announcer, Ray Lynott, closed down the station from Henry Street Continuity for the last time. A large crowd of colleagues had gathered to see off the old place. Mike Murphy and I attempted to liberate the Continuity microphone but were prevented by wiser heads. I did, however, manage to rescue the old non-working fire extinguisher that served as a hat rack. Any insomniac listeners, who had left their radios on after the sign-off, would have been regaled by a selection of ballads, anthems, rhapsodies and recitations from the assembled announcers and colleagues, as we went out singing. There may have been drink taken.

One of the practices that survived the demise of Henry Street was Lord Moyne's Soup Kitchen. It had grown out of Christmas drinks parties one year when Seán McCasey and his wife Bridie, Lady Moyne, had offered to supply soup to soak up the copious amounts of drink consumed by the technical staff and announcer colleagues. Eventually, it had become not an afterthought to the festivities, but the high point of the Yule social calendar, with invitations much prized and sought after. Iron lungs of porter were supplied and Lady Moyne put up a buffet supper, starting at midnight and ending at dawn, when we all drove home. How we weren't all killed is a mystery.

Something similar had happened at home in Lower Kilmacud Road. Andy, Dermot, Peter and I usually spent Christmas Eve in Davy Byrne's Pub in Dublin City, where we teamed up with Jimmy Wogan and his friends. The four of us then rushed home to Midnight Mass in Mount Merrion Church. One year, my father and sister suggested we come back for a cup of tea. Sandwiches were produced, then bottles of beer, then my mother got up and the party started at one o'clock in the morning. As the years went by, it became a regular event, with my sister Joan providing a late supper and my father opening bottles until near dawn. Christmas came late to the Balfe Household most years, with eyes opening at midday.

At this time we were all in our mid-twenties and all living at home. Dermot, Andy and I decided that we were big boys now and should be thinking about leaving home, if only for a while. We looked around for a flat for the summer months of 1972 and Dermot found a suitable one through an agency. It was a recently renovated mews house off Brighton Avenue, Monkstown. It was let to the model Suzanne Macdougald and she wanted to sub-let it while she went to Europe for the summer. It suited us perfectly, although we had to pretend to be friends of Suzanne, as the landlord would object to a formal sub-let; we were ostensibly minding it for her. Peter didn't move with us, as he lived around the corner anyway. When I told my mother I was leaving for the summer, to my surprise she was most upset. The summer season passed in civil fashion, with a few parties and late nights, but, by and large, only at weekends.

I left a few weeks before Dermot and Andy, to go on holidays with Peter and we drove all across Europe in Peter's MGB sports car all the way down to Dubrovnik, then in Yugoslavia. When we came back, I was intrigued to hear of a strange incident in the mews, recounted by the other two.

Andy had been out on a date, came home and went to bed. He had been sharing with me and my bed was at the other end of a long room, beside a window. He smoked a cigarette, turned out the light and continued sitting up in bed. Looking over to where my bed was, expecting to see the moon through the window, he saw nothing but darkness. He then had the strange sensation that someone was looking at him in the darkness. The feeling was exacerbated when he felt warmth on the left side of his face, as if someone had their face right up to his. It was a distinctly unpleasant feeling.

Then he heard Dermot come in downstairs and start to clump around. The sensation passed and he fell into a deep sleep. He thought no more about it until the next evening, when Dermot and he were having a pint in Goggins.

'By the way,' said Dermot, 'what were you doing in my room last night?'

'I wasn't in your room. I heard you come in and went asleep. Why?'

'Well,' said Dermot, 'I woke up and thought there was someone in the room. I thought it might be you. I looked at my watch, but couldn't read it. Then I looked up and saw a big figure in a black cloak and wide hat—just like the Sandeman Port man—standing over me. I thought for a moment it was some-one playing a joke, but it felt pure evil. I hit out at it, and then I fell back asleep.'

Andy gulped a little and told Dermot what had happened to him in the other room. They left that night. This could have been one more ghost story, except for the postscript. I was working on a television show in 1982 when news came into the studio that the RTÉ designer, Charles Self, had been dis-covered dead, brutally murdered. Nobody was ever charged, but it happened in his house in Monkstown. In a mews off Brighton Avenue. In the same house where the boys had had their nocturnal visitor ten years earlier.

A much more benign visitor to the mews that summer was introduced by Andy. Eileen Hogan was from Dun Laoghaire, and was beautiful, bright and intelligent with long dark hair and sparkling eyes. Reader, I married her. The ceremony in Foxrock Church on 7 June 1974 was officiated by Fr Martin Tierney, and John Skehan did the readings. A party in the Mirabeau Restaurant fol-lowed, the main course being Irish stew. Dermot was Best Man, and Andy and Peter were Groomsmen. The photographer didn't turn up, Paddy Gibbons for-got the tape recorder to capture the speeches and we all had a wonderful time.

A few nights before the wedding, I had my stag party in the downstairs disco of the Coliemore Hotel in Dalkey, one of our regular venues for pursuing the Terpsichorean arts, while consuming warm beer and cold chicken curry. We held a Maurice O'Doherty Impression Competition, with first prize going to Dermot Moynihan of Tommy Ellis Studios, while Frank Kelly came a close second. Maurice O'Doherty also took part and came in third. Donal Stanley was the only one there from RTÉ management and during the festivities, emboldened by drink, I asked him a question.

'Do you remember years ago, Donal, when you auditioned me for *Morning Melody*? You put me on the panel and I was the only one you picked out of lots of other well-known names. I've often wondered why me and not the other fellas?'

'I remember it well,' Donal replied, 'and let me tell you one of my Laws of Broadcasting. You'll find it in no book or manual, but it's this: Nice guys come over as nice guys, and bastards come over as bastards—and there's damn all you can do about it. I picked you because you qualified.'

'Thank you, Donal.' I've never forgotten his immutable rule of broadcasting.

We spent our honeymoon in Crete and when we returned, we hadn't yet got the keys to our house, so we spent a few weeks with our generous friends, Pat and Barbara Duffy in Greystones. Gay Byrne thoughtfully offered us the use of his cottage in Donegal for a break and, with Pat and Barbara, we headed to Dungloe. We understood how Gay and Kathleen liked it so much. The scenery was spectacular and the light crystal clear. Gay's friends and neighbours adopted us and in the mornings left gifts of vegetables or freshly caught fish hanging outside on the door.

A few years later, I got a phone call from one of our new friends to ask me to open the Dungloe Regatta. I said that nothing would please me better, but as I was working late Friday evening and also early Monday morning, the timing was too tight to drive there. I wouldn't arrive until late Saturday afternoon and would have to leave again by lunchtime on Sunday. 'Don't worry about that,' they said. 'We'll send a helicopter for you.' Eileen and I left Dublin early Saturday morning and were in Dungloe in time for lunch.

'What do you want me to do first?' I asked after a delightful lunch, feeling I should be doing something.

'Take your time, there's no rush. We'll go for a drive.'

They drove us around the town and its outskirts. Then back to declare the regatta open on the public address. I started a kiddies' race down by the shoreline, but could see no sign of activity out on the water. There were yacht races listed, children's boat competitions, currach racing, but no sign of anything actually happening. 'A slight miscalculation,' they said. 'We made out the schedule in great detail, spent weeks organising the events, but we forgot one tiny thing: we forgot to check the tides.'

And sure enough, the tide was now out as far as Boston. They were completely unfazed, our enjoyment of the event their only concern. There was a huge supper that night in the hotel, and the next day we were taken on a picnic in a motorboat to one of the outlying headlands. Meanwhile, the helicopter was pressed into service for the weekend, taking people on pleasure trips round the bay. What made the weekend so enjoyable was the carefree, happy-go-lucky attitude of the organisers. It was the only waterless regatta I'd ever seen, where the highlight was an air show.

We moved into our house in Dun Laoghaire, one road away from where Eileen used to live. I had bought it by auction, my solicitor, Paul Hayes, doing the bidding because I was too terrified. One year after the wedding, almost to the day, our daughter Eleanor was born. I played an entire programme for her on the radio and, even though it was spelled differently, 'Elenore' by The Turtles became her song, as did the second half of 'Soliloquy from Carousel', sung by Frank Sinatra from the first LP I'd ever bought, *The Concert Sinatra*: 'My Little Girl, pink and white as peaches and cream is she...' She was, and still is, a beautiful child, the apple of my eye.

Her first broadcast was in the RDS while I was doing a programme at the Horse Show. Eileen brought her in to see me in the studio. I carried on presenting while four-year-old Ellie sat on my lap and chatted away. 'I saw hens and chickens,' she told me, oblivious to the radio surroundings. Like all little girls, Ellie loved clothes and, in particular, high heels. She would clunk around in Eileen's high heels until, one year, she got a kiddie-sized pair of her own. She was so besotted with them that she wore them to bed.

She heard me on the radio regularly, but seemed to assume that it was just a thing that dads did: they went to work and, a little later, their voice was heard on the little black box in the kitchen. She was quite surprised later when she found out that her friends' dads weren't on the radio as well. One day, she came home from junior school with a puzzled frown.

'Dad, are you famous?'

'Why do you ask?'

'A girl at school said that her mummy said you were.'

'No, I'm not famous. It's just my job—a lot of people hear me, but I'm not famous.'

That seemed to make sense. A couple of years later, I was presenting a television quiz and I purposely put El on my lap to watch the programme on transmission. She looked at me on the screen, then looked up at my face, then back to the screen, then back to me. She seemed a little perplexed, but then seemed to accept that it was another thing that some dads did.

More programmes followed. *Beat the Band* was a quiz idea I'd had for a while. It was based on live music and featured a quartet and the RTÉ Concert Orchestra. It was produced by Frank Lawlor and recorded before a large audience in the theatre of St Patrick's College, Drumcondra. Contestants had to answer questions based on music played by the RTÉCO. If they won a round, they could challenge the quartet to play a tune. The four players were chosen for their musical range and comprised Jim Doherty on piano, Charlie Devanney on saxophone, Martin Walsh on bass and Jack Daly, drums. With their combined musical knowledge, they were hard to defeat, but if the contestant succeeded in beating the band and the other contestants, the top prize was the opportunity to conduct the Concert Orchestra. I had always thought that standing in front of an orchestra and waving a baton must be one of the best jobs in the world (who hasn't done it with a knitting needle in the front room?) and I guessed that it would be an irresistible attraction. And so it proved; the conductor, Proinnsias Ó Duinn, would conduct the piece, as it should be heard, then handed over the baton to the contestant. The results were often hilarious as the orchestra followed the tempo and cues exactly, producing a memorable mishmash. Other times, the contestant was so good that it sounded, if not superb, not bad at all. It was a good-humoured quiz and I could use my deviser's licence to cheat blatantly on behalf of the contestants.

Not so with *Hot Line Quiz*, a live phone-in series devised by Noel Jones, based on listeners answering questions on readings and sketches they had just heard. There was money at stake, a whole £50 as top prize, and any favouritism would be unfair. As more that one radio critic pointed out, I needed all my good humour to deal with the vagaries of the Irish telephone system, as contestants suddenly vanished off air or could not be contacted at all. Again, the old continuity training proved useful, with a good deal of extemporising and adjustment required on the part of the compere.

Even the word 'compere' was beginning to be replaced. 'Presenter' was now the preferred option in RTÉ Radio. Dermot Doolan, one-time writer of *Living with Lynch* and *The Maureen Potter Show*, was Secretary of the Irish Actors' Equity Association. He had recruited announcers into the union and was now trying to ensure a fair deal for presenters. In an attempt to put out fires before they became conflagrations, he had persuaded RTÉ to agree to a Presenters' Working Party to discuss and agree matters, rather than call in the Personnel Department every time a contentious issue arose. It was an early example of what in EU-speak was called 'subsidiarisation', meaning the more decisions made at local level, the better. RTÉ fielded Kevin Roche, Donal Stanley and P.P. Maguire, while togging out for Equity were Mike Murphy, Larry Gogan and I. It proved a highly effective device. Kevin and I were joint chairmen, taking turns to moderate or call meetings. Our roles became defined: Mike was the belligerent one, regularly proclaiming, 'How dare you even attempt to put that proposal on the table? That's an insult to our intelligence.' Larry was the agreeable one, 'I know you're trying to do your best for us, Kevin. It's just that it's hard to live on that sort of money. You know that yourself, Kevin, being a freelance musician once.' I came in somewhere in the middle with a logical argument based on facts and comparisons. I found that keeping an eye fixed firmly on what we wanted to achieve, regardless of side issues, was effective; most times, having gone through the ritual, we reached agreement amicably.

We decided on a fee structure for presenters, based on types and durations of programmes, and agreed terms and conditions for contracts that are still in use today. I learned that, in union matters, money is not always at the centre of the argument. Most people want respect and appreciation of good work, but money is the most tangible and visible proof of respect, hence invariably becomes the main topic of the negotiations. But many disputes, in my experience, could have been headed off by simple good manners and courtesy on the part of the management.

Mike's forthright approach sometimes got him, and others too, into trouble. He was having a heated debate with Kevin Roche on something connected to his personal career. Matters seemed to get out of hand and the meeting in Kevin's office was ended summarily. Mike strode to the door and, as a parting gesture, told Kevin exactly what he thought of him, his department, his organisation, and, probably, his musical prowess. He slammed the door. A moment later, he opened it again. 'And I know Brendan Balfe agrees with me,' he said, and slammed the door again. Generous of him to think of me as an afterthought, but I could have done without it. Kevin was distinctly frosty next time we met.

Another experience, incidentally, shared by my wife happened some time later. Mike and I had met at a reception in town one night. I was on *Morning Call* the following morning and was anxious to get home. Mike decided to pay me back for bringing him home years before after a Hotel Crawl and bringing him into work the morning after. He now insisted on driving me home, saying that he'd be back in the morning to bring me into the station. 'No need,' I said. 'I'll get a taxi.'

The next morning, I called a taxi and got to work, bright-eyed and bushy-tailed, and presented the programme. Meanwhile, Eileen was still in bed at home. After I'd left, she heard a ring at the door. She ignored it, thinking it was possibly another taxi but knowing that I was already gone. A short time later, she heard a tap on the window. This left her nonplussed, as the bedroom was on the second floor. She opened the curtains to see Mike Murphy clinging precariously to the window ledge.

'Good morning, Eileen,' he said. 'Is Brendan there?'

'No, he's gone to work,' Eileen said, and closed the curtain. She heard a scraping noise as Mike slid down the outside wall.

Not getting an answer to his ring at the doorbell, Mike had gone around to the road next to ours. He had climbed over the gates of the building behind us, over their back wall, through a lane, over our back wall and somehow managed to climb on to the window ledge on the second floor. It was typical of the man to want to repay a favour from years before. It was like getting a present of the complete works of the Spice Girls: completely unnecessary, a nice thought, but you really shouldn't have. Really.

I had now been voted to the Executive Committee of Equity. Every year, the union honours one of its members by awarding Life Membership. One of the first proposals I made was to bestow the award on Joe Linnane, during Irish Radio's fiftieth anniversary year of 1976, to mark his contribution. Joe was regarded with huge affection by his colleagues, as well as by the public, and it was agreed immediately. The award was publicly presented on a special *Late Late Show*.

In May that year, in the midst of a dispute with RTÉ, Equity hosted an international conference of FIA, the International Federation of Actors. The key topics were fees and the payment of royalties by a new-fangled American institution, Home Box Office, a television station that came on a cable and was now big enough to produce dramas. Many felt then that it would be of only minority interest and that the big network companies, ABC, CBS and NBC, would never be replaced. How wrong they were.

Local Equity topics were the fees for television and radio commercials, particularly the vexed matter of the use of British voices on Irish television commercials. There already was an agreement to re-dub commercials made in Britain, but it was loosely policed. The Irish advertising agencies didn't want the bother of replacing the voice-overs, while RTÉ believed that the cost of doing so would be much better spent on buying airtime, so they would be the beneficiaries. That is why we heard so many voices recorded in London on Irish television commercials; Patrick Allen, Robert Beatty and Fergus O'Kelly were particularly prevalent. It was a constant battle to hold the parties to their agreements, sometimes threatening them, sometimes persuading them. It's now an academic exercise anyway, as EU rules don't allow such chauvinistic behaviour; all voice-overs and all nationalities are equal. I suspect, though, that Irish voices connect better with an Irish audience.

It's well to remind you that in 1976, there was only one radio station in the country. Through the councils of Equity, representing my presenter colleagues, I tried to start a debate about a long-overdue second radio station. In July of that year, in the Montrose hotel, Equity hosted a special meeting of interested parties from the music, advertising and studio sectors, to press for a new radio channel that concentrated on light music and entertainment. The Minister for Posts and Telegraphs, Conor Cruise O'Brien, was called upon to give the green light to such a station 'because of the deliberate policy of RTÉ Management to phase out light music programmes in general, as well as dropping sponsored programmes'. The newspaper reports of the meeting said that 'it was felt that RTÉ's emphasis on current affairs and programmes of a minority interest was alienating huge numbers of listeners and forcing them to turn to the BBC or Radio Luxembourg for entertainment.' As the organiser of the meeting, I was quoted as saying, 'The new station should be based on the old Light Programme formula, with plenty of music, quiz shows, comedy and news.' We were generally in favour of RTÉ supplying the second channel, but if they were not in a position to do so, or was unwilling, it should be given to commercial interests to run. I became the Equity representative on a team to draft a feasibility study to present to the minister.

Feasibility studies are the usual fallback in these importuning initiatives, but the main object had been achieved: to get it into the public forum and start the debate. In retrospect, the model I had proposed is the one that became the most listened-to radio station in Europe, BBC Radio 2, where once I had worked and where Terry Wogan now holds the highest audience figure in Britain.

While waiting for a new station to materialise, the current station continued to provide openings. I proposed a series of music documentaries on the evolution of popular music. Like most young people, I knew something about contemporary music but I was curious about what came before. *A History of Pop* started in the summer of 1977, running for twenty-five weeks. It was a large undertaking, requiring lots of research and reading, and reliant, in those pre-internet days, only on books, articles and magazines. Neither was the music easy to access; there were few compilation albums around then. I viewed it almost like writing a thesis; I had to inform myself before informing the listener.

It started back in Tin Pan Alley, so named for the crashing of tinny pianos in the music publishing houses around 42nd Street in New York. In one episode, I set out the groundwork for what became popular music through Broadway theatre and Hollywood films, defining the mores of The Establishment, so to speak, before Rock 'n' Roll came to re-write the rulebook. I found out that pop music may be evolutionary, but, conversely, it is also cyclical. The evolution is in the development of styles as black music crashed into white music, as Rhythm 'n' Blues met country music to produce Rock 'n' Roll. The cycle is in the recurring trend of the Pioneers to become Settlers, as those who were once the Anarchists become the Management.

Nobody epitomises it better than Elvis Presley. A white southern boy, he had been exposed to hillbilly and country music as well as blues and gospel, but his favourite singer was Dean Martin. As he said, 'I don't sound like nobody.' And he was right. He was an original. But after a while, he grew fat and satisfied and other young bucks took over. So, the new trends always come from the streets (or the cornfields), and the Establishment is constantly being surprised, usually imitating, rarely initiating.

Elvis died on 16 August 1977. A couple of weeks earlier, I had broadcast an episode of *A History of Pop* on Elvis, under the chapter heading 'The Man Who Would Be King'. One of the radio critics reviewed it as 'an obituary' on Elvis, because I had spoken about him as if his best days were over. It was a prescient observation, nonetheless, and two weeks later it became RTÉ Radio's tribute to him as 'The Man Who Was King'.

Speaking of tributes, 'We've a slot on Saturday morning that needs filling,' said Billy Wall. It was between the end of one series and the start of another. An unintended gap, I gathered, that Light Music had to fill. I usually have a few programme ideas in my head, wheezes in embryonic form that could be brought to fruition fairly quickly. I had done a five-minute version of one on a magazine programme some time before and thought it could be profitably fleshed out. It was a send-up of a programme type that I abhorred: those smug, sycophantic, unctuous programmes that the BBC used to broadcast under titles like 'Drury Lane Memories' or 'Hits From The Blitz', evoking memories of showbiz troupers valiantly putting on wartime musical comedies against great odds, not least a complete lack of talent. I decided it should be a Tribute to Nobody, a paean of praise to somebody who never existed, a singer and entertainer called Ted LaVern.

Fittingly enough, I was appearing in a musical comedy myself at the time, as *Playin' Porter* was running in the Gaiety Theatre. I utilised my fellow cast members, Rosaleen Linehan, Tony Kenny and Des Smyth, to play a number of parts and also persuaded Maureen Potter, Noel Purcell and Noel Kelehan to record contributions. I wrote pieces during the day and recorded them in dressing rooms during the show. Through their heartfelt tributes, and using a deadpan narration style, the story of Ted LaVern unfolded in a restrained fashion and gradually became more ludicrous: born in Dublin, friend of milkmen and sailors who yearned for the glamour of California films but emigrated to Holyhead because of a mistake on the ticket, arrived in America via China, invented the talking film, wrote songs, pioneered scientific developments that led to television, sang a duet with Tony Bennett and Count Basie and was the reason why Howard Hughes bought an airline to see him opening his new show in London...

'And you should have heard him,' said Noel Purcell. 'Never appeared in a musical before, never mind write one, but you should have heard him. Was he good?...

'He was brutal, bloody brutal!'

We Remember Ted was entered in the Ondas Radio Prize in Barcelona in 1978. The task of translating some of Des Smyth's incomprehensible Dublinese into French was a major headache for Liz Wogan, but she got it eventually. The programme and scripts were despatched to Spain and no more was heard until a telegram arrived for me on Saturday afternoon in RTÉ. It was written in French, so I couldn't be sure what it said until I rang Liz and spelt it out over the phone. I had, apparently, won first prize for the idea and script. Joy was unconfined and, as I had written the programme, I was to accept the prize.

I travelled over with producer Colin Morrison. The organisers were particularly pleased that RTÉ had entered and regarded the Irish presence as something of a *coup*. I was more pleased that I had beaten the BBC's £3,000 entry, a musical version of Cinderella, with a hoax programme that cost £40 for my fee. Bernard Krichefski was the BBC producer and Colin and I found him almost Irish in character as we enjoyed the many receptions and lunches. Our own Seán Mac Réamoinn arrived, in a flurry between EBU junkets. He didn't deign to talk to us, as he was representing RTÉ as Head of External Relations and had to keep in contact with his EBU colleagues as they continually traversed Europe, attending meetings and festivals, from Bratislava to Geneva, from the Golden Rose of Montreux to the Silver Slug of Knokke, in search of relations to be externalised. He reminded me of one RTÉ executive who complained that because he had so many festivals to go to, he hadn't had time to take his holidays yet.

I was reminded of my little radio practical joke about six years later when the film *This is Spinal Tap* was released, creating something of a fashion for 'mocumentaries', as they came to be known. Like my Prix Jean Antoine entry a few years before, *We Remember Ted* was broadcast by all the participating countries, including BBC Radio. Imagine my surprise a few months later when I spotted a programme billed in the *Radio Times* that bore more than a passing resemblance to my modest effort. *Atkinson's People* was a new series of pro-files of fictitious people—an actor, a bishop, a statesman, a writer—presented by Rowan Atkinson and produced by Griff Rhys Jones. Both later went on to become household names in the BBC television series *Not the 9 O'Clock News*. If I can help somebody....

The year 1978 also saw the first strike in Equity's history. It arose out of a report by Mr Justice Brian Walsh of the Supreme Court, who had been asked by RTÉ and Equity to act as an independent assessor of the 'artistic, economic and social factors involved in fixing the place of the actor in RTÉ'. He made a number of important findings, not least of which was that 'RTÉ was one of the creators and custodians of artistic standards in the state' and that the REP actor in his work 'can have the effect of helping to enrich the working vocabu-lary of the listening public and to make it more articulate'. Because the status of the actors should be made tangible, he recommended an increased salary scale, tied to that of producers. It was an erudite and wise document, befitting its author, and Equity was delighted that it captured on paper the role and value of an artist in society, relating the ephemeral to the practical.

The problem was that RTÉ refused to accept it. Equity voted for strike action and all members were withdrawn on 1 December 1978. Programmes and news bulletins were cancelled. Actors, presenters, newsreaders and announcers were on picket duty outside RTÉ and the sight of familiar faces like Gay Byrne, Mike Murphy, Vincent Hanley, Cyril Smith and Colette Proctor in freezing conditions ensured gifts of champagne, smoked salmon, chicken, wine and coffee from a sympathetic public. Even the Director-General sent down refreshments. It was the best-catered strike in living memory.

Management personnel were putting programmes on air and were limp-ing on, with huge gaps to fill. To concentrate the minds of the management, the Irish Congress of Trade Unions granted Equity an 'all-out' strike picket, which would have closed down the entire output of radio and television. Before it came into effect, the Congress got the two sides together in its head-quarters. We faced RTÉ across a long boardroom table. Michael Carroll, the Controller of Programmes, was adamant. They would not accept the Walsh Report; they couldn't be tied into its assessment; there were things in it they didn't agree with. Dermot Doolan, Maurice O'Doherty and I got the impression that the money elements were soluble, if we could only get some acceptance of the report.

In an example of 'an acceptable form of words' being arrived at, I didn't ask Michael Carroll to agree with Mr Justice Walsh, but regarding the point where the report re-valued the actor asked if he 'took the point'. Michael Carroll took the point. And on the role of the actor? He took the point. An agreement was hammered out that day, where 'RTÉ accepts there is much validity in what Mr Justice Walsh says' and 'it identifies the valuable contribution that the radio actor makes to radio broadcasting' and 'as has been said by Mr Justice Walsh, salary scales are probably the most tangible way of indicating the status of a person, RTÉ is prepared to negotiate a revised salary scale for actors'. Case closed. Strike over. The actors got their salary increase. I had cordial relations with Michael Carroll ever since and the supreme irony was that when he retired from his role as Director of Radio, he found a late vocation… as an actor.

Six months later, there were more negotiations prior to RTÉ Radio 2 going on the air in May 1979. The Working Party was intensely involved in the preparations as Billy Wall, the Controller of Programmes for the new station, began to assemble a schedule. It became clear that, even though existing presenters had started the debate, they would not have the new schedule to themselves. Billy was intent on bringing in some of the DJs who had made a name on pirate radio and he took the matter to a Presenters' Working Party meeting. Pat Kenny had replaced Mike Murphy on our side, but Larry Gogan was still the third man. I was inclined to agree with the injection of new blood, on the basis that you can't hold a person's sins against them forever. My colleagues concurred, but there was a degree of antagonism from some of the other established presenters. 'We couldn't go off and appear on pirate stations,' they said. 'RTÉ would never hire us again if we did, but those guys who broke the law are now being rewarded for it.' It was a view that was hard to argue against, but my response was that every enterprise needs refreshing and, anyway, there weren't enough 'legit' DJs on the books to meet the demands of the Radio 2 proposed schedule.

We also had a responsibility to ensure that, however distasteful this new hooligan element was to the established order, they were paid a fair price. The programme rates were agreed and updated regularly, but adjustments were needed for the added element of the compere-operated console, or 'comp-op desks', where presenters play their own records and commercials. Only continuity announcers were permitted to do so, up until then. The negotiations dragged on, resulting in us still talking at length the day before the opening of the station. Pat, Larry and I met with Billy Wall and Donal Stanley during the afternoon and the crux of the matter was the percentage fee increase due to us conceding the principle of 'comp-op'. (The fact that the presenters had been agitating for it for years was irrelevant.) I left the meeting at 4.30 to present *Music on the Move*, which I'd been doing for a while. This, however, was the last edition (it was being replaced the next day by *Slán Abhaile* with Liam Ó Murchú) and I had asked Gay Byrne and Joe Linnane, the two people most associated with the programme, to come in and co-present, after a fashion. They were, as you'd expect, both superb, and an enjoyable programme of badinage and mild insult marked the demise of the teatime show. For the last time, I played the signature tune I'd picked many years before, 'Fish and Sticks' by the Eric Delaney Band.

Then, back over to Donal Stanley's office for the continuation of the negotiations. We had got nowhere in the interim. Billy Wall had been moved from a 10 per cent fee increase to an 11 per cent one, and it had taken three hours to move him and he was proclaiming that his last offer was final. I was insistent that the increase wouldn't do and that, even though Michael Carroll had asked me to open the new station the following day, there might be no station to open, if we couldn't agree. Donal was taking a back seat, but I caught his eye. He suggested we take, in recent parlance, 'a restroom break'. While the others chatted, I followed Donal to the men's room.

'What have you got, Donal?' I asked.

'Billy is stuck on eleven. I can approve twelve and a half per cent without going back to the DG. Otherwise, I'll have to consult tomorrow.'

'Done,' I said.

Donal went back to meet his colleagues. I had tea with mine. The meeting resumed. Billy made a final offer of 12.5 per cent. We agreed to it.

'Do you have to have it approved by your members?' they asked.

'No. Consider it approved.'

The next day, 31 May 1979, I introduced all the new presenters in Studio 1 before an invited audience. The Minister, Pádraig Faulkner, did the honours and then I formally identified the station for the first time and handed over to the first programme:

'So, let us begin. This is RTÉ Radio 2 and here to present *Pop Around Ireland* is Larry Gogan.'

I have since been privileged to become an answer in 'Trivial Pursuit' (Irish Edition), in reply to 'Whose was the first voice on RTÉ Radio 2?' (A signal honour, Ma'am.)

That afternoon, the *Evening Herald*, over a picture of Larry, carried on the side of the front page an article on the station opening. The main story across the top of the page referred to a previous Minister for Posts and Telegraphs, Conor Cruise O'Brien, whom we had petitioned three years previously to approve a new station and who was now resigning from the Senate. The two stories were completely unrelated, but their juxtaposition on the front page read: 'Radio 2 is Airborne. O'Brien Quits.'

Our new presenter colleagues were a friendly bunch: Declan Meehan, Ronan Collins, Marty Whelan, Jim O'Neill, Gerry Ryan and Dave Fanning, while new producers included Ian Wilson, Robbie Irwin and Pat Dunne. Vincent Hanley, Pat Kenny, Ken Stewart, Larry Gogan, Arthur Murphy and I had all been on the Senior Service.

One or two were a trifle antagonistic towards RTÉ, as if it were the cause of their misery in some way, by not recognising their genius earlier. Others were so impressed to be working for the state broadcaster that they metaphorically put on suits and almost became civil servants, forgetting that they had been hired for their buccaneering spirit. Others got it right straight away, and all have long since become accomplished broadcasters of high renown, a credit to their profession.

I was assigned two programmes on the fledgling station: *Six O'Clock Rock*, an oldies show on Sundays, and *The Brendan Balfe Show* on Monday evenings. The first one subsequently moved through all the hours of the schedule, due, no doubt, to its handy title. I did occasional specials, on Buddy Holly and Elvis and the like, and it proved to be a popular show with the customers. It did, however, attract its fair share of anoraks (a descriptive phrase for those who take an obsessive interest in particular topics, inspired by the outer weather-proof clothing of those fans who took boats out to view the pirate ships). They would write to correct apparent inconsistencies: 'You said it was Ben E. King, but it wasn't. He hurt his knee that day and his place was taken by Johnny Brown, who is on the LP version but not on the US single release and you'd have to get the French compilation for that.' One hopes that with the improvements in mobile audio technology, these people can get out more. Occasional studio guests came in for interview, Tony Hatch among them and also Joe Linnane's airport friend, Andrew Oldham, The Rolling Stones' manager. We got on supremely well as it happened, and he spent the whole two hours with me in the studio. I had a pre-release advance copy of 'Satisfaction' with me that he remarked on. He never got a copy, he said, so I gave him mine.

In August 1979, Eileen, El and I we were visiting my sister, Jacinta, and her husband, Costas Mavrikis, who worked for Olympic Airways in Corfu. They lived at the end of the runway, but it's remarkable how you can get used to a jumbo jet apparently coming through your wardrobe, without waking up. After a week with them, we spent some blissful days in a *pension* on the beach in Glyfada, where El acquired a taste for black olives and feta cheese, exotic flavours for a four-year-old, I thought, but a taste that has stayed with her.

Then we heard that my mother was ill; she had not been well when we left, but had taken a turn for the worst. We got back in time and she died on 8 August, aged sixty-three. Dermot, Andy and Peter were a great comfort to us, as was my extended family, through Eileen.

When I went back to work, I was moved to offer my services to Pat McInerney, the producer in charge of organising commentaries for the Pope's visit. He assigned me to Seán McDermott Street in the inner city area, where the cause of Matt Talbot for canonisation was centred. It was thought that Pope John Paul II would stop to show solidarity with the parishioners. I was perched in a building opposite the church, with one side of a banner below me that stretched across the street and proclaimed: 'God Bless The Sacred Heart'. I was prepared for a long stay, but the cavalcade didn't stop and I described the scene for two or three minutes before he arrived, then followed him out of sight around the corner. Later, I saw him at a press conference for journalists in the convent where he was staying that night. A copy of his speech was handed out in advance. He came to the balcony to address the ladies and gentlemen of the press. He thanked us for the work in covering the visit and blessed our families and us. Then he continued:

'I used to be a journalist, too. And I know that not every speech is actually made. You have a copy. You know what I want to say. But the Pope is tired and I'm going to bed. Goodnight.'

He left to wild applause. No one ever reported that he never made the speech, but it was printed verbatim in all the papers next day.

Then it was back to Radio 2 to cover the overnight shift as thousands travelled across the country to the next venue. The following day, Sunday, I was in again for the overnight between 1.00 and 6.30 a.m. Just before the end, as I was visibly wilting, Gene Martin came in for a friendly visit. 'We're in Studio 5,' he said. 'See you in a few minutes.' I had, in the frenzy of the Papal Weekend, forgotten that I was also presenting *Morning Call*, so I couldn't go home for another two hours. The Announcers' Broadcast Log records that I presented the programme that Monday morning, but I had no memory of doing so. However, I wouldn't have missed being part of the papal coverage for the world.

Sounds of the Century was another documentary series I proposed in 1979. It was essentially the history of recorded sound since 1900, based on the voices, the events and the music of the twentieth century to date. It was another major research task that included searching for film soundtracks, news archives, music, comedy clips, historical speeches and radio and television footage. It was sliced up into half-hour segments, covering about five years at a time, in chronological sequence. There were two related difficulties in covering such a wide range of material: the first was assembling the audio material in the first place, from RTÉ's archives, from my own historical recordings bought over the years, and from commercial recordings; the second difficulty was in distilling the material down to thirty-minute programmes, dropping items that I had spent months trying to source, because they were now irrelevant, or another clip had made the point better. In writing, it's called 'killing your darlings'; in radio, it's 'not falling in love with your material'. If it's in the way, or breaks the rhythm, it has to go.

The producer assigned to the series was Brian Reynolds, my old pal from the announcers' course, who had just returned from Germany with his wife, Helga, having spent some years working for German Radio's world service, Deutsche Welle. The series was well acclaimed, providing an accessible history of the world over the previous eighty years. It ended on the Pope's speech in Galway, 'Young People of Ireland, I Love You'. The last three words were the basis of every pop song ever written, but when the youngsters heard them for real, the response was cathartic.

The year ended with *The Big Broadcast of 79*, a ninety-minute Christmas-night radio show that brought together elements of my recent experiences from radio, stage and cabaret. The hit songs and styles of the century were performed by my friends and colleagues from *Playin' Porter* and *Sing a Little Bing*, Tony Kenny, Des Smyth, Anne Bushnell, Pat Reilly, and Rita O'Regan, while Bill Whelan's Rooftop Ranchers acted as the house band, augmenting the RTÉ Concert Orchestra, conducted by Noel Kelehan. They sang everything from Al Jolson to Abba. (In the theatre, they call it 'versatility'; in RTÉ we call it 'economy'.) Later, much the same cast of vocalists took part with me in a live music series, *Radio Revels*, where I even sang a song or two, carefully chosen for their lack of musical merit.

I was one of the few presenters working on both Radio 1 and Radio 2 programmes. When John Lennon was shot on 8 December 1980, I was called in to talk to Jim O'Neill on his Radio 2 programme and found myself doing an ad-lib obituary, trying to drag up salient facts and biographical details out of the back of my head. In the days before the internet, human memory had to suffice. The following Sunday, I dedicated the whole *Six O'Clock Rock* to John. There was to be a memorial ceremony outside the Dakota Building, where he lived and died. There was also a worldwide three-minute silence at seven o'clock, our time. I observed the silence by playing string music and was able to provide a special commentary on the ceremony. It was by someone who knew John well and who gracefully described the poignant scene from high up in the Dakota Building. It was Andrew Oldham.

∼ *SOUNDTRACK* ∼

Laugh Out Loud
I've been playing comedy records for many years on many programmes, most recently on the Saturday lunchtime programme, *BalfeB@*ʀᴛᴇ́. These, in no particular order, are the **twenty comic cuts** that proved most popular.

✦ A Call from Long Island/Cast of 'You Don't Have to Be Jewish'
✦ Ajax Liquor Store/Hudson and Landry
✦ Introducing Tobacco to Civilisation/Bob Newhart
✦ One Leg Too Few/Peter Cook and Dudley Moore
✦ Punch Drunk Boxer/Allen and Rossi
✦ Incoming Call/Frank Kelly
✦ The Bricklayer/Gerard Hoffnung
✦ Hold On (Nicholl's Department Store)/Shelley Berman
✦ Party Singers/Billy Connolly
✦ Alleebees/Cast of *Not The 9 O'Clock News*
✦ Horses/Jerry Seinfeld
✦ The Devil/Rowan Atkinson
✦ Father of the Bride/Brendan Grace
✦ Phonetic Punctuation/Victor Borge
✦ The Toastmaster/Michael Bentine
✦ Party Political Speech/Peter Sellers
✦ Elderly Man River/Stan Freberg
✦ Mobile Phones/Noel Ginnity
✦ The Schoolmaster/John Cleese from *The Frost Report*
✦ The Sermon/Niall Tóibín

Chapter 14 ∿

| TV TIMES

A blond bombshell came into our lives when John James Balfe was born in Holles Street Maternity Hospital on 19 October 1981. Eileen and I were dark, so we couldn't understand where the blond gene came from, but he was a happy and vigorous baby and we were overjoyed to have our second child. The name John means 'a gift from God' and we asked our friend Larry Hogan to be his godfather.

Sunny-natured and mischievous, John was soon making programmes on the cassette recorder in the kitchen, acting as DJ introducing records and, whenever possible, insulting his sister. The sports gene seemed to have skipped a generation and John was, and is, fanatical about sport. He appeared on *Poparama* on 2FM at the age of six, to explain the intricacies of American football, in advance of a Notre Dame game in Lansdowne Road. Later in school, at the age of sixteen, he wrote the sports column for *Outlook Magazine*. My father would have been delighted at his huge interest in sport, but sadly, John had his paternal grandfather for only nine months, as my father died in June 1982, aged seventy-three.

It hits hard when the last parent dies. You're really on your own now, you feel. Before he died, I tried to help sort out his business. Years before, James (Jimmy) Balfe had been made redundant from Baxendales and had set up his own company with his long-time assistant manager, Cecil Martin. The company was called Balmar and specialised in architectural ironmongery — locks, window fasteners, door handles, door closers and all types of door furniture. Their good names and efficient service in Baxendales meant that they retained many major customers in building firms and architects' offices. Working out of a garage at first, they got credit from the major suppliers in Britain and Ireland, enabling them to supply customers without having to pay for the goods up front. All they needed was a head start, and soon business was booming as their reputation for service and prompt deliveries increased, sometimes getting foremen or site clerks out of a jam by dropping off urgent items themselves. Good service pays back and, within a couple of years, they had built a warehouse and offices in Tallaght out of their current account, without taking out a loan. They supplied the ironmongery for most of the local authority building schemes as well as major projects like the Irish Life Centre and UCD.

I must admit that I took no great interest in the intricacies of the business, but when my father's health started to fail and he had to attend chemotherapy sessions before driving to Tallaght, I took notice. They had been approached by one of their suppliers, Dorma, a German firm that made door closers, with an offer to buy the company. In fact, they were meeting them that week. I asked for a look at the paperwork. Even with my limited business knowledge from Marquis Productions, I could see that Dorma was getting a bargain; Balmar was cash-rich with a large surplus in the bank and a fully paid-for warehouse, all of which would accrue to the purchaser. Dorma was effectively buying Balmar with its own money. I argued against it and the solicitor was told to defer any decision.

I insisted that my father could no longer drive to work because I had seen a few marks on his car and tyres which indicated that he had made contact with an immovable object. I dropped him to Tallaght in the mid-mornings and collected him in the mid-afternoon.

One day, I took him on a tour of the old places: the Long Hill at Kilmacanogue, on to Glendalough, to Gorey, then past Hobbs' house where we stayed in Poulshone, down to the beach, and ended with a few drinks and dinner in the Taravie Hotel in Courtown.

Events overtook the sale of the business and my father was suddenly taken to St Luke's Hospital by ambulance, summoned by my sister, Joan, who lived with him in the family house. He recovered somewhat and paid close attention to the World Cup, but began slipping in and out of consciousness. The business worries were on his mind and while I was there with him one evening, he was losing consciousness intermittently, talking incoherently about invoices, bank payments, schedules, deliveries, meetings and all the detritus of running a business. Trying to relieve his anxiety, I said, 'Don't worry, Dad, I'll take care of it. I'll do it for you.' I don't know if he heard me, but he seemed to relax visibly and fell into a sleep. On 28 June, he slipped away.

If Balmar wasn't to collapse or be taken over, it needed a support for Cecil Martin, who was in danger of just walking away. Representing the family, I became a working director of the company, turning up every day to help run the business. I got to know the intricacies of the ironmongery profession and took a look at the systems.

We redecorated the showroom and made it more attractive, got proper invoices and delivery dockets printed (they had been using scrap paper and backs of envelopes), hired a stock handler to move the heavy orders and got to know the customers. Coloured door furniture was now all the rage for public buildings and our competitors were getting all the business, because none of our existing suppliers carried a coloured range. Cecil and I went to an ironmongery fair in Cologne and I secured the Irish agency for 'Eco' door furniture. On the success of that, Cecil asked me if we could track down some 'intermittent strip'. What? It was a seal that was stuck onto doors to prevent smoke from coming through in the event of a fire. New doors had them included in the manufacturing process, but old doors had to have them fitted later, so we needed some of the stuff. I phoned contacts in England looking for a supplier, to no avail. I tried Germany. 'We've never heard of intermittent strip,' they said. 'All we have is intumescent strip.' The penny dropped. 'That's the one,' I said. 'Send it over.' (In the interests of verisimilitude, 'intumescent' means 'swelling', indicating a material that swells in heat, blocking the gap between the doors and preventing smoke from passing through.)

I was now a full-time businessman, because for the first time in my career, I had no radio show to do. Suddenly, the phone had stopped ringing. So, when I met the Deputy Director-General of RTÉ at a funeral, and he asked, 'How's your little business getting on? Made any money yet?' I replied sharply, 'It's making a damn sight more than yours, Bobby. You've posted another deficit, I see.' He wasn't pleased.

I took over in Balmar to ensure that the company would continue as a going concern and that my sisters could access their legacy, the bulk of which was tied up in the company. The company had been split evenly between my father and Cecil. Our legacy was therefore a third each of 50 per cent of the company, in other words a sixth each. To release the funds, and to honour my commitment to Cecil, I had undertaken to take over the company by buying my sisters' shares and also Cecil's shares. I had raised the cash by presenting a business plan to the bank. The figure for Cecil's half had been agreed. Then, out of the blue, Cecil had second thoughts. A widower himself, he had just married a widow, complete with new stepson. I had even been his Best Man. Now, he wanted £10,000 more than we had agreed. It threw out all my careful calculations about repayments. I told him that I wasn't going to agree; a deal is a deal. Our solicitors exchanged letters, his side maintaining that the company was worth the extra £10,000; my side saying that an agreement had been made six months before and that it should be honoured.

Then, a miracle. I'll never know if this was my Guardian Angel working or a slip-up on their side, but a letter arrived with a well-worn legal stratagem to underpin the value of something. It said that, because Cecil believed that half the company was worth what he said it was, 'he was prepared to sell *or buy*' at that figure. I rang my solicitor. 'Is that an offer?' I asked.

'Only if they forgot to put the words "without prejudice" on the top of their letter,' he replied. 'And it's very unlikely. Check it again.' Unbelievably, the magic words were not there.

'Accept their offer to buy at their price,' I commanded authoritatively, feeling like MacArthur accepting the Japanese surrender. A few days later, we drew up an agreement for the sale of the shares, Cecil sheepishly gave me a cheque in his solicitor's office and I walked out. Instead of buying the company, I had sold the company, with the extra £10,000 attached. I never went back to Balmar, not even to collect my personal belongings.

I was delighted to be free of the burden, but I had enjoyed my eighteen months as a businessman. RTÉ had come back as well. Toward the end of the Balmar saga, Adavin O'Driscoll, the then Head of Light Entertainment, had asked me to present the drive-time slot on Radio 1. It was only a short-term arrangement, until the unions and management could agree on a new current affairs programme for five o'clock. It ran for years, eventually giving way to *Today at Five*, with Pat Kenny.

An offer came from Billy Wall to resurrect the old 'Beat the Memory Man' formula on Radio 2, where contestants try to beat a panel of experts on tests of knowledge. I came up with a new format called *The Panel Beaters*, an appropriate title for a re-spray job that put new number plates and retreads on an old crock. Using experts like Michael Dwyer on film and Ken Stewart on music, and allowing them to reverse the process by asking the contestants questions as well, made it sound like it was as good as new, but I think it had too many miles on the clock.

Apart from pop music and personality shows, Radio 2 also produced what could be called minority programmes on folk music, current affairs, traditional and country music. In the early 1980s, its first attempt at an arts programme fell to producer Pat Dunne and me. It was called *The Audio Visual Show*, on the basis that all art is received through either the ears or the eyes. Well, mostly, anyway; it may be possible to appreciate art by feel or smell, but we couldn't cater for it. It was all the things arts programmes should be: edgy, iconoclastic, spunky, and unpredictable. We covered the funeral of Christy Brown, interviewed the Virgin Prunes, did features on cowboys, demonstrated how to play Spanish guitar, and reviewed the usual film, theatre and concert offerings by sending unlikely critics — B.P. Fallon to a string quartet recital, for instance.

One item is seared on my brain, though. I came down to the studio ten minutes before live transmission at eight o'clock, having gone through the running order earlier with Pat.

'Change of plan,' he said. 'Anthony Burgess is coming down for an interview. We'll put him at the top of the show.' Before I could say, 'Anthony who?' a tall distinguished man appeared beside us in the studio. Pat introduced us and I led him into the studio and settled him into the guest chair. I nipped back out to the control room, ostensibly to get a pen, but really to get some idea of who Anthony Burgess was. Pat briefed me in five seconds flat: 'Joycean scholar, here for the celebrations, author, wrote *Clockwork Orange*, musician, wrote screenplay for *Jesus of Nazareth*.'

I returned to the studio dreading another Flower Show interview and, as we went live, decided that candour was the best policy: 'Mr Burgess, you're an expert on Joyce. We're a youth station. How would you convince our young listeners to check out James Joyce?'

Rising to the occasion magnificently, Anthony talked about the comedy of Joyce, the musicality of Joyce, the anti-establishment career of Joyce, and quoted lines at random; then I led him into *Clockwork Orange* and why the film was banned, screenplays, Christianity, Jesus, the Rosicrucian Movement, popular music and on and on. The whole piece ran twenty minutes and he was remarkably complimentary, saying that appearing on a pop station was the highlight of the year so far.

I proposed a comedy show for the Drama and Variety Department, set in a non-existent radio station (today it would be a 'virtual' one), called *Balfe's Broadcasting Company*. The half-hour show was written by me and Brendan Martin, a young journalist with a surreal sense of humour I had drafted in from the RTÉ *Guide*. There were send-ups of radio's more predictable formats — sports, current affairs, news, household hints, an egomaniacal disc jockey, Billy Cann (that was me), and a drama serial called 'Heartbreak Hotel', where nothing ever happened. My buddies from Tailors' Hall, Bill Whelan and Stacc, were the resident band and I persuaded other colleagues to take part in the final drama production: Mike Murphy played a song and dance man on the make, Gay Byrne played a Sam Spade-like Private Eye, Maurice O'Doherty played Robin Hood and Larry Gogan an ancient retainer in a French farce. Rodney Rice, Ruth Buchanan and Jimmy Magee also featured, against their better judgement, in a variety of roles (Ruth in particular sending up her *Poparama* kiddie image with some bloodcurdling children's stories).

The regular cast was Anita Reeves, Brendan Cauldwell and Jonathan Ryan, a newcomer to radio. I had discovered him during a Saturday lunchtime series when I ran a phone-in competition for impressionists. Frank Kelly judged it and Jonathan won first prize. He came in to the studio the following week and did some live turns with the hardy annuals: Columbo, Humphrey Bogart, James Stewart, Jimmy Hill. So when the comedy series was given a green light, I brought Jonathan in as a cast member. The producer, Paul Murray, later cast him in some straight plays and he joined the RÉP on contract. He didn't stay too long as he moved into the world of commercial voice-overs, expanding his range of characters into a one-man voice bank, and his clean, crisp baritone is heard today on hundreds of commercials. When he bought his first new car, he went for a Volvo, because it was paid for by 'Voice-Overs, Lotsa Voice-Overs'.

Another new talent came onto my radar by a circuitous route. Fr Michael Paul Gallagher knew Eileen and rang her one day to see if she could persuade me to come and see a young student in UCD, where he taught. He was trying to break into comedy and would welcome the attention of someone, anyone, in RTÉ. Because I had a sort of a name for comedy, would I come and see him the following week? We both went along to one of the lecture theatres in Belfield to see his lunchtime stand-up routine. He was good and had complete control of the audience. The one that stood out was his take on a pop priest who desperately wanted to relate to the kids and spoke only in clichés.

Speaking to him afterwards, I suggested things that might improve the act, editing in particular, and advised him to keep at it, but to shorten the individual pieces.

A short time later, Adrian Cronin, Head of Light Entertainment in Television asked me if I had any ideas for a comedy show. He had a day's studio time coming up and could use it for a pilot programme. The idea I suggested was a show built around an obnoxious TV host, who was smarmy and patronising on air and cruel and vindictive off air. I would insist on overpowering the guests, cheat playing the piano by miming to a record and interview people without letting them get a word in. This character was the linking thread, while the other elements were slightly bizarre sketches: a send-up of American beach movies, a parody of a black-and-white prison film, complete with a Barry Fitzgerald-style priest and Brush Shiels and his band performing a punk version of Tom Lehrer's 'Masochism Tango' ('I ache for the touch of your lips, dear, but much more for the touch of your whips, dear').

As an added spot, I remembered the young comedian from UCD and asked him to perform his pop priest routine. Up to then, the priest was nameless, but when asked in advance for a name for the caption to be superimposed on the screen, I recall suggesting 'Father Brian Trendy'. Dermot Morgan's first TV performance was never seen by the public but the producer, John Keogh, was much taken by Dermot and suggested him for *The Live Mike* series, where he later made his name. The pilot programme was never developed. I don't think I had the acting chops to sustain the character of a grievously unlovable TV host, but I think of him whenever I see Alan Partridge or Larry Sanders.

Another radio series followed. *The Jaundiced Eye* was a series of pseudo-current affairs documentaries, which parodied the earnest, self-important style of journalism. It was really a device to string together a series of sketches on a single topic. I wrote programmes on topics like Advertising, Travel, Radio Made Easy (an instructional self-improvement LP for embryonic broadcasters) and the Irish in America. The latter was a send-up of those solemn investigations into the Irish soul and hardships suffered by the poor bedraggled Irish immigrants who tried to make a few dollars in the New World. One scene I remember vividly was 'The Night Before The Saint Valentine's Day Massacre' where Al Capone, Bugsy Moran and Dion O'Bannion were on the telephone discussing plans for the next day. The convoluted arrangements were made even more confusing by the fact that all three characters sounded exactly the same, like Marlon Brando in *The Godfather*. It was the height of nonsense, but it took on surrealistic proportions, as Dermot Morgan, Jonathan Ryan and I couldn't keep going without bursting into laughter. It was a classic case of 'corpsing'. We tried again and again, much to the chagrin of the sound operator. The more he suggested that we try not to laugh, the more we obliged. It took a half-hour break, lots of coffee and a walk around the Radio Centre before we could record it, the microphones re-arranged so that we had our backs to each other and couldn't catch each other's eye.

In that same programme, I used a song written by a friend of mine, Johnny Devlin. Johnny had been a musician and bandleader in Dublin, before running away to sea in his fifties to play on the cruise ships. When he returned, he took up a job in RTÉ as a radio producer, working with presenters like Tommy O'Brien and Joe Linnane, as well as with the RTÉ Concert Orchestra. He was well read and literate, with a surreal sense of humour, often slipping into gobbledegook while meeting people for the first time. Eileen fell victim to him on more than one occasion. Every fourth word was discernible, but the rest was nonsense. He gave the impression that he was talking perfect sense, leaving the other party with the feeling that their mind, as well as their hearing, was on the blink. He could also do a perfect drunk act, grabbing the hand of the victim in a vice-like grip while singing incomprehensible Irish ballads into their ear.

The borrowed song, to be sung by Jonathan Ryan, Dermot Morgan and me, was 'for the delectation of the professional patriots' and was performed in the style of the more fanatical ballad groups:

> From Britain's towns they came to raise
> Our country from the mire
> And braved with true crusader's zeal
> The Rebels' murderous fire
> To bring the Pax Britannica
> To savage Gaelic Clans
> They fought and bled, but never fled
> The Gallant Black and Tans
>
> They murdered them by stealth and guile
> They stabbed them in the back
> Their only crime was loyalty
> To the grand old Union Jack
> But their spirits burned unquenchable
> By dastard Fenian plans
> And bomb or mine ne'er broke their line
> The Steadfast Black and Tans
>
> We cry in pain 'Come back again,
> Come back Brave Black and Tans.'

That episode of *The Jaundiced Eye* went on to win the Monaco Radio Prize that year.

Parallel to my career in radio, and occasional forays onto the stage, cabaret or business, was a career of sorts in television. Some people regarded radio as some sort of penitential rite to be endured before the green pastures of television came into view. Not I. I loved radio, but thought that I could contribute something to television as well as, not instead of, radio. One programme straddled both media. In the early 1980s, I was presenting a successful television panel game that had started on radio. *Off the Beat* was originally a summer series I had come up with on Radio 1. It was more an entertainment than a serious inquisition, involving two teams and a music group. I had persuaded Frank Hall to be one team leader; he knew his music, having written the *Evening Herald* dance column for years under the pseudonym 'Tempo', and, as he was also the film censor at the time, he was *au fait* with films. Hugh Leonard, the playwright and novelist, who also knew his onions in the world of the silver screen, led the other team. Celebrity guests made up the other two places and the band was the old reliable Jim Doherty Trio with Des Smyth, whispering vocalist.

The attraction of the game was largely in the playing, with some blatant cheating permitted, as long as it was done with some aplomb. The questions were quirky and eccentric, as in our Book Round: 'What two songs contain references to *Webster's Dictionary*?' (Answers at the end of the chapter.)

My friend John McColgan had recently been made Head of Entertainment in the new television channel, RTÉ 2. He asked me if I had any ideas for a half-hour entertainment programme for the station. I mentioned that *Off the Beat* was working well and would probably transfer successfully to television. I gave him an audio copy of one edition. He liked it and, with the minimum of fuss, gave it the green light. It went on almost immediately with the original team captains, Frank and Hugh, and places for celebrity guests. We never had prizes on radio, but as we were adding a member of the public to each of the teams, I thought that there should be some modest incentive to win something. Michael Murphy, the former newscaster, was assigned to produce and the show became a great hit, topping the TAM Ratings on RTÉ 2.

Hugh Leonard, in particular, became known as a film buff and one week, I asked each team captain to set a question for the other captain. Hugh's wasn't correctly answered; try it yourself: 'Name the film star who was male but always played females and, although he appeared in the Talkies, never said a word?'(Answer at the end of the chapter.)

Looking back, my first attempt could not be described as auspicious. It was in 1969 and it was a quiz game called *Eye Cue*, devised by the journalist Tony Butler. As you might imagine from the title, it was a visual quiz, with two teams of contestants representing their county. The Good Lord has mercifully erased the more horrific elements from my mind, but, unfortunately, some of the grisly scenes still remain etched in the memory. Like when the director, a certain John A. Murphy, ordered a kind of Perspex blackboard, so that the camera could point through it at the contestant writing on it. Everyone was surprised to discover that when you shoot though the opposite side of a Perspex screen, the writing and the figures are back-to-front. No problem for John A. He electronically reversed the shot, so that we now saw a mirror image of the shot, but the writing went in the wrong direction, from right to left, and the contestants seemed to have parted their hair on the other side and worn their breast pocket on their right.

He also wanted to copy the split-screen effect of *University Challenge*, where one team appears to sit on top of the other. This is simple to do, but it depends on both teams being physically on the same side of the quizmaster, as you've probably seen on television with Jeremy Paxman. On our set, there was a team on either side of me, so when you put them on top of each other, one team was looking right and one team was looking left. John A. persuaded one team to look in the opposite direction, but they couldn't always remember, so the viewers got the effect of one team engaging with me, the other pointedly ignoring me. Halfway through the series, the talents of John A. Murphy (I sometimes suspected that he wasn't using his real name, with good reason) were needed elsewhere and a new director, Jeremy Swann, was assigned to finish the series. To make things run more smoothly, he equipped me with an earpiece so that he could talk to me continually from the control box. His instructions were of the 'Oh My God, we've lost VTR, keep talking' variety, requiring me to improvise by chatting to the contestants about their holidays and hobbies, unsettling them further.

Mary Casey acted as hostess and Norman Metcalfe was the resident organist for the musical rounds, one of which in particular is deeply ingrained. Contestants had to identify the name of a county by looking at the slide of a landmark, while Norman played a tune with the county in the title. Unfortunately, the slides and Norman got out of sync and when the slide showed Glendalough in Wicklow, we heard 'The Green Glens of Antrim', and when we saw the Cliffs of Moher in Clare, we heard 'The Homes of Donegal'. Gloss over it though I might, it descended into a débacle and I had to stop the recording ten minutes from the end. In those days, video recording was still fairly rudimentary and wouldn't allow us to pick up from the last good bit; we had to go back to the beginning and start again. Alas, we had no second set of questions, so Jeremy came onto the floor and made the teams promise that they would answer the same questions again, exactly as they had on the first take, even the ones they got wrong. They swore to do so, on their honour, no bother, sir. And for the first ten minutes they did, but County Pride got the better of them and it took only one to break the agreement before they were all at it, answering questions correctly with wild abandon. As the guy out front, I took the rap and *Eye Cue* joined the long list of television turkeys.

Jeremy had been a floor manager before he became a director and the stories about him and his colourful style are legion. He was working on a programme celebrating the centenary of Edmund Ignatius Rice, the founder of the Irish Christian Brothers.

Having been told that there was a guest at Reception, he went out to bring him in to the studio and saw a Christian Brother waiting. Jeremy greeted him, cheerily.

'Brother Rice, I presume?'

'No,' said the startled cleric. 'I'm the current Brother Superior. Brother Rice died one hundred years ago.'

'Must have been a dreadful loss to your little community,' said Jeremy, unperturbed. 'This way, please.'

I often wonder what contestants and studio audiences thought of Telefís Éireann and its exotic employees in the early days. Television was still regarded as a sort of nine-day wonder in the 1960s. I asked another floor manager, Tadgh De Brún, if the arrival of an Outside Broadcast Unit in rural Ireland was still the cause for general celebration. 'Not any more,' he said. 'But some people seem to think that everything on their screens comes from Dublin. Up in Co. Meath, one old man asked me, "Do you see much of that detective fella, Frank Cannon, up there in Telefís?" I told him that they are all Hollywood film series that we show; they're not made in Dublin. "And that Lucille Ball, what's she like to talk to?" he persisted. "Same again, from Hollywood, we don't actually make them." But he wasn't listening. "And that Jackie Kennedy one, on the news last night, going to marry that Onassis fella. If you're talking to her up there, you can tell her she's the talk of Nobber!"'

My television experience, such as it was, was good enough for a friend of mine, Ian McGarry. An accomplished drummer, he had played in the 1960s with Bluesville, The Action and other highly rated bands. He had applied for a job as Television Director and had been accepted for a training course that culminated in a final audition programme. Ian chose the life of Beethoven and asked me to write and narrate it on screen. I was delighted to do so, as any practice in the medium would be positive.

Ian was appointed and when he was producing *The Tony Kenny Show*, he asked me to work on it, writing scripts, suggesting songs, putting together production numbers. When the matter of my on-screen credit came up, I invented a title that was as vague as it was all-encompassing: 'Programme Associate'. And for years afterward, I did that job for Ian McGarry and Tony Kenny, then on *The Sandie Jones Show* with producer John Keogh and, *Patricia*, a series with Patricia Cahill, produced by John McColgan. A crucial element of the role was to work on the content, rather than the look, of the show and steer the performers towards music that they, perhaps, hadn't considered before. I wrote a condensed story of Hans Christian Andersen for Tony, persuaded Sandie Jones to perform a Supremes medley (for which John Keogh conjured up three of her) and convinced Patricia Cahill to expand her light classical and Irish range with more contemporary music like 'Disney Girls', 'I Write the Songs' and the one that became almost her signature song, 'At Seventeen'.

I became conscious that, with all the paraphernalia, equipment and technical operators involved in a television production, the performer can easily get lost in the maelstrom. It sounds like a paradox, but the star and performer can easily become the least important member of the production, under the pressure of getting it right technically. A case in point: a director was rehearsing The Nolan Sisters one morning for a programme to be recorded later that night. It was a difficult piece, 'Don't Sit Under the Apple Tree', where the singers reproduced the difficult close harmonies of The Andrews Sisters. When I arrived, they were on their fifth run-through of the song and were visibly wilting; singers don't like singing in the morning anyway, as the voice hasn't warmed up. By the time I got to the director's box, they were starting take six and now looking tense and fraught. I asked why they had to keep repeating the song.

'I'm getting a flare off the green lamp on the final shot and I want to correct it,' the director said. He didn't seem to appreciate that if he persisted, he would get a perfect shot, but a lousy performance. 'They're paid to sing, so let 'em sing,' he added.

I suggested that he ask the floor manager to explain that it was a technical problem and that all the girls had to do was stand there and pretend to sing, so that the lamp could be fixed. They did so. My sympathies were always on the side of the performer. I tried to make them sound good and look relaxed. That included giving them words that they could say naturally. The key in writing for performers on radio or television, I've found, is to listen to how they talk in normal life and try to replicate their style in the script; tidied up slightly, but recognisably themselves.

In the 1970s, the echoes of *Eye Cue* having died down, I was asked to appear as a permanent panellist on *To Tell The Truth*, a panel game presented by Mike Murphy and produced by the Eamonn Andrews Studios for RTÉ. The idea was American, a formula devised by Goodson and Todman, the duo who devised *What's My Line?* Eamonn Andrews had presented it in Britain and had launched the formula in Ireland. Three people came on and the panel had to decide which of them was real and which were the two fakes. I don't recall much about the contestants, other than the time when three Aer Lingus hostesses came on and I spotted the real one instantly, because she was the only one who took off her gloves when she sat down.

In 1976, that series led to my being asked to present another format from the Goodson–Todman Empire, called *Password*. A better game I thought, requiring a degree of literacy and word power. Good fun too, as contestants had to suggest a hidden word to their partner without actually using the word themselves. I recall intense negotiations with the Legal Affairs Department following the cancellation of some programmes, due to strike action by (I think) the cameramen. It was a short dispute that was resolved quickly and new dates were scheduled to record the *Password* programmes. I looked, reasonably, I thought, for a new contract for the new dates. I had been booked for the original dates, I kept myself available and I came in, as scheduled; the fact that RTÉ couldn't organise itself to honour the contract and record the programmes wasn't my fault. They owed me the original fee for the cancelled programmes and also a separate fee for the new dates. The Head of Legal Affairs was known for his parsimony and we argued for an entire afternoon. He eventually agreed. Having established the principle, in case it happened to other performers, I gave him back half the fee for the cancelled programmes.

A short time later, I got a phone call from the producer, John Kelleher.

'Your agent has been plugging you for a part,' he said. 'But I don't know if you can do it.'

What agent? What part?

'John McColgan thought you'd be perfect, after that *This is Your Life* on yourself last year,' he said. 'The part is Uncle Sam in a play written by Eoghan Harris called *The Greening of America*. It's to celebrate the American Bicentennial and it's going out on 4 July. But I'm not sure you're up to it.'

I don't know to this day if he was using reverse psychology, but the more he said he wasn't sure, the more I was determined to convince him that I could. I met him to discuss the part and I brought along still photos of me in the character shots from the sequence I'd done with John McColgan. The role of Uncle Sam was not unlike the role of the MC in *Cabaret*. I was a multi-faceted individual: the Master of Ceremonies and owner of a bar wherein the trial of Paddy was taking place for usurping these United States of America. I had to link the entire proceedings, occasionally sing and join company scenes. After much persuasion, John Kelleher cast me. No sooner had we agreed, than the dispute that had been fermenting suddenly erupted and our technical colleagues were out on strike. It looked like the show was doomed, but on the off chance, we continued rehearsals in the Scout Hall in Donnybrook.

It was a heavyweight cast: Godfrey Quigley and Jim Fitzgerald were permanent bar-flys in Dooley's Bar, using the words of the Irish-American writer Peter Finley Dunne. Arthur O'Sullivan was the Judge in the Courtroom, with Tony Doyle as the Prosecutor. Paul Bennett played Paddy, the symbolic Irishman on trial, and the all-purpose supporting cast included Bill Golding, Peter Caffrey, Susan Slott, Eamon Morrissey, Joe Cahill and Madelyn Erskine, while Earl Gill was the house band comprising mainly the folk group Spud, augmented by Dick Keating on keyboards.

It was my first time to rehearse in such distinguished company and I was taken aback to see that Godfrey had his lines already learned, more or less. The rest of us worked off scripts, as we blocked out the scenes around the floor plan. Then the word came through. The strike was fixed and we were in studio the following day with three days to go.

Studio 1 was turned into a huge Brechtian set, 'in the round', where no effort was made to separate the different performance areas, the bar, the court, the performing stage, the bar-room tables. It was described as a 'satirical extravaganza based on fact' as the Irish experience in America was re-enacted in a vaudeville saloon. As the linkman, I was everywhere, following the action, commentating on it in verse and, sometimes, causing the action. The whole thing was exhilarating, made more so by the camaraderie engendered by the actors and crew who pulled out all the stops to get it done under severe time pressure. When it went out, it looked superb and for the first time in a long time, RTÉ garnered rave reviews.

Kevin Marron, in the *Sunday World*, wrote: 'This show was probably the best thing Montrose has created since it first saw the light of a television set. When it was over, I felt like cheering. Dammit, I wanted the curtain to rise so I could shout encore.'

Peter Cleary, in the *Sunday Independent*, also felt like cheering: 'At long last RTÉ sent out a revue which didn't sound amateurish. This programme was a real honey... The Irish, I believe, are the only people who understand the Americans and RTÉ's programme went a long way to prove it.'

Vincent Browne, as 'Wigmore', wrote: 'Not alone the best American anniversary programme by any of the stations in this region, but perhaps the best show ever produced by the outfit.' And then, damning with faint praise, he continued: 'Brendan Balfe at last found expression for his very considerable talent, which is hardly contained in the vacuous role of disc jockey.' Thanks a lot, Vincent. *The Greening of America* is one of the few Irish television programmes to have a permanent place in the Museum of Broadcasting in New York.

I continued to have a strong association with the Eurovision Song Contest. In 1971, the year Ireland first hosted the contest in the Gaiety Theatre, the producer, Tom McGrath, asked me to present a new element of the contest. The EBU had decided that the audience and voting panel should get a chance to see and hear the songs before the show itself. Each country was asked to record a performance, which was sent to every other station participating. Tom asked me to link the songs in studio. The problem was that all the videos were in colour and RTÉ did not yet have colour cameras in studio. The only colour cameras were in the new Outside Broadcast Unit, to be used in the Gaiety, which had already clocked up its first colour transmission at the 1971 Railway Cup Finals. Tom, never one to take no for an answer, arranged for the OB Unit to be parked behind the studio building and a camera to be hauled up to Studio 3, the cable winding down corridors, through offices and downstairs to the unit. I read my linking pieces to camera and the whole thing was assembled later with the videos. A small thing, but quietly historic, marking the first colour transmission from the RTÉ studios.

Thereafter, for about fifteen years, I was the Jury Secretary on Eurovision Day, acting as host to the Irish jury and calling in the vote later that night on the live show. Jury members, we were informed by the regulations, 'should be half male and half female'.

The ritual was always the same: the jury secretaries took part in an electronic conference with the Scrutineer at the venue to alert us to any last-minute changes. Normally they passed off routinely, apart from one year when the BBC was running it, I think, in Brighton. They had invented a new voting system, whereby all the countries voted on each song individually. In other words, all twenty countries called in their vote on Song A, then all twenty countries on Song B and so on, right through the twenty songs. In the rehearsal the previous night, the voting sequence alone had taken four hours, making the entire show a six-hour endurance test. Even the most diehard Euro-fan, with the possible exception of Louis Walsh, would baulk at that. It was refreshing to see that even Homer nods, and the comments about the BBC from jury secretaries around Europe were pointed and acerbic. A new voting system was introduced there and then, one that exists today, which I had to explain to the jury.

During the day, we were locked away with the song lyrics and a tape machine, playing the songs in audio only, while the jury took notes. Come teatime, from their discussions and requests to hear particular songs again, I could get a good idea of how they were leaning. In the studio, we heard the dress rehearsal from the venue, without pictures. Then, after dinner, we watched the show. I collected the votes after each song and handed them to our own counter, Aeneas McDonnell. What was most surprising was that the early indications of the favourites went out the window when they saw the performers. 'I didn't like the look of him,' they would say, or 'I thought she looked a bit common.' It's true, of course, that it is a song contest, rather than a singer contest, but it's equally true that a song means nothing until it's interpreted and performed. The matter is moot, anyway, as it seems to have descended into a competition for circus acts. I acted as commentator only once, in Bergen, Norway, where the host country put on an excellent show and lavished every comfort on us, happy to be in the driving seat at last, after years of nil points. I, along with Larry Gogan who was doing the radio commentary, missed most of the week's festivities as we spent our time chasing information on the artists. It was the usual drawback in being a commentator, but the work comes first. No drinks for Lar and me, thank you. Not while we're on duty. Although it's very civil of you to enquire.

Then there was Twink. I worked on a lavish special with her in the early 1980s, acting again as Programme Associate, suggesting songs, working up production numbers, writing sketches and scripts. Produced and directed by John McColgan, it looked and sounded classy. Twink excelled in the production numbers, particularly in a 1930s nightclub scene, where she and John Kavanagh flirted, engaged and parted with just the songs telling the story. That in turn led to *The Twink Series*, where she was joined by Jonathan Ryan. I was the script editor as well as writer, taking meetings with the other writers, working up ideas and commissioning sketches from such as Paddy Murray, Tom Andrews, Eanna Brophy and Dermot Morgan. Paddy Murray was always terse and economical, stripping back the writing to its essentials, while Dermot Morgan was just the opposite, sending in pages of closely typed script that went in all directions. My job was to sub-edit the material to see if there was a usable joke therein. Eanna was a practised scriptwriter, but had an optimistic view of what could be done on the budget: 'We open on Paddy Moloney playing a set of uilleann pipes. Gradually, the pipes turn into a giant octopus which wrestles with him before chasing him out of the studio.'

Writing for television does give a writer a great feeling of power, as well as a contrasting feeling of fear. For instance, I wrote a sketch set in a chip shop. When I came in, there was a complete chip shop on the studio floor, with counter, tiled floor, tables and chairs, jukebox, fryer canopies, signs and neon lights, just as I had written it. That's the power bit; the fear bit is in thinking, 'This had better be funny.'

The two most famous characters from the series came about when I suggested we needed some running sketches with people who would appear regularly. Two charladies were decided on and I gave them a 'back-story', some biographical details so that we knew how to write them. Bernie was a charlady who was vocally brassy and glamorous in a gaudy way. She had been a Royalette in her day and still fancied herself as a draw to the gentlemen. She was inspired by some of the theatre staff in the Olympia and the Gaiety. Her char-colleague was Rose-Violet, so called because Jonathan looked anything but flower-like, low key, put upon and tended to repeat the last words of her colleague ('Colleague, that's right'). Bernie and Rose-Violet were contracted to clean in the RTÉ studios, giving them the rationale to pop up anywhere.(We had a cleaning lady named Bernie, incidentally, who helped Eileen one morning a week, but when she heard her name being used on television, she left.) I enjoyed writing the two characters and putting them into ridiculous situations. Once they were well drawn and their personalities established, it got easier.

Two other characters were dear to my heart, too. The Pirate DJs were inspired by the plethora of half-witted jocks making a name for themselves in Dublin. They all had hairdresser names and our twosome were Cynthia Brewster St James and Justin Adrian Warrington Junior the Second. They were a superb vehicle for spoonerisms and malapropisms: 'Josephine is in hospital for a hysterical rectum', 'a special request for her mother who is 111. (Pause)...Sorry, who is ill.'

The Twink Series was immensely popular with the audience and, even now, when programme guests are asked to choose a favourite piece from the archives, Bernie and Rose-Violet or The Pirate DJs invariably appear. For all their bravado, they had a certain charm. I've worked with Twink on many occasions, on television, stage and cabaret and writing stand-up routines for public appearances. I wrote a Margaret Thatcher routine that was given new number plates regularly, by Twink ringing me for a topical opening gag. I would give her some lines based on the evening news and, as we discovered in Jonathan's Restaurant, if the opening is topical, the whole script becomes topical. She is a superb performer in the operatic style; she likes to make entrances, she doesn't rate punctuality very highly, she always looks like she is ready to go on, her nerves manifest themselves at the dress rehearsal but are never obvious on stage, she will leave you in no doubt as to what she thinks of you. All these qualities are those of a star, a career she embraces fervently. But she is, and always has been, an engaging and versatile performer with a warm heart. Her dog bit me once, but I've forgiven her (Twink, that is; not the dog).

Towards the end of the 1980s, John Williams asked me to help out on a new series of live shows, *Sunday Night at the Gaiety*. They were traditional variety shows compered by Brendan Grace. My Programme Associate duties were to come up with scripts for Brendan and to help and advise John Williams, who had a great regard for variety artists and also a keen sense of what an Irish audience likes. He arranged for CIÉ to run trains every week from different venues around Ireland, virtually filling the theatre from those alone. We both agreed that money should be spent on big stars as top-of-the-bill performers, but equally agreed that we had some Irish stars who were well up to filling the slot. He also insisted on engaging a 'dumb act', as they were known in the business—the acrobats, gymnasts and speciality performers who were a vital part of the traditional bill. I also had to come up with a production number each week, to close Part One. These were costumed with specially designed sets, and performers were engaged for these alone. Ones I remember with some affection were a potted version of *My Fair Lady* with Patricia Cahill and Alan Stanford as Eliza Doolittle and Professor Higgins, Val Joyce recreating Ian Priestly Mitchell's style of presenting an Old Time Music Hall, Brendan Grace himself doing a Burl Ives scene and Twink and Fran Dempsey performing a Rock 'n' Roll scene, 'Rock Frolics'. The latter was taken from the Braemor Rooms production I had put together earlier.

Let me digress for a moment. On Monday mornings, we had the regular production meeting that settled into three phases: the first was a post mortem on the previous night's live show. At this meeting, I took issue with one director who had a penchant for avant-garde artistic shots. He would shoot the plasterwork, the chandeliers, the lamps or the audience, when all we wanted to see was the performer, particularly one we had flown in specially, like Howard Keel. The second part of the meeting was arrangements for next week's show and plans for future shows. The final part was when I took a meeting with Brendan Grace and our two gag writers, Val Fitzpatrick and Chris Casey. Both had come from the variety stage and both were comedians.

For the rest of the afternoon, we would swap gags, one leading to another as memories were triggered. It was a most enjoyable session and I became very fond of the two old pros. I would take notes of the jokes and work it up into a monologue for Brendan. Occasionally, he would try out the gags on his own cabaret shows during the week. This had two benefits; we knew that the gags worked and Brendan got barrels of new material for the act. In fact, Val and Chris made a couple of appearances in the production numbers when they played the Scarecrow and the Lion in a *Wizard of Oz* production scene with Anne Bushnell, from the aforementioned *Judy Garland Show*. Val and Chris also appeared as Cecil Sheridan and Jimmy O'Dea in a Dublin Variety Scene along with Seán Mooney and Cecil Nash.

For the Twink and Fran Dempsey Rock scene, we borrowed a Yamaha motor bike on which Fran made his entrance, and Michael Grogan designed a magnificent set, with a street scene exterior, including a cinema and a drugstore. When the scene moved into the dance sequence, the frontage flew out to reveal a fully dressed dance hall. To the right of the stage was Michael's *pièce de résistance*: it looked like a sparkling red chevvy, but it was actually a Triumph Herald, split in half down the centre and with the wings and fins embellished with filler. Angled slightly, it looked like the real thing from the front, but from the perspective of the performers looking outwards, it looked different. Because there was just half a car, there were no seats and the performers were sitting on scruffy kitchen chairs. Holding the whole thing upright was a rough iron frame with a few poles stuck into stage weights. I complimented Michael on the design. 'Thank you,' he said, 'but with our luck, that stupid so-and-so will shoot it from the rear.' And that's exactly what the director did; using his hand-held camera, he started on the back of the car, with the kitchen chairs and poles, and pulled back to reveal the audience looking at the stage and then swung around to look at the action.

Whatever sense of mystery or illusion the set conjured up, this director was going to shatter it. 'It's deconstructed, dear boy, avant-garde, don't you know, showing the inherent contradiction between style and substance.' I always believed that directors should get those shots out of their system at producer training school, as well as the undressed set with ladders in the background.

For the next two series, we moved down to Dame Street, as the show became *Sunday Night at the Olympia*, with much the same format, although I recommended that we change the production numbers, mainly because we were finding it hard to come up with a new one every week. My idea was to hire a permanent repertory company of singers, who would perform the hits of a certain year in an appropriate setting. It would still look stylish, but would be easier to cast. Des Smyth, Tony Kelly, Damian Smith, Helen Jordan, Kathy Nugent and Angeline Ball, in her television debut, formed the permanent company, a versatile bunch who could handle any style. The format worked well, with Brendan introducing a quick rundown of the year in question, then, on his cue, 'That was the year and this was the music', the curtain rose on a colourful scene with the hit songs of that year.

I later worked on the Sandy Kelly series and wrote the script for a special featuring her and the Jordonaires, *The Voice of Sandy Kelly, The Songs of Patsy Cline* which became a successful theatre show in London. Daniel O'Donnell was hard to fathom at first, as I worked with him on his first TV series, produced by John McColgan. I picked songs and wrote the script, but I could never quite get to grips with his music taste when suggesting songs. The 'If you liked that, you'll like this' approach didn't seem to work and he seemed to like and dislike songs for no discernible reason. It made life difficult when trying to choose material. He was, though, the complete professional, always on time, always familiar with the script, always knowing the song lyrics. He was strangely downbeat in person but came to life when the audience came in. He seemed to know everyone by name: 'Did your mammy get the pension all right?', 'Did your brother come back from America in time for Christmas?',

'How's your sister? Did she have the baby yet?' I saw Daniel after a show in Castlepollard, which we had recorded for radio, talking to the fans for almost two hours. The gear had been stashed away, the bar was closed, but still he talked, until they had to put the lights out. Over fifteen years later, I was back guiding Daniel through the intricacies of interviewing as well as talking to camera, on his recent series directed by John McColgan's son, Justin.

Saturday Live was a more recent series on RTÉ television that used a guest presenter each week. I was billed as the MC, doing a piece to camera with the fake news of the week and introducing the guests. I suspect I was also there in case the guest presenter panicked or refused to go on. I thought that the premise of the programme was inherently confused, if not flawed. Guest presenters were chosen from the ranks of sometime television presenters— Tracey Piggott, Pat Spillane, John Daly—who had been in a TV studio before and knew the grammar, so to speak. They were rehearsed, scripted, briefed and taken through their paces at great length during the week, so that on the night they were competent. That's all, competent, but no sparks were lit and no glass shattered. It seemed that RTÉ wanted a professional, capable, safe presenter who wouldn't embarrass themselves or the station. My view was that it should lean towards the opposite pole and that presenters should be chosen because they were edgy, unpredictable and contentious. It might look untidy, but it would be fascinating to watch. The only one who came near the ideal was the comedian Seán Hughes. He was himself and didn't behave as if he were auditioning to present *The Late Late Show*.

I was involved with a television show that turned out to have all those qualities: unpredictable, edgy and untidy. It wasn't planned that way; it just happened. It was 31 December 1984 and I was co-presenting the New Year's Eve Show with Mike Murphy. 'Co-presenting' is not strictly correct; I was engaged to write and present six or seven pieces to camera reviewing the year through a sceptical lens, sitting in a large leather armchair, for all the world like a slightly groovier Cyril Fletcher. We were due to go on air at around 11.30 p.m. Reviewing the running order, I remarked to Mike that it looked a bit light for the thirty-minute slot before the midnight bells; there were three musical acts and three of my bits. Mike explained that, because so many of the guests were working in pantos or plays, the director had decided to accommodate them in the second half. Fair enough, so. After the rehearsal, I went to make-up and ambled back to Studio 1 at about ten past eleven. John Cooke, the floor manager, asked me to sit in my chair and give a sound level. As I was doing so, the camera framed me in shot. As I was reading casually from my script, I saw John Cooke freeze to the left of camera and make the universal mime for 'stretch'. Not knowing what was going on, I kept reading anyway. To my slight dismay, John disappeared completely, but I noticed that the other cameramen had suddenly taken up position and a slight frisson was noticeable in the studio.

I had been talking for about five minutes and had reached Margaret Thatcher's infamous 'out, out, out' speech of only a month before, when I saw John reappear with Mike Murphy in tow. He gave me a thumbs up, so I took a chance and said something like, 'that's the sort of year it was and to put a proper end to it, over to you, Mike.' Mike picked up with smooth aplomb and introduced the first musical act, during which I tried to find out from him what had happened. Apparently, Presentation had come to us twenty minutes early. They swore that they had told the producer during the week. He, conversely, swore that they had not and left the control room to take issue with them, preparing to settle the argument, if necessary, through means of a clenched fist, firmly applied.

Meanwhile, Mike and I ploughed on, impressing on John Cooke the need for more performers, as we had used up those assigned to the first section and had fifteen minutes to fill. Get anyone, we said, the first one you see. Twink was found and hurriedly forced onto the floor to chat to Mike and me. We talked until midnight. It might, on the other hand, have been five minutes past midnight, because I called the time from my own wristwatch, the battery for which was running down, but it was the only timepiece in the studio. The second section was fine, with plenty of performers, and in the hospitality suite afterwards, the producer complimented all of us on a fine performance, not least his own.

He was right, to an extent. The audience didn't know what was planned, so they assumed that what they saw was meant to happen. The trick from our side is to make it look as if everything is intentional. The fundamental thing applies: don't embarrass the audience. So, don't feel mortified if you didn't know that the two songs that refer to *Webster's Dictionary* are 'Too Marvellous for Words' and 'The Road to Morocco' and that the film star's name is Lassie.

～ SOUNDTRACK ～

Favourite Standards – most from the *Great American Songbook*

- 'The Very Thought of You'/Tony Bennett
- 'I Have Dreamed'/Frank Sinatra
- 'At Last'/Etta James
- 'Mack the Knife'/Ella Fitzgerald, live in Berlin
- 'The Folks Who Live on the Hill'/Peggy Lee
- 'Mountain Greenery'/Mel Tormé
- 'Thou Swel'/The Supremes
- 'Younger Than Springtime'/Bing Crosby
- 'Let There Be Love'/Nat 'King' Cole & George Shearing
- 'I've Got You Under My Skin'/Frank Sinatra
- 'Guess I'll Hang My Tears Out to Dry'/Frank Sinatra
- 'Granada'/Frank Sinatra
- 'Every Time We Say Goodbye'/Ella Fitzgerald
- 'September in the Rain'/Dinah Washington
- 'Mood Indigo'/Nina Simone
- 'All the Things You Are'/Sarah Vaughan
- 'At Long Last Love'/Buddy Greco
- 'In the Chapel in the Moonlight'/Dean Martin
- 'Baubles, Bangles and Beads'/Kirby Stone Four
- 'Birth of the Blues'/Sammy Davis Jnr

Chapter 15 ∽

| LOOKING FOR AMERICA

It looks like a film set. Coming in on the plane over the skyline of New York City for the first time takes the breath away. I've been here before, in a hundred films, and it looks so familiar. Black-and-white cop cars, drugstores, cocktail bars, delicatessens, yellow cabs, steam coming from the manhole covers. The cold air is like a slap in the face. The atmosphere seems to be pumping with positive energy; there is palpable electricity in the streets; anything is possible here. There are eight million stories in the Naked City and this is one of them.

One of the offshoots of producing the Aer Lingus sponsored programme was that Marquis Productions was asked to tender for the inflight audio entertainment system in the new Boeing 747s, joining the fleet in 1971. An American company had the contract to provide the inflight films and also pitched to supply the audio programmes. Its submission for the main speech channel, 'Three Hundred Years of Shakespearean Theatre', may have damaged its chances with an Irish company, however. We put together proposals for eight hour-long audio programmes, including a pop show, a traditional Irish programme, a classical music programme, an easy-listening programme and so on, but the key channel was the speech programme.

It was called 'Ireland from the Air' and was designed for visitors coming to Ireland from America. On the first edition, I presented a feature on 'The One Man Show', as exemplified by Mícheál Mac Liammóir, Ulick O'Connor and Jackie McGowran; Valerie McGovern presented a travel guide; John Skehan told a ghost story; Petula Clark and Tommy Steele talked about their new film *Finian's Rainbow*, while Niall Toibín took us on a tour of the real Irish accents, as opposed to the Oirish ones besmirching Finian and his pals. The programmes were received well, and writer and broadcaster Proinnsias Mac Aonghusa wrote that 'to praise the aircraft would be an impertinence, but I must single out the audio channels as being first class and a credit to the company'. Because the audio channels were the same in both directions across the Atlantic, they had to cater for incoming passengers as well as outgoing ones. It was a good discipline, though, addressing one audience without alienating the other. We refreshed the programmes once or twice a year and then suggested that we should do some New York stories, for Irish passengers going westwards. Besides, for contractual reasons, we had to record the classical and the easy-listening programmes with the inflight company, in its studio with its catalogue of music. I therefore had to go to New York.

Dermot Herbert and I went over with our Aer Lingus client, Phil Newport. I went to Cue Recording Studio to record two programmes, Dermot went to a meeting and Phil went shopping. We agreed to meet at the corner of Fifth Avenue and Fortieth Street. We hailed a cab, Phil got in with loads of shopping, Dermot followed and I squeezed into the back seat last, and assumed that Phil had called the destination. He hadn't; he was waiting for us to do it. After a good thirty seconds, the New York cabbie turned around and said, wearily, through hooded eyes: 'Hey Mac, do ya give clues?'

That was just the ticket. Damon Runyon was alive and well. More than somewhat, in fact. To source stories and interviews, Seán Carberry, our friend from the *Irish Permanent Programme*, was a valuable contact. He was now Press Officer for the Irish Tourist Board and knew the Irish-American New York community well.

Over the years, he gave help unstintingly and, through him, I arranged interviews with people like Dennis Smith, the fireman who became a best-selling author; Jimmy Breslin, the hard-boiled newspaperman who reviewed the Abbey Theatre production of *The Plough and the Stars* and told me, 'I couldn't understand a damn word they were sayin''; the famous author and playwright Marc Connolly, who entertained us in his apartment overlooking Central Park; and Brendan Gill with whom I had a fascinating conversation in the dark offices of the *The New Yorker* Magazine. He was insightful and thoughtful in his memories of Brendan Behan in New York. Of Dorothy Parker and the Vicious Circle at the Algonquin Round Table, just across the street, he said, 'They weren't as important as they thought they were. None of the great writers were there; Baldwin wasn't there, Hemingway wasn't there' (Marc Connolly was).

Gill had just published a biography of Charles Lindbergh and he told me that he had been secretly employed by the Irish Government to advise on the airport that eventually became Shannon. 'He came upon an old man who had been looking out for him when he had crossed the Atlantic in a solo flight. Without giving his name, he asked the man if he had seen Lindbergh's plane. The old man, with eyes glinting, said, "No, but I heard him. I heard him." If

Lindbergh had identified himself, he would have made the old man's life. But he never did. Bastard.'

On later trips I flew down to Washington, Seán having made contact with Senator Ted Kennedy. I interviewed him in his office in the Capitol and went to have a look at the Senate and the House of Representatives in session. Tip O'Neill, the Speaker of the House and third in line to the presidency, later gave me an interview in his palatial office and spoke about his Irish ancestry.

These New York trips always seemed to happen just before or after St Patrick's Day. I was there for only one of them, but one was enough. Monsignor Jack Barry, Chaplain to the Emerald Society of the New York Police Department, brought me to an early breakfast attended by the Mayor, Ed Koch. I got police clearance to walk the route with my tape recorder, interviewing friendly New Yorkers ('Jeez, I love your accent') and standing on the steps of St Patrick's Cathedral talking to the Cardinal. It was freezing and I eventually ended at the reviewing stand, with hizzoner The Mayor, the TV celebrity Merv Griffin and some thick-necked Sons of Old Érin. Frozen to the bone, I headed back to my hotel room at six o'clock, looking forward to the food and drink promised at the Aer Lingus reception at eight. All day, I had avoided the green-hued drink that was in plentiful supply. I was, after all, a good little professional.

Back in the room, I checked my recordings, lay down on the bed, woke up at a quarter to eight and hopped into the shower. I had told Dermot that I'd meet him in the bar downstairs. But the bar was closed. Funny. The coffee bar was full, but there was no sign of Dermot. I headed outside to the dark freezing air and hailed a cab for Fifth Avenue. It was eight o'clock, but strangely the sky was getting lighter. Not wishing to antagonise another New York taxi driver by changing the instructions, I got out at the Aer Lingus office, looked inside to confirm my worst suspicions and got another cab back to my hotel. Dermot was in the lobby and I joined him for breakfast.

'You missed a great night last night,' he said. 'Where did you get to?'

'Oh, I was very tired, so I just went asleep.' Which was perfectly true.

New York bars are exactly how I had pictured them. Some are manned by just one barman, who can keep a whole bar supplied by himself with nobody kept waiting. Down in the corner, you half expect Frankie to call, 'Set 'em up, Joe.' Downtown, the bars in business districts, like P.J. Moran's, offered a buffet, absolutely free, to entice customers to have a few drinks before getting the train home. If you look like you're going to stay a while, the barman buys every third drink. We tended to end up at Eamonn Doran's, where you could see tangible proof that the intensity of nationalism is in inverse proportion to the distance from home. One evening, a gentleman straight out of Central

Casting, dressed in trench coat and trilby hat pulled down over the eyes, came around collecting for 'The Cause'. I declined politely. He insisted. I declined again.

'Do ye not care what's goin' on in the Old Country?' he asked vehemently.

'I know exactly what's going on in the old country. Which is more than can be said for you. It seems you'll do everything for Ireland, except live there.' I said that in a voice I didn't quite recognise as my own. I then noticed that two or three regulars had come near me, as support, rather than intimidation. The professional patriot retired.

In New York, I always stocked up on records, particularly in the comedy, spoken word and historical categories. I loved visiting the Museum of Broadcasting, which I had covered on its recent opening. I don't like shopping and, apart from gifts for the family and the records, didn't go near the shops. I did, however, buy something for Bill Whelan from Manny's famous music store. In fact, it took most of my trip to organise, calling Bill back home with payment details, checking import licences, and persuading Aer Lingus to classify it as a personal carry-on item, even though it was stowed away. I don't think many pianos came from New York as hand luggage, but Bill's did.

One year, I crossed the Atlantic twice in as many days. I had come home from one of the trips, jet lagged and weary, when Seán Carberry rang. They needed to do a television commercial urgently and he wanted me to come back over. My mother said that she never thought she'd hear me utter the words, 'No, not New York again?' but I presented myself the following morning for the jumbo to JFK. The short notice on the TV commercial had come about because Joe Malone had just been appointed Head of the Tourist Board in America and had vetoed the TV campaign proposed by the Board's advertising agency. It was full of shamrocks and shillelaghs, and Joe thought that it was time to bury them forever and promote a more contemporary Ireland. I was to be the face of that New Ireland.

The lawyers had cleared me with the Screen Actors' Guild, because my visa classed me as a journalist, able to appear in that capacity. It was a bit of a stretch, but it was acceptable. We went to a studio, purposely hidden behind dirty doors covered with graffiti to disguise the millions of dollars of equipment inside. The young director, Steve Katz, explained that first we had to record an audio track which would be used to cut pictures to; the following day we would come in and record me speaking live to those pictures. 'We have all morning to get the audio right, don't worry about it, but we're trying to get the script to run twenty-eight and a half seconds exactly. No pressure,' he said. 'We'll do it as many times as it takes.'

'Fine,' I said, thinking that they certainly knew how to make a big deal out of a mundane matter. (Maybe they didn't realise that Ireland now had electricity as well as running water. Maybe the old commercials had this effect on Americans. Maybe they should have been changed long ago.) I recorded one take; it was twenty-nine seconds. No problem; take two was twenty-eight and a half. They were a little surprised but I had, after all, been talking to the split second for years on continuity and, like most presenters, had developed a sort of internal clock in the brain. I left them to fill in the long session they had reserved and came back the following day to record the visuals. The commercial offered a free Guide to Ireland and was playing in six key cities, quoting a toll-free number to call. I recorded six different endings as voice-overs, one for each city. To my delight, I was told that they qualified as six different commercials and I would be paid accordingly, with repeat fees. For the rest of the year, I got a substantial cheque every month from the advertising agency.

In 1973 I went to New York with Andy. We stayed with Seán and Barbara Carberry and it was a scorching summer. The only way to see the city in daylight was to zigzag down Fifth Avenue to avail of the air conditioning in bars and restaurants. Cold beers were purely for medicinal purposes. After a week, we headed off on the second leg of our journey to Music City USA, Nashville Tennessee, to visit our friend Shay Healy.

He was host and manager of a restaurant called Tara, just outside the city, which, although famous for its country music, is more a centre for the insurance and printing industries. Music Row is not a large area and downtown is like any other industrialised city. The people are hospitable and friendly and, while we were talking to a southern gentleman at Shay's place, he asked us casually to drop on over the following evening, as he'd like his family to meet the Irish guys. I instantly forgot about it until he rang us at Shay's house the following evening to enquire as to our whereabouts.

We headed out to his place to find a huge mansion and up to thirty guests gathered to eat a buffet and meet his new friends from Ireland. They were particularly taken by the idea of a radio station with a million listeners that boasted a drama company, two orchestras, classical singers and a string quartet.

In New York too, people are friendly and hospitable; I was offered the loan of a car and an apartment from someone I'd just met an hour previously. One of Shay's friends was a disc jockey named Dick Downes, who worked for WLAC Nashville, a famous station in the evolution of pop radio, one of the first to plug Elvis Presley intensely. Dick asked me over to have a look at the studio and, even though it was September, he asked me to record greetings in Irish for the next St Patrick's Day. I was happy to do it and he later sent me a tape of his programme with its bizarre WLAC station identifications in Irish.

The Grand Ol' Opry was broadcast from the Ryman Auditorium, an old church in the lower part of town. I loved its informality, as acts went on and off and announcers read commercials on stage during the changes. Backstage, it was exactly like the Television Club, Harcourt Street, with musicians swilling warm beer, complaining about the money and enviously comparing how much more of a crowd Conway Twitty got the night before. I was delighted to meet Bob Luman, the singer of one of my favourite songs from the 1960s, 'Let's Think About Living'. I recalled how I had traipsed into Grafton Street every few days to see if it had come into Switzer's record counter. He was quite impressed.

Shay, with his likable personality and his try-anything-once attitude, was highly popular around Nashville. He would sing a few songs of an evening in the downstairs bar in Tara ('where there are no strangers, only friends you haven't met yet'). Some were his own compositions and some were parodies. One that was instantly topical was his take on 'Ode to Billie Joe', which was adjusted to honour a tennis champion and became 'When Billie Jean King beat the bejaysus out of Bobby Rigg'. One night, despite his best efforts, his audience was agog with indifference so I suggested that he sing a parody he had written for me to deliver in Jonathan's Restaurant. It was to the tune of 'Matrimony' and told of the exploits of one Charlie Haugh-Hee. It got huge applause from the Nashvillians, even though they didn't understand a word.

In 1987 I was back in the USA to record a series of interviews for radio. With the help of researcher Carol Louthe, I had lined up a list of performers, aiming principally at those I liked myself. I knew from experience that there was a certain etiquette to be gone through and I wanted to write to the artists first to explain the programme, who I was and who I worked for. In the Aer Lingus interviews, I was used to arriving in town, getting on a phone and asking if I could come over—now.

So, the first problem was tracking down the addresses, and that's where Carol came in. In the days before the internet, websites and e-mails, we wrote in the old-fashioned way, saying that I would be in the States in September and asking if I could be fitted in. We got more refusals than acceptances, for legitimate reasons—filming, not in town, or, in the case of Elizabeth Taylor, launching a new perfume.

The one name I couldn't track down was the musical satirist Tom Lehrer. The standard biographical references all said 'keeps a low profile', 'notoriously secretive', 'doesn't welcome press enquiries'. All I could glean was 'thought to reside in Cambridge, Massachusetts'. Not to be beaten, I used the famously efficient American telephone service. Sitting in RTÉ one night, I asked the Irish operator to give me the information operator in Boston. I asked for the telephone number of Tom Lehrer, possibly in Cambridge. Within seconds, she gave me the number. Good to have, but I wanted to write to him first. I got back to the Boston operator, said, 'I have a phone number; do you have a Reverse Directory to give me the address?' She gave me a street and a house number in Cambridge. I wrote away immediately and got back a letter which first asked, 'How did you find me?' Nonetheless, Tom was agreeable in principle and told me to call when I was over. I set up other interviews in New York, Nashville and Los Angeles, arranged flights and accommodation and, at the beginning of September, set off for a month in the USA.

By coincidence, our friends, the Healy family, were travelling at the same time to attend their daughter's final vows as a nun. They're a wonderful family, warm, open-hearted, musical and great fun. I am a friend of the parents Des and Peg and also of the four brothers, Paul, Michael, Mark and Des Jnr. At the airport, they went over to Queens while I went into Manhattan. My first priority was to try Frank Sinatra. I had been trying to get a contact for weeks and had got a contact number for his secretary, Dorothy. I rang her and found, to my surprise, that Frank was in New York that week in Carnegie Hall. She wasn't hopeful, but she said that she'd refer my request to his press agent.

Meanwhile, the toast of Broadway that month was an Irishman, and that couldn't be missed. Colm Wilkinson in *Les Misérables* was the hottest ticket in town. I arranged to meet him in his dressing room and did an interview while he prepared for his role. A far cry from the Four Keys and Terenure Tennis Club, he agreed, when I reminded him of his earlier days. After the interview, I made to get out of his way.

'Have you seen the show, Bren?'

I confessed that I hadn't been able to get a ticket. He rang the box office immediately, but there was no seat, not even standing room.

'Can't have that. Just stand there in the wings and look at it from there.'

Colm went to the opposite side of the stage for his first entrance. A man in a suit appeared beside me.

'You can't stay there, sir.'

I explained that I was a friend of Colm's, that I was from Irish radio, that Colm had put me there. With the robotic stare of a Secret Service man, he ignored my entreaties.

'Please leave the theatre, sir.'

So there I was, thrown out into the alleyway, tape recorder over my shoulder, all dressed up and nowhere to go. Determined to see a show—any show—I went to the ticket kiosk in Times Square to look for cancellations. *Starlight Express* had some seats available. I can understand why. It was dire. As Jim Doherty put it about another tuneless spectacular, 'It was the only show I've come out of, whistling the set.'

The following day, I was booked to interview the King of Broadway, Harold Prince. He had directed *Phantom of the Opera* and *Evita* by Andrew Lloyd Webber, but in the 1950s had been apprenticed to the celebrated producer George Abbott, and had produced classics of the American musical theatre like *The Pyjama Game, Damn Yankees, West Side Story, Cabaret, Company,* and *Pacific Overtures.* We met in his office high up in the Rockerfeller Centre. He was an effusive, effervescent man who knew his business and talked fondly about George Abbott, Stephen Sondheim and Lloyd Webber. He said that he would love to work with the Abbey Theatre, which may even be true. I normally wear headphones to monitor what's going on tape, but on this occasion, I didn't. Back at the hotel, I was astonished to discover that my recorder had acted as a radio receiver and had picked up the local radio station, WABC, whose transmitter was on the roof. Hal Prince was talking along happily while The Eagles chugged along in the background. I excised most of it when I got home, but it's still clearly audible. I explained to our listeners that there was a radio in the background, which was strictly correct.

My business in Manhattan finished, I accepted the Healy's invitation to attend the final vows of Mary Healy. I got a train to Queens and a cab to their house and thence deep into New York State to the well-appointed convent. Before I left the hotel, the Statler-Hilton (whose telephone number gave Glenn Miller a huge hit, 'Pennsylvania 6-5000'), I got a message that Frank Sinatra's press secretary had rung but hadn't left a number. Maybe it was to say no. Maybe it was to say yes. Maybe it was, 'Come in and see the show as our guest and talk to Mister Sinatra afterwards.' Most probably it was 'get lost'.

I flew from New York up to Boston and found Tom Lehrer's house, near to the campus of Harvard University. A small, wooden building, sparsely furnished, with a grand piano in the living room. He was strangely nervous as we started the interview, but relaxed as we proceeded. We talked about his seminal works, 'Poisoning Pigeons in the Park', 'The Irish Ballad', 'The Vatican Rag' and his hymn to nuclear Armageddon, 'We Shall All Go Together When We Go'. He had actually worked in Los Alamos and is a mathematician by profession. He was now teaching the Philosophy of Maths ('there isn't one') in Harvard and Math and Musical Appreciation in California at UCLA. 'Our school of satire was called "sick"—Lenny Bruce, Mort Sahl, a few others—but actually I'm a sceptic.' He is also an accomplished pianist—that's not just vamping he does—and 'once a week, I invite some friends around and we sing through one of the great American musicals like *Oklahoma!* or *Carousel*.'

He has not much time for Mr Lloyd Webber and none at all for the revivals of shows like *Camelot* 'where you can see the remains of Richard Burton before your very eyes'. Why did he retire? 'Because my objective was to get a good recording of my songs on my own record label. After that, there was no need to do them again.'

He was pleased that a new show based on his works, *Tomfoolery*, had been produced in Dublin by Noel Pearson. As I left, we shook hands and he asked, 'How did you get my number again?'

Next stop was Nashville, where I had already lined up Waylon Jennings and Chet Atkins. I stayed in a motel near Music Row. The interviews were two days apart and I mooched around in between appointments. Waylon was an interesting character, happy to be called an outlaw. He had been part of Buddy Holly's band playing bass and was nearly on Buddy's last flight, but had given up his seat at the last moment. When I talked with him, he had recently released *The Highwayman*, making up a quartet with Johnny Cash, Kris Kristofferson and Willie Nelson. Chet Atkins, far from being an outlaw, was a gentleman through and through. A guitar player with an original style, he had turned to production for RCA records and had produced and played on the early records by Elvis and the Everly Brothers. His uncanny knack was for finding talent and matching it with the right song. With friendly rival Owen Bradley, he was responsible for 'The Nashville Sound'. I asked him to describe it. He put his hands in his pocket, pulled out a handful of coins, jingled them in his hand and said, 'That's the Nashville Sound'. We talked about poetry and classical music and Jim Reeves and Perry Como and, when we finished, I thanked him for the interview. 'The pleasure was mine,' he said. 'You're a very good interviewer.' Southern manners, gentlemanly courtesy.

I had lined up Johnny Cash from Dublin and his press agent, Dean (I think), had arranged a specific time and place. It was a field near Hendersonville, his home, where he was performing at a charity event to raise money for an animal shelter. Mr T from the A-Team was also billed. 'Come along at twelve,' Dean said. 'John will see you then.' I was there well ahead of time. There was a big stage and a huge sound rig.

Dean introduced himself, a young man in a smart suit. 'John's in the caravan there. I'll get you in soon.' The support acts were playing, but it seemed that the animal shelter day was a well-kept secret around Nashville and Mr Cash was not going to play to fewer than two hundred people. He was going back to the house for a rest and he'd be back later. It was overcast and clammy, and standing in a field in Hendersonville was not my idea of how to spend my birthday, for that's what it was.

It seemed that my interview was now coupled with the size of the crowd. Johnny wasn't going on until more people arrived. It was now six o'clock and my normally sunny disposition was darkening, just like the skies over Hendersonville.

Dean said, 'He'll certainly do it later tonight.' Johnny eventually went on stage at nine o'clock for an hour. At ten, Dean was back.

'He won't do it now; he's tired,' said Dean trying to look apologetic. 'But he will do it in the morning. Promise.'

'Tell Mr Cash I'm tired too and the request for an interview with RTÉ is withdrawn.'

I turned on my heel, as much as one can in squelchy mud, and strode off manfully toward the lights of Nashville and my single room at the end of Lonely Street.

Dean, at least, had the good grace to look embarrassed.

There was another reason why I couldn't interview Johnny Cash in the morning, apart from pure exasperation. I was booked on an early flight to Los Angeles. I had booked a hired car from the airport and at the desk they had a device where you could enter the name of your hotel and it would print out a customised route. I hit the streets. If you're not used to driving on the right, LA is no place to experiment. The customised route presupposed a navigator and I was so intent on not crashing into one of the local maniac drivers that I could consult it only at traffic lights and try corrections. On the multi-lane free-way, I saw my hotel gliding by on my right. I tried to correct by manoeuvring through an over-pass; now the hotel, like a ghost ship, was serenely passing on my left. There was nothing else for it but to get off the freeway system entirely and get down to the lower street level. If you've seen the Tom Wolfe movie *Bonfire of the Vanities*, you can picture the scene perfectly. I was now in a slum rundown area, with the occasional burnt car on the sidewalk and collections of surly youths at the corners. Luckily, it was broad daylight. I could see the sign for my hotel in the distance and headed for it with all speed, commensu-rate with my personal safety and well-being. I put the car in the hotel car park, intending never to use it again.

Having arrived at my room in the Universal Hotel, Hollywood, up high, overlooking the film studios, I manned the phone for a full day, tying down interviews that had been loosely arranged from home and now needed dates, times and places. The sun was splitting the stones and I looked longingly at the swimming pool twenty floors below, but I couldn't get near it because I was expecting return phone calls. American efficiency is a myth; they are not good at it. At last, a schedule emerged that I could work to and I could at least get the occasional swim in.

I met the comedian and actor Bob Newhart in his trailer on the lot of Paramount Studios. He was filming his own situation comedy series, set in a New England Hotel. A welcoming and generous man, he pointed out that he was a mixture of Irish and German, 'so I suspect the humour comes from the Irish side, as the Germans are not one of the great fun nations of the world.' He had been in Ireland many times and recalled that while he was staying in the Shelbourne Hotel, a group of radio actors had approached him in the dining room to enquire if he was who he sounded like. He was indeed, and they took him off to the Abbey Tavern in Howth for a few songs and, possibly, a few drinks. Famous for his one-sided monologues, he peoples his sketches with an assortment of characters you can't hear or see, but everyone can see the woman in the Driving Instructor sketch or Sir Walter Raleigh trying to introduce tobacco to civilisation: 'You stick it in your ear, right Walt?'

Pat Boone was another delightful guest who told me that when The Beatles came to knock him, and dozens of other singers, off their soft pop perches, he cleaned up by selling portraits and images of the Fab Four. He was oft ridiculed for his gleaming teeth, wholesome manners and anodyne songs, but he sold more records than everyone except Elvis, another southern boy. 'The funny thing is that the people who bought my records, also bought Elvis's records. Everyone thought that there were two separate groups, but they were the same people. Maybe I represented the safe, gentle part of a person, while Elvis represented the rebel side. But it's perfectly possible for the two sides to exist in the same person.' Pat Boone is one of the great survivors and when I was with him in his Beverley Hills office suite, his company was busily involved with his syndicated radio show, personal appearance and more records. A bright and intelligent man, Pat Boone knows his place in pop history, doesn't rest on it, but is always on the lookout for new projects.

When I called to the house on Bellagio Drive, a young woman opened the door. She was the secretary and they had been expecting me. The hallway opened onto a large room with a sunken floor. A woman was moving slowly across the floor with the aid of a walker. Her long, straight hair was perfectly groomed. It had once been blonde, but now it was white and shining. 'Pleased to meet you,' she said. 'Do you mind if we do it in the bedroom? I've hurt my hip and I like to lie down.' The bedroom was off the main room, furnished in the grand style, with lots of cushions and satin. All along one wall was a full bookcase. She lay down on the bed with the help of her secretary. I took up a position at the bedside table and started to interview Miss Peggy Lee, one of the most popular song stylists in the world. Her cool, laid-back voice could handle jazz, folk, swing, ballads, standards and contemporary pop.

I had done my homework and knew her career; it's always a good idea to know the research, rather that continually consulting notes. We talked about her days with Benny Goodman, her marriage to guitarist Dave Barbour and about the songs she had written. Of her most famous record, *Fever*, she wrote more than half of the verses, the ones with the literary and historical connections, but received no royalty or acknowledgement. 'I co-wrote the songs for *Lady and the Tramp* for Walt Disney, but never got proper royalties. As well, I appeared on the soundtrack as the two Siamese Cats and as Peg, the singer. I only got paid the session fee for those. Mr Disney was a nice man, but he wasn't Santa Claus.' We spoke about her reading, her love of art and her famous recording of 'Is That All There Is?' She was worried about recording it. 'I thought it could be taken as the viewpoint of a world-weary cynic, a pessimist. Then I thought it could be sung from the viewpoint of an optimist, Is that all there is? Is it as harmless as that? That's not so bad. And that's the way I sang it.'

The interview finished. Her butler brought me a drink. We chatted on. She asked me would I like to stay for dinner. We had Mexican tortillas and scotch, Peggy still lying on the bed, me in the chair beside her. I stayed for an hour or so. Miss Peggy Lee. You always use 'Miss'.

Billy May had told me by letter to Dublin that he lived in South Laguna, about eighty-five miles south of Hollywood, but said to phone him when I got in. I was prepared to drive down to him and rang him for directions to his house. 'As it happens, I have to come up to Hollywood tomorrow, so I can see you in my condo there, if you like.' His apartment was only a short distance from my hotel, so I walked over, a practice rarely engaged in around LA. Billy had been a trumpet player with the Glenn Miller band, took his own band on the road and then swapped the touring for a life in the recording studio. Along with Nelson Riddle, he was one of the most famous arrangers in the world, known particularly for his orchestrations for Frank Sinatra. 'His greatest gift? Well, Frank's a fine musician. He knows a lot about music and what makes a good recording. He's knows the trick of circular breathing, so that he can take in air while still breathing out. He learned that from Tommy Dorsey's trombone playing. He can come to the end of a phrase and carry the note right into the next phrase of music. It's a thrilling thing to hear.'

Billy's first album with Francis Albert was *Come Fly With Me*, and his arrangements were both swinging and sweet. He was known for little break-aways in his arrangements, little musical jokes, and his habit of keeping his tongue firmly in his cheek. 'Well, the musicians liked it, and Frank liked it. It added to the fun of the session.' He had arranged for all the greats, Nat King Cole, Ella Fitzgerald, Bing Crosby and had written the theme for the TV cop show, *The Naked City*, among many others. 'I'm sorta retired now, but I did a movie score lately and it's still a thrill to tune into the Boston Pops Orchestra and hear them doing my arrangements.'

Billy was like any of the professional musicians I'd met in Ireland, low-key, self-deprecating and humorous. That humour was evident in the charts he'd written for the comedian Stan Freberg: send-ups of 'The Yellow Rose of Texas', 'Banana Boat Song', 'Heartbreak Hotel' as well as original arrangements. 'Stan would come over with a guitar and sing a song, I'd write down the melody and write the arrangement.' Just like that. When you listen to an intricate big band arrangement for Sinatra or any of Billy's instrumental recordings, it's hard to believe that they were written on paper in a small room in Hollywood. No piano. No trumpet. Billy May heard the orchestra in his head and wrote it down.

Billy invited me to a reunion of the Stan Kenton Big Band that night in Coldwater Canyon, organised by the Big Band Academy of America (Billy is a board member), featuring such Kenton alumni as Pete Rugolo, June Christy, Short Rogers and Laurindo Almeida. Before we left, I mentioned that I had been trying to track down the aforementioned Stan Freberg, without any luck. 'Leave that to me,' he said, and picked up the phone. 'Stan, I've got a guy here from Irish radio. Nice fella. You should see him.' We arranged to meet later that evening at his house in North Beverly Drive. Unfortunately, I was going to miss the Kenton night.

Stan Freberg had been a hero of mine for many years. He had more or less invented comedy on record, stretching the medium of sound to best advan-tage, and was a firm believer that the pictures are better on radio. 'I was the last of the network radio comedians,' he said. 'I took over from Jack Benny in 1957 and after me, there were none.' His house was comfortable in the Hollywood style, but not large. His curly hair had gone white and his horn-rimmed glasses gave him the look of a mature schoolboy, probably a swot. 'I started on cartoon voices and my first record for Capitol was a parody of the radio soap operas, where all that is said are the two words, *John* and *Marsha*. Then I took at swipe at the Rock 'n' Roll crap, but I heard that Elvis kinda liked my take on 'Heartbreak Hotel' and sent one of his guys out to buy it quietly.' He firmly believed that good satire comes from outrage, 'but outrage in its natural state is an indigestible commodity. It has to be made palatable with a candy coating of humour.'

He was delighted to hear that I had played his 'Green Chritma' every year for the previous twenty. 'That was a shot at the advertising industry that nearly didn't get out. The Capitol lawyers didn't like the reference to whose birthday we're celebrating. I almost left the company, but they relented. I've always said that my records aren't released, they escape.' He was much taken by my telling him that a friend of mine, Oliver Barry, had laughed so much at his 'Elderly Man River' on the radio that he had crashed into a tree. Stan recalled that he had been told that the authors who compile *The Book of Lists* called him to tell him he was included in the section People Who Died Laughing. A man collapsed with a heart attack while listening to a Freberg record. As the ambulance men took him away, they asked his daughter, heartlessly enough, 'By the way, which record was it?' It was 'Wunnerful, Wunnerful', the parody on Lawrence Welk, the bandleader who mangled both music and the English language equally effectively.

Stan Freberg's ambivalence towards the advertising industry was taken to fruition in the formation of a company specialising in producing humorous commercials for radio and television. It's called Freberg Limited (but not very), and its motto is "Ars Gratia Pecuniae", which means "Art for Money's Sake". If you use good artistry to make good commercials that treat the audience as intelligent, you will make money. I've been telling that to Corporate America for years now and they're beginning to believe me.' The proof is all over his house with awards and statuettes for his satirical commercials dotted casually around the living room. Among them is a Pulitzer Prize for Best Radio Script of the Year 1957 for 'Incident at Los Voroces', a twenty-minute sketch from his radio show that mirrored the Cold War in the rivalry between two casinos, the El Sodom and the Rancho Gomorrah. 'You will recognise the biblical connections—my father was a pastor.' It was a chilling sketch and when it ended on a desolate wind with a lone coyote howling in the distance, the studio audience was unsure whether to laugh, or cry or applaud. That's the thing about radio; that's why I call it 'The Theatre of the Mind'.

Back at the Universal Hotel, I was getting used to the menus. I had been there a week and the food was coming around again, just like the tunes on the mood music system. 'Enjoy your water,' Tad said brightly as he plonked a glass on the breakfast table with an incandescence improbable this side of medication. Or it could have been Brad or Chad or any of the blond, blue-eyed, white-toothed server persons assigned to my table. I was having a running battle over the breakfast menu. All the offerings were made up as designed dishes and I wanted the American breakfast; it being similar to the Irish variety, with bacon, sausage, eggs, tomato, strawberry (yes) and grits. The grits turned out to be a hurdle that had to be overcome. They sounded like a pota-to hash, so I ordered them on the first morning. They were, to put it mildly, a disappointment: a glutinous porridgey concoction, only cold. 'Hold the grits,' I said the following morning to Brad. 'It comes with grits,' he said. I was aware of that, I told him, but I didn't want any. 'You're paying for them, anyway, so you might as well have them.' Not required, I replied, thank you all the same. This boy didn't give up easily. 'Why don't you just leave them on your plate?' Because I find them offensive, I told him, and asked him if he was familiar with the concept of Customer Service. 'Sure, and in our customer surveys, grits do all right.' I found the solution by asking for grits as a side order. They came in a separate dish and I covered them with a side plate. One of America's least attractive qualities is the inability to improvise, or amend the regulation to allow for compromise. Or it might just be something in the space and sun-shine in Los Angeles that encourages airheads. Enjoy your water.

It's no fun exploring restaurants when you're by yourself, so I stuck to the hotel restaurant. I needed to be near a telephone and left word with the switch, so they were aware of my whereabouts all day. In the cocktail bar, I nodded to Dustin Hoffman and had a drink with Telly Savalas. Well, he was beside me. We didn't actually talk.

My last quarry was Bob Hope. I became very friendly with his secretary and spent many hours on the phone in LA, settling dates and times for the interview that had originally been agreed in Ireland. I had even braved the traffic in my little car and practised driving the route to his house, visible from my hotel room. I had an offer of an interview with Sammy Davis Jnr in Las Vegas, a short plane hop away, but it clashed with the fourth and final firm arrangement to meet Bob Hope. I cancelled Sammy; then Bob cancelled me. I had already extended my departure date with Aer Lingus. It was time to go home. I arranged for my hired car to be picked up in the garage of the hotel, took a cab to the airport and headed for New York. When I saw the Aer Lingus 747 and talked to the friendly hostesses, I felt I was already home.

Back in Dublin, Eileen and El were waiting at the airport and five-year-old John took a running jump into my arms and told me that we had got a cat.

There are a few postscripts to my American Saga.

I played Niall Toibín's inflight piece on Irish Accents to Gay Byrne and suggested that it would make a good item for *The Late Late Show*. Noel Pearson was also on that night and, on the basis of the performance, agreed to manage him. It was the kick-start to Niall's comedy career.

Peggy Lee's lack of royalty payments from Walt Disney went to law and the studio was forced to make a multi-million dollar payment in settlement for her work on *Lady and the Tramp*.

There was no Cash and no Hope, but the rest of my American interviews were made into programmes and broadcast as a series called *Showpeople* on Radio 1, all except for the interviews with Waylon Jennings and Chet Atkins. They were never heard.

A sound operator wiped them before transmission.

∼ SOUNDTRACK ∼

My Personal Top Thirty Chart of All-Time Hits

- ↭ 'Runaway'/Del Shannon
- ↭ 'You Don't Know Me'/Ray Charles
- ↭ 'Strawberry Fields Forever'/The Beatles
- ↭ 'Dream Lover'/Bobby Darin
- ↭ 'Whiter Shade of Pale'/Procol Harum
- ↭ 'A Forever Kind of Love'/Bobby Vee
- ↭ 'Like a Rolling Stone'/Bob Dylan
- ↭ 'Mr Tambourine Man'/The Byrds
- ↭ 'Good Vibrations'/The Beach Boys
- ↭ 'At Seventeen'/Janis Ian
- ↭ 'Lipstick on Your Collar'/Connie Francis
- ↭ 'Into My Arms'/Nick Cave
- ↭ 'Carey'/Joni Mitchell
- ↭ 'Cathy's Clown'/the Everly Brothers
- ↭ 'Layla'/Derek and the Dominos
- ↭ 'White Flag'/Dido
- ↭ 'I Don't Know What to Do with Myself'/Dusty Springfield
- ↭ 'Sorry Signs on Cash Machines'/Mason Jennings
- ↭ 'Crying'/Roy Orbison
- ↭ 'I Put a Spell on You'/Nina Simone
- ↭ 'I Only Have Eyes for You'/The Flamingos
- ↭ 'A Change is Gonna Come'/Sam Cooke
- ↭ 'Both Sides Now'/Dion
- ↭ 'Goodnight Saigon'/Billy Joel
- ↭ 'Waltz No. 2'/Elliott Smith
- ↭ 'Sunshine of Your Love'/Cream
- ↭ 'Hallelujah'/Tim Buckley
- ↭ 'I Count the Tears'/The Drifters
- ↭ 'He's A Rebel'/The Crystals
- ↭ 'The Future'/Teddy Thompson

| THE LATEST CHAPTER

Noel Purcell died in March 1985, almost as old as the century. I knew two of his sons and rang to see if I could come down to the house with a tape recorder. I wanted to do an obituary programme and felt the best way was to attend a real Dublin wake. His widow, Eileen, graciously received me and I joined the throng in the house in Sandymount. Chris Curran was playing the piano and Jim McCann was singing. I moved around the friends and family, gathering memories of one of the stalwarts of the Dublin variety stage, as well as one of Ireland's most recognisable film actors. As his son Mike was recalling how Noel had been brought to hospital in an ambulance, and how he had insisted that it stop to buy a bottle of whiskey, the crowd started singing Noel's theme song, 'The Dublin Saunter'. I caught it on tape and it made a moving end to the obituary programme on 'The Auld Brown Son', as he was known.

I was speaking afterwards to my producer colleague, Maura Clarke, and remarked that the Variety era was fast disappearing and if it wasn't captured soon, there would be nobody around to talk about it. I proposed a series to document it, called *The Spice of Life*. I trawled the radio and television archives for old material and drew up a list of possible interview subjects. There was little or no written information, apart from newspaper clippings, so I had to start with a clean page, so to speak. One interview led to another, as people suggested other possible contacts. Over a couple of months, I inter-viewed more than seventy survivors of the era, while Maura Clarke transcribed the content onto cards and made cross-references. Gradually, a shape for the series emerged. I would build it around the main theatres: the Royal, the Gaiety, the Olympia, the Capitol; then the travelling fit-up companies and cir-cus; then dance halls and ballrooms; the cabaret stage; and profiles of three individuals, the famous theatre owner and impresario 'Mr Louis' Elliman, producer Noel Pearson and the Queen of Irish Theatre, Maureen Potter. In the course of it, I met some delightful people whose contribution had not been adequately recognised—Seán Mooney, Cecil Nash, Paddy Dunlea, Chris Casey, Hal Roach, Roy Croft, Harry Bailey and dozens more, including my next-door neighbour, Cyril Cusack, and Eamonn Andrews.

'The Quarry' was Eamonn Andrews' house in Portmarnock and was the height of modernism, designed by Sam Stephenson and built, as you might guess, in a disused quarry. Eamonn welcomed Maura Clark and me warmly and invited us up to his study with its spectacular view of the garden through a circular window. He recalled his days in Radio Éireann and a device he invented to promote his own programme. 'I'd talk to anyone in the lift on the way up to the third floor and make the comment that I'd heard a wonderful interview the previous night. It was one of mine, of course, but they weren't really sure who I was. By the time the day was over, people were compliment-ing me on a wonderful programme, saying that they had heard great things about it.' He was adamant that broadcasting stations should be gentle in encouraging new performers and treat them with courtesy. Meanwhile, they should take on everything—the church raffle, the charity concert, compering talent shows—for the experience.

'To get your face in front of an audience, I suppose,' I said.

'No,' he replied. 'To get their face in front of you. To be able to walk out on stage and address a live audience without panicking. To look them in the eye and make a connection. To know how to get on and, just as important, how to get off.'

Eamonn's big break came not from radio, but from compering the *Double or Nothing Quiz* on the stage of the Theatre Royal, where bandleader Joe Loss discovered him. His touring with the Loss Band eventually led to a radio audition in the BBC. I brought up Denis Meehan's theory that Eamonn's distinctive 'mid-Atlantic accent' was the result of seeing too many cowboy pictures as a kid.

'Not so,' he said, 'What I've got—and what you've got too—is one of the Dublin accents. There are many; mine happens to come from the south city. To English ears, it sounds mid-Atlantic, somewhere between Britain and America. But you must remember, we gave the Americans their accent, so we're not copying them, they are probably copying us. The reason why my voice was acceptable on the BBC was that it was classless; it didn't betray any roots, because they didn't know where it came from. It's much the same with Terry Wogan.'

The Spice of Life won a Jacob's Radio Award that year and in my acceptance speech, I recalled that Brendan Behan had been at a funeral of a minor Irish writer who had shown promise but never made the premier division. Looking at the wreaths at the graveside, Behan remarked, 'Isn't it a pity that they didn't give him the flowers when he could still smell them?' So, on behalf of all those artists who had added the spice to Irish life, I was pleased to accept the bouquet.

In 1986 I proposed to Michael Carroll, the Director of Radio, that my position be upgraded. Since I had been suggesting, compiling, scripting, timing and presenting all my own programmes for years, I had effectively been producing them. Added to that, I had been producing sponsored programmes for the previous twenty years as well and some recognition was overdue. 'What have you in mind?' he asked.

'Presenter/producer is the grade that should be invented, combining both roles,' I said.

He came back to me few days later and said, 'You will have to do a Producers' Training Course.'

Without thinking, I asked, 'Give one, or take one?'

He meant take one. I also had to apply formally and be interviewed, my first-ever interview after twenty-three years of broadcasting. At the interview, it was clear that the Head of Light Entertainment, Adavin O'Driscoll, found the very idea of a presenter/producer anathema. It was, in her mind, like giving first-class status to a third-class passenger. She pushed me on whether, because I had produced stage shows, RTÉ might see a conflict of interests there. On the contrary, I replied, RTÉ should be delighted with the extra experience I'd bring. Brian Mac Aongusa, the Controller of Radio 1, seemed genuinely surprised at the amount I seemed to know about radio.

In 1986 RTÉ Radio was celebrating its sixtieth anniversary, with documentaries and features. I had an idea with which to wrap up the year and I sent a note to Michael Carroll, suggesting a whole day of vintage programming during the week after Christmas. From my familiarity with the archives, I had a good idea of what I wanted and drew up a draft schedule to cover a day's broadcasting, set in no particular time frame, but what you might have heard on Radio Éireann in, say, the early 1960s. In *A Day by the Wireless*, there would be no people remembering how it was. We were going to demonstrate how it was, in a combination of archive programmes and live broadcasts. The draft schedule essentially stood up. Old sponsored programmes were assembled with the celebrated voices of Niall Boden, Patrick Begley, Denis Brennan, Arthur Murphy, Cecil Barror, Frank Kelly, Frankie Byrne, Leo Maguire and Gay Byrne, who also returned as a continuity announcer. The news would be real and the once-anonymous announcers were back to show that news doesn't have to be sold, just told: Una Sheehy, Ivor Kenny, Liam Devalley,

Tom Cox, Jim Sherwin, John O'Donohue, Pádraic Ó Raghallaigh, Michael Herity, John Skehan and Bernadette Plunkett. There were comedy and entertainment programmes from Joe Lynch, Paddy Crosbie, Din Joe and Joe Linnane, and music programmes from Noel Andrews, Tommy O'Brien, Larry Gogan, Roy Croft, Harry Thuillier and Jimmy Magee.

Terry Wogan presented a new edition of *Hospitals Requests*, while Eamonn Andrews came in to introduce some vintage recordings from his series *Microphone Parade*, including the famous 1947 interview with Sir John Barbarolli, when he so memorably described the long corridor in Henry Street. I produced Eamonn in the programme, my first time as an RTÉ producer and his last time as an RTÉ presenter. He died the following year and I also found myself producing his obituary programme. As the first chairman of RTÉ, he set up the television service and had to defend it against those who wanted to use it either as an arm of government or as an elitist service to promote the Irish language or the arts. 'There were many lobby groups and pressures', he told me, 'but I wanted a station that people would watch. It's hard to educate, uplift and inform if they aren't watching in the first place.' On New Year's Day in 1992, I put together a television version of our radio marathon called '30 Years a-Glowing'.

The RTÉ monopoly was broken with the introduction of the Independent Radio and Television Commission. They advertised for submissions for twenty-five local stations and, to the surprise of most, a national service as well. John McColgan rang me. The PR consultant to one of the applicants wanted help with their submission to the IRTC and wanted to know if I would come on board. Absolutely. John and I had been talking about some commercial ventures anyway. It turned out that the clients were Oliver Barry and James Stafford, and Muiris MacConghail was advising them on programming.

We met the principals and gave some advice on the schedule, which at this stage contained every ingredient, except a cure for the common cold. There were arts, job lines, Irish language, sport, household hints mentioned, but no names attached. The immediate problem was their submission in person to the IRTC, which was due shortly. I suggested that the argument be put on tape, a sound submission for a sound licence. I also wanted to show that they could use the medium effectively and set the scene in a sort of cyber station, as if Century were already up and running. To drive home the message to any radio professionals, I used Stan Freberg's famous commercial for radio itself, produced for the National Association of Broadcasters in which he intended to fill Lake Michigan with tons of whipped cream while the Royal Canadian Air Force dropped a giant maraschino cherry on top, to the cheering of 50,000 extras. I changed the location to Croke Park as Jonathan Ryan gave directions, but it was recognisably Freberg's famous sketch. It worked well, to all but those with a humour bypass.

I didn't attend the hearing in the National Concert Hall, but we all met for lunch in the Shelbourne Hotel afterwards. I asked how it had gone and Mr Stafford was supremely confident that the licence would be awarded. We all found out since that his confidence was well founded, as they had bribed the Minister, Ray Burke. Terry Wogan and Chris de Burgh were investors; they tried to lure Gay Byrne to no avail, but some did leave RTÉ, including Marty Whelan and my friend Pat Dunne. A chief executive with no radio experience was appointed, coverage ranged from patchy to non-existent and it lasted only a couple of years. I always thought that if Oliver Barry, with his instincts for the tastes of an Irish audience, had run it himself and dispensed with his UK and Australian radio doctors, it would still be a going concern.

When the national licence was re-advertised some years later, John and Moya McColgan applied to run Radio Ireland, which transformed itself into Today FM.

We were at the Eurovision Song Contest the night that *Riverdance* made its debut. After the event, Eileen and I, along with John and Moya, Bill Whelan and his wife Denise, Jean Butler and Michael Flatley, tried to get into Lillie's Bordello, a night club in Dublin, but the security people told us that only celebrities were welcome. We spent the evening in Jurys Coffee Dock, eating onion soup. I haven't been back to Lillie's, nor do I intend to return. I know my place.

But I'll never forget the seven minutes of *Riverdance* itself. The primal roar from the audience at the end seemed to come from a deep recognition in the Irish psyche that the time had come to celebrate who we really are. The play *Dancing at Lughnasa* had the same spiritual resonance. It's a topic I hope to explore in my next radio project, *The Irish Voice*.

Out of the Century submission, I was asked to help out with the submission for the Wexford station. I spent a week or so with them and asked Noel Andrews to act as Station Manager in the submission. They too were successful as South East Radio.

In all this commercial activity, my agreement with Kevin Healy, the new Director, was that my voice belonged to RTÉ, but my body could do what it liked.

Though sponsored programmes had long since been abolished, I felt that there might be a need for syndicated programmes for the local radio sector. Mike Murphy suggested that I work in conjunction with his Emdee

Productions to try out the market. I produced a farming programme with Peter Murphy and Mairéad McGuinness for FBD Insurance, and an oldies show called *Pop Go the Years* for ESB shops. Ken Stewart presented it and I brought back Maurice O'Doherty to the air, as a newsreader, to deliver the news of years gone by. He had left RTÉ to live in France, but had since come home and had suffered a stroke, affecting his speech. He was reluctant to do the programme, but I persuaded him and after a few weeks of stops and retakes on each sentence, he became a fluent reader again. Pat Dunne, now without a job due to the demise of Century, came to help me in production. We introduced a training component for local stations and trained and advised presenters in Shannonside Radio, including Ciarán Mullooly, later Midlands Correspondent with RTÉ.

Mike was proving himself an excellent businessman and dealmaker and was advising an Irish-American investor on cable television opportunities in Ireland. Along with cable, he suggested that they get involved with local radio as a possible investment. Northern Sound was in trouble and needed investment. The previous management was no longer around and someone was required to revamp the station and keep it on the air while investors sorted themselves out. I became acting Station Manager.

There were many bad habits prevalent and some of the presenters were not susceptible to training or production. I got their attention by a simple expedient. I ordered a pre-recorded announcement on the hour to the effect that Northern Sound was about to revamp its schedule and would welcome submissions and audition tapes from anyone who fancied themselves as a broadcaster. The announcement was satisfyingly stimulating for the existing presenters and attracted new voices and contributors, enough to revamp the schedule. Gareth O'Connor was brought in to present the mid-morning magazine as a prelude to his time with RTÉ.

One bad habit I had to address before he came was a bizarre, and probably illegal, practice. During a political discussion programme, I kept hearing the Sinn Féin line being put forcefully by the presenter. Section 31 was still in force and Sinn Féin spokespersons were not allowed direct access to the airwaves, but the local SF representative, Caoimhghín Ó Caoláin, was seated in Reception listening to the monitor. Every now and then, he would write a note, which the receptionist would drop into the presenter, who would read it out as a SF riposte to a panellist. I told the SF man that the practice had to stop, that we would read any newsworthy statements, as long as they were faxed in on Sinn Féin notepaper from Head Office as an official party statement. It solved the problem.

When Taoiseach Albert Reynolds made it his political priority to attempt a resolution of the Northern Ireland conflict, I saw a way in which radio might play a positive part in reconciling the two traditions in the north as well as creating understanding in the south. The Downing Street Declaration, the forerunner of the Good Friday Agreement a few years later, was issued by Albert Reynolds and Prime Minister John Major in December 1993. It set out the principle of mutual consent, that the people themselves should solve the problems and that each community should be accorded 'parity of esteem'. I thought that radio might play a part in helping the communities to get to know each other better and worked out a detailed plan for an all-Ireland radio service as a joint effort between RTÉ and BBC Northern Ireland. It was called *Harmony FM* (from the musical definition of harmony: 'the simultaneous sounding of different notes to make musical sense, the absence of discord'), and it was based on the sharing and alternating of RTÉ and BBC radio programmes on the FM transmitter recently vacated by Century Radio and now lying dormant.

It was a 'virtual station' in that it didn't really have a physical home, other than in cyberspace, but I worked out a daily schedule whereby northern and southern programmes took turns on the new service, *Liveline* alternating with *Talkback* every second day, for instance. In this way, I was convinced that mutual suspicion and enmity could be ameliorated to some degree.

The plan for *Harmony FM* went to the Taoiseach's office via his press secretary, Seán Duignan. I also met with the RTÉ Chairman, John Sorahan, who was convinced that, while it was a good idea, BBC Belfast would never go for it. The proposal went no further, due perhaps to Albert Reynolds' unexpected resignation shortly afterwards. It's still a good idea, however, in these more agreeable times between north and south and would still have many benefits in underpinning good neighbourliness between the different parts of the island.

Another international radio opportunity came along when I was working with Mike Murphy in developing syndicated radio programmes. Paul Dubsky contacted me, saying that my name had been recommended when he enquired who was a good radio man in Ireland. Paul was an Irish businessman with a Czechoslovakian family background and was convinced that the countries formerly in the communist regime were ripe for investment opportunities. Radio, he said, was one of the areas ready for development and he had contacts in Prague anxious to set up a radio station, but didn't know how to proceed. Would I act as consultant? Delighted.

We flew to Prague and met Paul's contacts. Some of them were radio enthusiasts who ran a pirate radio station out of a block of flats near the university. They wanted to broadcast rock music and provide radio access to what had been the underground student movement. They were cheerfully confident, if still lacking the technical wherewithal to accomplish their ideals. Others, of a more deliberate mien, were more calculating about the costs and finance needed. Perhaps owing to years of suspicion and circumspection, they spoke in metaphors and codes, lest the person behind us in the café be part of the Secret Police. I was also conscious of a lack of initiative or a fear of change, as if it hadn't quite dawned on them that they were free to say and do what they liked. 'We still have to be careful. The people who were big in the Party are now big in business. Gangsters once, gangsters always.' The government was about to advertise radio franchises for Prague and our contacts wanted to apply.

Back in Dublin, I worked on the Prague application by the tortuous exchange of faxes, made all the more difficult by the obliqueness of the exchanges, in case their mail was being monitored. When I asked, for instance, what arrangements they envisaged for a news service, I'd get a reply along the lines of 'regarding the thing of which we spoke, the man who is aware of it is correct in his assumptions, bearing in mind that we have no further need of the first situation, but this could change, but not until later, when the situation will be clarified.' Perfect English, but incomprehensible.

This looked like it was going nowhere. We had access to funds through Mike's business contacts, but to make it succeed, a presence in Prague was required to steer it through and we weren't prepared to make such a commitment. Paul Dubsky organised a planeload of businessmen to come to Prague and among them was Denis O'Brien of 98FM, who took up the reins and eventually opened a station there.

Back in RTÉ, having always wanted to present a two-hander show, I suggested a replacement for *The Gay Byrne Show* that would use a guest co-presenter who would stay with the programme for a week at a time. I wanted Pat Dunne to produce, but RTÉ was reluctant, as some sort of *cordon sanitaire* would have to be enforced to cleanse him from his time with Century Radio. No one knew how long his time in the desert was to last, but no one would make a decision, even though he was back helping, unaccredited, in 2FM. I suggested that, in an exercise of appearance over substance, if he acted as producer, he would become producer. Whenever I was asked about facilities, technical arrangements, billings for the schedule, names of guests, I always said, 'Ask Pat Dunne.' Eventually someone said, 'I see you're the producer; we'd better organise a contract.' *Two for the Show* ran for that summer with guests like Maureen Potter, Phil Coulter, Terry Keane, Niall Toibín and Hugh

Leonard. We did a live programme from Cathal O'Shannon's kitchen, and breakfasted with Michael Noonan in the Castletroy Hotel.

Michael Noonan's week was eventful. The Monday was a bank holiday and we were in the cramped Limerick studios. There had been a major development overnight with Britain and the European Monetary Union. Because we were the first live programme—there had been no *Morning Ireland*, it being a bank holiday—I asked Michael to comment on the development and what exactly it meant for Ireland. He gave a short, lucid account of the implications and we continued the programme. At ten o'clock, he got a call from *The Irish Times* asking him to write a piece on the financial news; it was published the following morning. On Tuesday, he was asked by RTÉ television to do a piece for them. On Wednesday, *The Irish Times* pointed out that Michael was commenting outside his brief, as he was not the Fine Gael Spokesman on Finance. By Thursday, the papers were saying that this signified a major split in Fine Gael and, by Friday, they reported that Michael was obviously using his week-long exposure on radio to make a play for the leadership of the party. On *This Week* at Sunday lunchtime, Nora Owen, the Deputy Leader, was blaming me for the whole thing, saying that 'Michael was trapped into it by a trick question from Brendan Balfe'. That's how journalism eats itself.

In later editions of *Two for the Show*, I was joined by the then Tánaiste, Dick Spring, in the studios of Radio Kerry in Tralee, the first live RTÉ broadcast from a commercial local station. The Station Manager, Dan Collins, described my approach as one of 'studied gullibility'. He was being complimentary, explaining that by asking the simple question and not overtly pushing interviewees, I got them to say things that they hadn't meant to say. I have no particular technique for this, but I found one approach effective: when politicians launch into party-speak or policy statements, I suddenly change the subject, thereby interrupting their train of thought. Then I came back to the topic from a different direction. They don't like it, y'know.

The series came back the following year and a few years later came back on Sunday mornings for a year, when I interviewed all the party leaders, including the Taoiseach, Bertie Ahern. Former Tánaiste, Mary Harney's approach to radio is a little disconcerting. She is an excellent extemporary speaker with a sound grasp of her brief, but in order to concentrate, she looks at the carpet somewhere to the interviewer's left. It's a normal thing when people are collecting their thoughts, but the lack of eye contact meant that I couldn't signal that enough was enough and I would have to interrupt her to stop the flow. The series ended when the new editor of Radio 1, with a BBC background, hired Gloria Hunniford to present the programme. It wasn't, I'm afraid, a success.

I produced and presented other programmes and, as executive producer of the specialist music programmes in the *Sounds...* series, organised traditional music programmes, country programmes, personal choice programmes and live music programmes, recording musicians at venues around Dublin. *Sounds Different* with Ken Stewart was the template for the programme that replaced the series *Mystery Train.* There was a well-orchestrated outcry when the traditional music programme was about to be curtailed, but no discernible listenership was measurable. It seems that a particular constituency wanted the programmes to be done, but they didn't want to listen to them. A bit like the Irish language; they like to know that someone is trying to save it, but don't want to speak it themselves.

I continued to pour out documentary programmes on topics like the closing of Radio Luxembourg, the labour leader Joe Hill, the film actors John Wayne and Gene Kelly, and dozens more. I produced a two-hour obituary programme for George Harrison as well as local personalities, Maurice O'Doherty and Niall Boden. On the night of Frank Sinatra's death, my three-part series *The Sinatra Story* was broadcast back-to-back over three hours on Radio 1. I never got to meet him, but I included part of my interviews with Peggy Lee and Billy May, as well as contributions from Barry Norman, Alan Dell and Frank Sinatra Junior.

My Saturday programme, *On Balfe Street*, was a fast programme with some magazine elements. It carried a satirical component with 'Pathetic Newsreel', which delivered the news of the week in the style of a 1950s cinema newsreel, narrated by Joe Taylor, complete with references to Southern Éire and its Teashack and the crazy exploits of the fun-loving U2 Pop Group. Then Omagh was bombed. The new Director, Helen Shaw, asked me to mark it in some way on my Saturday programme at lunchtime. I asked the announcer, Catherine Hogan, and Joe Taylor to read pieces of poetry and prose and I played music to match. Sometimes outrage needs to be given time to sink in. *Remembering Omagh* was born out of cold anger and was meant to be heartbreaking.

More recently, I have presented RTÉ Radio's response to the 9/11 atrocity with a two-hour programme of music, *To America, with Love.* When no words are adequate, sometimes music is all we have. Likewise, on the death of Pope John Paul II, I compiled a programme to catch the mood of the nation. It was recorded before his death, so I had to imagine the outpouring of grief that would result. Many said that it would be low-key, but I felt that his death would have an enormous effect on Ireland and tried to capture that in the music and archive clips. It was broadcast in my Saturday afternoon slot, where I had been mixing comedy with music. It was called *BalfeB@RTÉ* and had developed a devoted audience, particularly among younger listeners. I used a sort of multi-layered approach to the format and the audience could listen on three levels: first, at the surface level, a fast-paced programme of comedy records interspersed with pop music; on the second level, the music comments on the comedy and moves it onwards; on the third level, the comedy and music both comment on the events of the week.

Despite the programme's success with listenership figures, RTÉ has a motto on these occasions: if it ain't broke, break it. The programme was taken off the air, summarily, and I learned about it when our Press Office was sending out a press release announcing its replacement. It's one of the things that big organisations don't do well. When I applied for Director of Radio on two occasions and Editor of Radio 1 on another, I learned the result of the interviews on the corridors of the Radio Centre. It was some consolation, I suppose, that many of my plans and suggestions were implemented. RTÉ seems to veer between internal and external appointments, much as a pendulum swings one way and then another. Sometimes, they cook it themselves; other times they buy a takeaway. The effect on the digestion of the staff is not a consideration.

I have to say, though, that I was an admirer of Helen Shaw as Director of Radio. For the new millennium, she asked me to devise a programme for New Year's Eve. I knew that we would be deluged by pictures from around the world, but one firework display looks like another and I was looking for something with some heart and soul. *Soundtrack of the Century* was conceived as the echo of our lives over the previous hundred years: music and speeches, poetry and prose, film and television, technology and inventions, war and peace, and all the reverberations of 36,500 days, through which the voice of humanity struggled to be heard. Over twenty-four hours, from noon on New Year's Eve, there came a selection of sounds, unannounced, apparently in random order. They appeared just to happen fortuitously, but like the technique with comedy records, I constructed a multi-layered approach with oblique connections between the items, if you wanted to hear them. For example, President Truman's announcement of the dropping of an atomic bomb on Hiroshima, was followed by Maria Callas singing 'One Fine Day' from *Madam Butterfly*, longing for the return of her American lover, Lt Pinkerton. At certain points, the lighting of an evening candle, the time just before midnight, I arranged for an appropriate item. As the sun rose on New Year's Day 2000, Ciarán MacMathúna read the old poem 'Dawn on the Irish

Coast', followed by the soaring Symphony No. 2 by Sibelius. The whole thing ended twenty-four hours after it started, with a warning by Holocaust survivor Elie Wiesel on the perils of indifference and the strains of 'Fanfare for the Common Man' by Aaron Copeland. There was no narration; I appeared only at the beginning and end.

I thought of it as a tapestry, possibly a mural, to be revealed without someone telling us what we should think or feel. Hang it up, let them in, and trust the audience to get it. My family thought that it was the best thing I had ever done.

The creative streak also seems to have been passed on. My daughter Ellie is a leading make-up artist with her own business, teaching and training others, as well as being in huge demand in the world of fashion and photo-shoots. John's interest in radio and broadcasting continues, as well as his love of sport, music and films. He loves New York, too, and studied for a few months in the New York Film Academy as a scriptwriter. He has two screenplays under his belt, at this writing. Both Ellie and John have beautiful personalities and sunny dispositions and we love them madly. Nice voices too, in case you wondered.

My assistant on the New Year programme was David Byrne, an efficient and helpful young man, who was a student of mine on the Radio Broadcasting Course in the Dun Laoghaire Institute of Art, Design and Technology. I had been teaching on it since 1993, when my old pal Brian Reynolds set it up. I have taught about a hundred students since then, including my son John, and many are now in broadcasting, or a related business. At last count, six of them were working in RTÉ Radio alone, and many are working in local radio stations all over the country. It's true that the tutor learns as much as the student, because I have had to rationalise things that I had always done from instinct. There's a plaque hanging on the wall in front of me as I write, given to me by Ellie. It's a quotation attributed to Michelangelo, creator of such masterpieces as the sculpture of David and the ceiling of the Sistine Chapel. It says 'Ancora Imparo'—'I am still learning'.

As technology moves onwards, we all had to learn self-operated digital editing, new methods of getting programmes on air and living in a more competitive environment, always conscious of the fact that novelty is sometimes just gimmickry in disguise and what is new isn't always better. I have always had a jaundiced view of Mission Statements and Visions; they tend to be either unattainable or too vague to be measured. Most of them beg the question, 'How will you know when you get there?' RTÉ's vision, printed on the glass walls of the staff restaurant, is 'to grow the trust of the people of Ireland as it informs, inspires, reflects and enriches their lives'. You may think it slightly Orwellian, or even lacking in a key ingredient, but I couldn't possibly comment.

There are, however, some eternal verities in broadcasting and I tried to capture some of them in 2001, when I was asked to give a Thomas Davis Lecture on Radio Entertainment to mark seventy-five years of Irish radio. I laid out the history of how Irish radio had tried to entertain the Irish nation and I tried to encapsulate whatever insights I had gained from my experience. Radio can be serious, and should be, but it ill-serves the listener when it tries to be solemn or self-important. Entertaining in its broadest sense means to engage, to attract, an audience. It is noble work, because if the programme doesn't connect, it doesn't succeed. The essence of public service broadcasting is to balance the light with the heavy and to do both with equal success; to make what is good popular, and to make what is popular good. The wheel came full circle with the Thomas Davis Lecture when I thought back to the man who originated the series, the man I never met, Francis McManus, who wrote me an encouraging letter to say, 'Please believe me that you will get on, but you must have patience.'

I think back to that year, a few months after his letter. I am on a hill in Courtown, in the café, drinking fluffy coffee for breakfast, on a bright and sparkling sunny morning. It is still early and there are few people about. I can see the harbour and our tent over in a field behind the ballroom. It's the summer of 1965 and the jukebox is playing the perfect summer song, 'I'm Alive' by The Hollies. It's a good time to be young and I am about to start my announcer training course in radio.

In the years since then, everything I thought it would be, it was. I have been blessed with a beautiful family, the whole reason I do what I do. I have trusted my audience to make sense of my offerings, knowing that if I trust them, they will trust me. I have learned new things and met new people. I have become part of all that I have met, the community of broadcasters and professional colleagues whom I've known and admired all my life. It has been a career that still continues to be satisfying and exciting, this love affair with radio, this chance—to be there.

THE END

INDEX